Walter Ha

Emeritus Professo
University of Zurich

The Swiss Constitution in a Comparative Context

DIKE

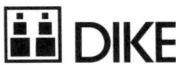

Cover page: The Swiss Parliament, Berne
              The Parliament Building: The South Façade

Bibliographic information published by ‹Die Deutsche Bibliothek›.
Die Deutsche Bibliothek lists this publication in the Deutsche National-
bibliografie; detailed bibliographic data is available in the Internet at http://
dnb.ddb.de

All rights reserved. No part of this book may be reproduced by any means,
or transmitted, or translated into machine language without the written permission of the publisher.

© Dike Zurich / St. Gall 2009
   ISBN 978-3-03751-189-3

www.dike.ch

Acknowledgments

A number of people helped me with this book, and I wish warmly to thank them. My brother-in-law Dr. Michael Robinson, a natural born British citizen and a Swiss by conviction, generously read a first version of the manuscript, corrected my English and was a helpful critic even with regard to the content of this book. Dr. Alison Wiebalck, who specialises in legal English, scrutinised and carefully corrected a second version. We had stimulating discussions on questions of legal terminology. The responsibility for any errors in the text remains, however, entirely my own. My friend and colleague Prof. Dr. Helen Keller read substantial parts of the book and made many valuable suggestions.

A long-standing cooperation unites me with the publishers Werner Stocker and Bénon Eugster. They also encouraged me to write this book, and ensured its professional production.

Zurich / Switzerland, 29 July 2009　　　　　　　　　　Walter Haller

Contents

Acknowledgments		III
Select Bibliography		XI
Abbreviations		XIII
Introduction		1

Part I – Fundamentals			7
1.	Historical Development		7
2.	The Constitution of 1999		12
3.	Comparative Context		14
4.	Other Sources of Constitutional Law		17
	A.	International Law	18
	B.	Statutory Law	18
	C.	Case Law	19
5.	Constitutional Interpretation		20
	A.	Verbal Analysis (wording)	21
	B.	Systematic Analysis	21
	C.	Historical Analysis (legislative intent)	22
	D.	Topical Analysis (contemporary understanding)	23
	E.	Teleological Analysis	24
	F.	Combination of Methods	25
6.	Basic Principles		26
	A.	Rule of Law	26
	B.	Democracy	27
	C.	Federalism	29
	D.	Social Justice	31
	E.	Other Principles	32
7.	Switzerland as Part of the International Community		34
	A.	Constitutional Guidelines	35
	B.	Switzerland and Europe	35
	C.	Membership in the United Nations and other Global Organisations	40

Contents

Part II – Federation, Cantons and Communes		41
1.	Three Levels of Government: Overview	41
	A. Federal Diversity	41
	B. The Federation	42
	C. Cantons	43
	D. Communes	48
2.	Federal Guarantees	50
	A. Existence and Territory of the Cantons	50
	B. Cantonal Constitutions	53
	C. Protection of the Constitutional Order in the Cantons	55
3.	Distribution of Competencies	56
	A. Methods of Allotment in a Comparative View	56
	B. Swiss Method of Assigning Tasks	59
	C. Competencies of the Federation: Overview	65
4.	Primacy of Federal Law	76
5.	Federal Supervision and Federal Coercion	78
6.	Intercantonal Treaties	80
Part III – Citizenship and Political Rights		85
1.	Swiss Citizenship	85
	A. Main Features	85
	B. Distribution of Competencies	86
	C. Acquisition of Citizenship by Law	87
	D. Ordinary Naturalisation	88
	E. Facilitated Naturalisation and Reinstatement of Citizenship	91
	F. Loss of Citizenship	92
2.	Legal Status of Aliens	93
3.	Right to Vote	96
	A. In General	96
	B. Prerequisites in Federal Matters	98
	C. Prerequisites in Cantonal and Communal Matters	99
4.	Instruments of Direct Democracy: Overview	101
	A. Definitions	101

	B. Federal Level	103
	C. Cantonal Level	104
5.	Freedom of Decision as the Essence of Political Rights	105

Part IV – Parliament, Government and the Judiciary — 107

1.	System of Government in a Comparative Context	107
	A. Parliamentary System	107
	B. Presidential System	108
	C. Semi-Presidential System	110
	D. Swiss System: Overview	110
2.	Bicameral Parliament	113
	A. In General	113
	B. In Switzerland	115
3.	The National Council	116
	A. Composition	116
	B. Eligibility and Incompatibilities	116
	C. Mode of Election	117
	D. Term of Office	119
4.	The Council of States	120
5.	Parliament at Work: Organisation, Procedures and Powers	121
	A. Institutional Framework	121
	B. Meetings	123
	C. Powers	125
6.	The Federal Council	128
	A. Composition	128
	B. Election	129
	C. Collegiate Principle and Administrative Units	132
	D. Powers	134
7.	The Federal Supreme Court	136
	A. Comparison with other Federal States	136
	B. Composition and Election	138
	C. Organisation	139
	D. Duties	140
	E. Court Proceedings	142

Part V – Fundamental Rights 145

1. General Considerations 145
   A. Definitions 145
   B. Comparative Context 147
   C. Sources in Swiss Law 150
   D. Implementation 153
   E. Restrictions 157
2. Human Dignity: Basic Value, Guiding Principle and Civil Liberty 162
3. Civil Liberties and Freedoms 164
   A. Right to Life and Personal Liberty 164
   B. Right to Privacy 168
   C. Right to Marriage and Family 170
   D. Freedom of Religion and Conscience 171
   E. Freedom of Expression 175
   F. Academic Freedom and Freedom of the Arts 182
   G. Freedom of Assembly and Association 183
   H. Freedom of Domicile 187
   I. Protection against Expulsion, Extradition and Deportation 188
   J. Right to Property 189
   K. Economic Freedom 191
4. Equality before the Law and Other Principles 194
   A. Equality before the Law 195
   B. Protection against Arbitrariness and Observance of Good Faith 201
5. Basic Procedural Rights 202
   A. Procedural Safeguards in General 203
   B. Guarantee of Access to the Court 205
   C. Special Guarantees for Judicial Proceedings 206
   D. No Deprivation of Liberty without a Due Process 208
   E. Criminal Proceedings 210
6. Basic Social Rights 211
   A. Right to Assistance when in Need 212
   B. Right to Primary School Education 213

Part VI – Rule-Making, Treaties and Constitutional Jurisdiction — 217

1. Revision of the Constitution — 218
   A. Distinction between Total and Partial Revision — 218
   B. Total Revision — 219
   C. Partial Revision — 221
   D. Barriers to Constitutional Amendments — 225

2. Statutes, Decrees and Ordinances — 227
   A. Form of Legal Norms and Other Acts — 227
   B. Federal Statutes — 228
   C. Federal Decrees — 232
   D. Ordinances — 233

3. Treaties — 234
   A. Definitions — 234
   B. Treaty-Making Procedure — 235
   C. Relationship between Treaties and Domestic Law — 238

4. Constitutional Jurisdiction — 240
   A. Essence and Forms — 240
   B. Comparative Context — 242
   C. Swiss Model: Overview — 245

Index — 249

Select Bibliography

Further references are made in connection with specific topics.

AUBERT JEAN-FRANÇOIS, Bundesstaatsrecht der Schweiz, 2 volumes, Helbing & Lichtenhahn, Basle 1991 and 1995

AUBERT JEAN-FRANÇOIS / EICHENBERGER KURT / MÜLLER JÖRG PAUL / RHINOW RENÉ / SCHINDLER DIETRICH (eds.), Kommentar zur Bundesverfassung der Schweizerischen Eidgenossenschaft vom 29. Mai 1874, 4 volumes, Helbing & Lichtenhahn, Schulthess, Stämpfli, Basle / Zurich / Berne 1987–1996

AUBERT JEAN-FRANÇOIS / MAHON PASCAL, Petit Commentaire de la Constitution fédérale de la Confédération Suisse du 18 avril 1999, Schulthess, Zurich 2003

AUER ANDREAS / MALINVERNI GIORGIO / HOTTELIER MICHEL, Droit constitutionnel suisse, 2 volumes, 2nd ed., Stämpfli, Berne 2006

BIAGGINI GIOVANNI, Bundesverfassung der Schweizerischen Eidgenossenschaft, Kommentar, Orell Füssli, Zurich 2007

EHRENZELLER BERNHARD / MASTRONARDI PHILIPPE / SCHWEIZER RAINER J. / VALLENDER KLAUS A. (eds.), Die schweizerische Bundesverfassung: Kommentar, 2 volumes, 2nd ed., Dike / Schulthess, Zurich 2008

FLEINER THOMAS / MISIC ALEXANDER / TÖPPERWIEN NICOLE, Swiss Constitutional Law, Kluwer, Stämpfli, Hague / Berne 2005

HÄFELIN ULRICH / HALLER WALTER / KELLER HELEN, Schweizerisches Bundesstaatsrecht, 7th ed., Schulthess, Zurich 2008

HALLER WALTER / KÖLZ ALFRED / GÄCHTER THOMAS, Allgemeines Staatsrecht, 4th ed., Helbing & Lichtenhahn, Basle 2008

HANGARTNER YVO / KLEY ANDREAS, Die demokratischen Rechte in Bund und Kantonen der Schweizerischen Eidgenossenschaft, Schulthess, Zurich 2000

KIENER REGINA / KÄLIN WALTER, Grundrechte, Stämpfli, Berne 2007

KLÖTI ULRICH / KNOEPFEL PETER /KRIESI HANSPETER / LINDER WOLF / PAPADOPOULOS YANNIS / SCIARINI PASCAL, Handbook of Swiss Politics, 2nd ed., Neue Zürcher Zeitung, Zurich 2007

KRIESI HANSPETER, Direct Democratic Choice: The Swiss Experience, Oxford: Lexington, Lanham 2005

Select Bibliography

LINDER WOLF, Schweizerische Demokratie: Institutionen, Prozesse, Perspektiven, 2nd ed., Haupt, Berne 2005

LINDER WOLF, Swiss Democracy: Possible Solutions to Conflict in Multicultural Societies, 2nd ed., Macmillan Press, Houndmills 1998

MERTEN DETLEF / PAPIER HANS-JÜRGEN (eds.), Handbuch der Grundrechte, volume VII/II: Grundrechte in der Schweiz und in Liechtenstein, C. F. Müller, Dike, Heidelberg / Zurich 2007

MÜLLER JÖRG PAUL / SCHEFER MARKUS, Grundrechte in der Schweiz im Rahmen der Bundesverfassung, der EMRK und der UNO-Pakte, 4th ed., Stämpfli, Berne 2008

RHINOW RENÉ / SCHEFER MARKUS, Schweizerisches Verfassungsrecht, 2nd ed., Helbing & Lichtenhahn, Basle 2009

RHINOW RENÉ / SCHMID GERHARD / BIAGGINI GIOVANNI, Öffentliches Wirtschaftsrecht, Helbing & Lichtenhahn, Basle 1998

THÜRER DANIEL / AUBERT JEAN-FRANÇOIS / MÜLLER JÖRG PAUL (eds.), Verfassungsrecht der Schweiz / Droit constitutionnel suisse, Schulthess, Zurich 2001

TSCHANNEN PIERRE, Staatsrecht der Schweizerischen Eidgenossenschaft, 2nd ed., Stämpfli, Berne 2007

TSCHANNEN PIERRE, Stimmrecht und politische Verständigung: Beiträge zu einem erneuerten Verständnis von direkter Demokratie, Helbing & Lichtenhahn, Basle 1995

SWISS FEDERAL CHANCELLERY, The Swiss Confederation – a brief guide 2008 (appears every year)

The Homepage of the *Swiss Confederation* www.admin.ch contains a lot of information relevant to constitutional law. The website www.ch.ch provides further useful information.

The Swiss Constitution in English

The first English translation of the Swiss Constitution was provided by Dr. Pierre A. Karrer, LL.M. Professor Thomas Fleiner and his co-authors included a full text of the Swiss Constitution in English in their book on Swiss Constitutional Law based on Karrer's translation, but up-dated and refined. The Homepage of the *Swiss Confederation*, mentioned above, also contains a non-official English version of the Swiss Constitution. The University of Berne provides another translation at www.servat.unibe.ch/icl/sz00000_.html. For the constitutional provisions in English in this book, all available translations were consulted, albeit rarely adopted verbatim.

Abbreviations

Am.	Amendment
Art.	Article
BBl	Bundesblatt = Federal Gazette. Contains, inter alia, bills proposing new legislation and statutes subject to a referendum. www.admin.ch/ch/d/ff/index.html
BGE	Entscheidungen des Schweizerischen Bundesgerichts = decisions of the Federal Supreme Court. Citation: BGE 129 I 217 (2003) = volume 129, part I (constitutional law), page 217, decided in 2003.
BGG	Bundesgesetz über das Bundesgericht (Bundesgerichtsgesetz) = Federal Law on the Federal Supreme Court of 17 June 2005 (SR 173.110)
BPR	Bundesgesetz über die politischen Rechte = Federal Law on Political Rights of 17 December 1976 (SR 161.1)
BüG	Bundesgesetz über Erwerb und Verlust des Schweizer Bürgerrechts (Bürgerrechtsgesetz) = Federal Law on the Acquisition and Loss of Swiss Citizenship of 29 September 1952 (SR 141.0)
BVerfGE	Entscheidungen des Bundesverfassungsgerichts = decisions of the German Constitutional Court
CCPR	U.N. Covenant on Civil and Political Rights of 16 December 1966
cf.	see, compare (confer)
Const.	Federal Constitution of the Swiss Confederation of 18 April 1999 (SR 101)
Const. 1874	old Swiss Constitution of 29 May 1874
E.	Erwägung = consideration (in a judgment)
ECHR	European Convention on Human Rights of 4 November 1950
ed.	editor / edition
eds.	editors
EEA	European Economic Area
EFTA	European Free Trade Association

Abbreviations

et al.	and others (et alii)
et seq.	and the following pages (et sequentes)
EU	European Union
i.e.	that is to say (id est)
n.	number (refers to numbering in this book)
p.	page
par.	paragraph
ParlG	Bundesgesetz über die Bundesversammlung (Parlamentsgesetz) = Law on the Federal Assembly of 13 December 2002 (SR 171.10)
RVOG	Regierungs- und Verwaltungsorganisationsgesetz = (Federal) Law on the Organisation of Government and Administration of 21 March 1997 (SR 172.010)
SR	Systematische Sammlung des Bundesrechts = systematic compilation of Federal Law (statutes, decrees and ordinances) as well as Treaties ratified by the Federal Government. Decimal classification; published in loose-leafform and regularly up-dated. www.admin.ch/ch/d/sr/sr.html
U.N.	United Nations
U.S.	United States / United States Report (decisions of the U.S. Supreme Court)
WTO	World Trade Organization

Introduction

Switzerland has one of the most recently formulated constitutions. It has only been in force since January 2000. But the main features of the Swiss constitutional order are the result of a long development, reaching far back in history. A turning point was 1848, after a civil war, when a new constitution created a federal state instead of the hitherto rather loose confederation, strengthened democratic structures and fundamental rights on a national level and introduced the organisational pattern of three top federal authorities which has basically prevailed until to-day.

The influence of thoughts and concepts developed in the U.S. Constitution by the Founding Fathers and later during the French Revolution on the Swiss Constitution of 1848 is obvious, though quite a number of characteristics are national peculiarities, especially with regard to the political system. More recently, foreign and international influences are most apparent in the field of fundamental rights, mainly due to the great impact of the European Convention on Human Rights (ECHR). The Swiss Federal Supreme Court often determines the scope and limits of a fundamental right by taking into account the relevant provision of the ECHR, and references to the case law of the European Court of Human Rights are commonplace in Swiss judicial decisions. Works of foreign constitutional scholars and decisions from constitutional courts in other countries have also left their mark on Swiss legal doctrine and constitutional jurisdiction. Some articles of the new Swiss Constitution, for instance the respect for human dignity or the inviolability of the essence of fundamental rights, are modelled after provisions in other constitutions[1].

---

[1] Cf. Art. 7 Const. with Art. 1 par. 1 of the German Basic Law, and Art. 36 par. 4 Const. with Art. 19 par. 2 of the German Basic Law.

Introduction

3 The adoption of foreign ideas has not been a one way affair. There are strong indications that American states were influenced by Swiss law when they introduced the popular initiative and the legislative referendum, beginning with South Dakota in 1898. An American journalist, J. W. Sullivan, studied the Swiss system of direct democracy on the spot and published a series of articles about the initiative and the referendum in the 1890s. His publications stirred the imagination of reformers in the United States[2]. Nowadays parliamentary delegations and experts from abroad quite frequently visit Switzerland to gather information on the functioning of the instruments of initiative and referendum or our federal system in general. Direct participation of citizens in political decision-making seems to be on the march in Europe, if we consider the number of referendums in connexion with the European Union as well as developments in Central and Eastern Europe following the collapse of the iron curtain. In addition, federal structures can help to maintain a certain degree of unity when diverging minority interests threaten to destabilise a national community.

4 If you ask a foreign tourist what he or she regards as typically Swiss, the answers may be: the Alps, products like cheese, chocolate or watches, the children's book «Heidi» translated into many languages, bank secrecy or perhaps – in the case of a more politically inclined observer – neutrality, federalism or direct democracy. As to the last, the most typical features of the Swiss constitutional and political order can be summarized in five points:

5 1. *Federalism* is a basic constitutional principle and a vital element of our political life. It fulfills an important function in safeguarding linguistic and cultural minorities, Switzerland

---

[2] Cf. THOMAS E. CRONIN, Direct Democracy: The Politics of Initiative, Referendum and Recall, Harvard University Press, Cambridge Mass. / London 1989, p. 48.

being a country with *four national languages* (German, French, Italian and Romansh). The Swiss federation consists of *26 cantons*, i.e. 26 constituent states of very dissimilar size and population. The cantons themselves are made up of over 2700 communes i.e., units of local government with a great deal of autonomy.

2. Unlike most European countries but similar to the United States, Switzerland has a *non-parliamentary system of government* and basically *separates powers* between a legislative, an executive and a judicial branch. But in contrast to the U.S. presidential system, the top executive power is not vested in one person, but in a multi-party collegiate body of seven members called the Federal Council *(Bundesrat)*, which is elected by parliament for a fixed term of four years. The federal parliament, called the Federal Assembly *(Bundesversammlung)*, was modelled on the U.S. bicameral system. The government cannot be forced to resign by a vote of no confidence. There is neither a Prime Minister, nor a Head of State nor an institutionalised parliamentary opposition.

3. Swiss citizens have a very direct influence on political decision-making by means of *referendum* and *popular initiative*. The electorate cannot only prevent laws voted by parliament from becoming effective, but even support binding plebiscites about new issues neglected by its representatives in the Federal Assembly. These instruments of direct democracy, which modify the representative system, are the main means of control and opposition. To some extent they compensate for the weak parliamentary opposition and the lack of a parliamentary vote of no confidence, making those who govern more directly accountable to the people. In cantons and communes the citizens have even more far-reaching mechanisms of direct participation.

4. With regard to *fundamental rights* the new constitution contains a systematic catalogue which meets the requirements of

the ECHR and in certain respects even goes further in protecting the individual. However, the constitution grants only very few directly enforceable social rights.

9 5. *Constitutional jurisdiction is severely limited,* especially in comparison with the situation in the United States and in the German Federal Republic. Art. 190 of the Const. provides that the Federal Supreme Court and other law-applying authorities are obliged to apply a federal statute or international law (irrespective of its conformity with the constitution). Nevertheless, the Federal Supreme Court has contributed greatly to the enforcement and development of the constitution, above all as far as fundamental rights and political rights are concerned.

10 The intricate networking of federal structures with a comparatively weak multi-party central government of co-equal members, combined with the citizens' potential to control, sanction or correct parliamentary decisions by means of referendum and initiative, makes it rather difficult for foreigners, sometimes even for politicians within the European Union, to understand properly how Switzerland is governed.

11 The aim of this book is to give an *introduction to Swiss constitutional law in a comparative framework.* Comparisons with other constitutions are meant to illuminate more clearly the essence and scope of Swiss institutions, procedures and rules for readers from abroad, to demonstrate common ground as well as differences, and maybe even to stimulate discussion in the search for solutions to constitutional problems which arise elsewhere. Comparisons will often focus on the U.S. Constitution and on the German Basic Law, because these constitutions are well known and, as is the case in Switzerland, embody a federal structure which grew out of a former confederation. A comparative analysis of diverse constitutional orders enables a more balanced evaluation of the advantages and disadvantages of different models and solutions that have been tested in practice. Sometimes it

can even provide the impulse for improving a given legal system by carefully adopting institutions and procedures that have proven themselves elesewhere.

Part I – Fundamentals

A survey of Swiss constitutional history, followed by a description of the concepts underlying the new Swiss Constitution, is the basis for understanding current Swiss constitutional law. A look at constitution-making in other countries will hopefully also contribute to discerning the characteristics of the Swiss Constitution. However, constitutional texts are only one source of constitutional law. International law, statutory law, case law, and methods of constitutional interpretation also have to be considered. Finally, basic principles that permeate the Swiss constitutional order, as well as Switzerland's position in the international community, will be discussed in Part I, before turning to specific elements of Swiss constitutional law in the following Parts II to VI of this book.

1. Historical Development[1]

Until 1848, the 13 ancient Swiss cantons (called «*Orte*») formed a *confederation* (the «*Alte Eidgenossenschaft*»), i.e. a league of sovereign states bound by a multitude of treaties reaching back to the 13th century. In addition, there were some affiliated entities and protectorates with subordinate legal status. The confederation was mainly a defensive alliance, combined with a system of arbitration to settle conflicts among the member-states peacefully. The only common institution was the Diet *(Tagsatzung)*, a non-permanent congress of representatives strictly bound by the in-

---

[1] Cf. in the first place ALFRED KÖLZ, Neuere schweizerische Verfassungsgeschichte, 2 volumes, Stämpfli, Berne 1992 and 2004. For an inspiring overview in English cf. JONATHAN STEINBERG, Why Switzerland?, 2nd ed., Cambridge University Press, Cambridge 1996, p. 8 et seq.

structions of the member-states. The influence of this body was further reduced by the requirement that as a rule decisions had to be adopted unanimously.

14 This confederate structure was completely replaced around the turn of the 19th century, from 1798 to 1803: under strong pressure from France, Switzerland became a *unitary state* called the *Helvetic Republic*. During this period the frontiers between the cantons were eliminated and Swiss territory was divided into administrative units called «cantons», which corresponded roughly to the French departments, i.e. they enjoyed very restricted autonomy. Under the influence of the French Revolution some important ideas were realized, many of which were to be taken up again later on when Switzerland became a federal state, for instance fundamental rights and equality, division of powers, popular sovereignty and compulsory primary education. However, the experience with a «one and indivisible republic»[2] also clearly demonstrated that a unitary state was irreconcilable with the traditional ideas and beliefs deeply rooted in Swiss political thinking.

15 Through the *Mediation Act* of 1803 Napoleon restored the sovereignty of the cantons, now 19 in number, while entities which had not enjoyed sovereign status in the old confederation were up-graded to full cantons. Central powers, focused on foreign relations and defence, were severely limited. Next to the Diet, a chief executive *(Landammann der Schweiz)* exercised mainly representative functions, the office rotating every year among the member-states.

16 Along with the decline of Napoleonic power a *restoration of pre-revolutionary institutions* occurred all over Europe. In Switzerland, accomplishments in tune with democracy and the rule of law were undone, and former bonds revived without, however, jeop-

---

[2] Art. 1 par. 1 of the Swiss Helvetic Constitution of 12 April 1798.

ardising the equal status of the cantons. Three new cantons that had belonged to France (Valais, Neuchâtel and Geneva) joined the confederation, which was held together only very loosely by the *Confederate Treaty (Bundesvertrag)* of 7 August 1815. At the *Congress of Vienna*, the Swiss frontiers as well as the perpetual neutrality of Switzerland received international recognition.

As of 1830 a *regeneration* happened in a number of cantons. Borne of the political movement of liberalism and partly with recourse to the achievements of the Helvetic Republic, some cantonal constitutions put into effect the idea of popular sovereignty by attributing the legislative power to parliaments elected by the people and introducing a constitutional referendum. Furthermore, these cantons guaranteed equal protection of the laws as well as civil liberties. 17

Attempts to amend the Confederate Treaty in accordance with the spirit of liberal cantonal constitutions, failed in the years 1832 and 1833. Subsequently, tensions between the mainly protestant liberal and the predominantly catholic conservative cantons steadily escalated and finally culminated in civil war. In 1845, seven conservative catholic cantons formed a secret defence alliance *(Sonderbund)* which soon became public. They refused to dissolve this union within the confederation. The Diet, dominated by the more progressive protestant cantons, declared the alliance null and void, as it seriously violated obligations deriving from the Confederate Treaty. The Diet's decision to dissolve the defence alliance was executed with military force in the *Sonderbund* war that lasted less than one month (November 1847). 18

The way was now paved for erecting a new constitutional order. Reconciliation had to be achieved between the advocates of state sovereignty and those who favoured a stronger union, as well as between conservatives and liberals. In view of the cause and the outcome of the civil war, special emphasis was placed on 19 strengthening the union and consolidating democratic and liberal ideas.

20 A unitary state was not a viable option, as the short experience with the Helvetic Republic, imposed by French rule, had shown. On the other hand, a confederacy did not meet the need for a tighter union. Under these circumstances, the architects of a new constitution looked to the United States, where the authors of the *Federalist Papers* had established the first theoretical foundation for a *federal state* as embodied in the U.S. Constitution of 1787.[3] The *Constitution of 1848* apportioned important tasks such as foreign policy, defence, customs and currency to the federation. The cantons retained all residual power.[4] National authorities with legislative, executive and judicial powers, namely the Federal Assembly (parliament), the Federal Council (government) and the Federal Supreme Court (judiciary) superseded the Diet. The Federal Assembly was thereby *modelled on the bicameral system of the United States* with a National Council *(Nationalrat)* composed of representatives of the people and a Council of States *(Ständerat)* consisting of two delegates from each canton.

21 The constitution was also strongly influenced by the *achievements of the French Revolution*, some of which, such as a strong emphasis on equality and democratic structures, had already been tested in the Helvetic Republic and adopted by liberal cantonal constitutions in the 1830s. ROUSSEAU'S ideas fell on fertile ground.[5] In addition, the demands for a division of powers and the protec-

---

[3] See ALEXANDER HAMILTON / JAMES MADISON / JOHN JAY, The Federalist Papers, a collection of 85 letters to the public that appeared in the newspapers of New York City between 1787 and 1788.

[4] This method of allocating competences between the federation and member-states corresponded to the U.S. Constitution, Am. 10 in conjunction with Art. I section 8.

[5] JEAN JACQUES ROUSSEAU, Du contrat social ou principes du droit politique, first published in 1762.

tion of fundamental rights advocated by LOCKE[6] and MONTESQUIEU,[7] which also underlay the U.S. Constitution and its first ten amendments, were reflected in a pragmatic way in the constitutional text. However, those who drafted the constitution tended to conceal the French influences, thus giving the impression that the relevant innovations were of Swiss origin.[8]

The new constitution was not based on any antecedent. Its enactment implied – to use the terminology of the famous ABBÉ SIEYES – the exercise of original constitution-making power *(pouvoir constituant originaire)*, as in the case of a revolution. The Confederate Treaty was not to be replaced with any other document by a mere majority. Almost one third of the cantons, mainly those that had been defeated in the *Sonderbund* war, repudiated its contents and were not willing to comply with a majority decision. Nonetheless, the Diet declared the constitution as adopted. It came into force on 16 November 1848.

A first complete revision of the constitution succeeded in 1874, after a failed attempt two years earlier. Although the text of the basic law was completely rewritten and inserted into new articles, the *Constitution of 1874* brought only few innovations. The most important was the introduction of an optional legislative referendum: 30,000 citizens (raised in 1977 to 50,000) or eight cantons could request a binding vote on federal legislation passed by parliament. When a referendum was called for, a statute could not enter into force unless approved by the voters. Other major reforms included an expansion of federal powers and of civil

---

[6] JOHN LOCKE, Second Treatise of Government, first published in 1690.
[7] De l'esprit des lois, first published in 1748.
[8] Cf. ALFRED KÖLZ, Die Bedeutung der französischen Revolution für das schweizerische öffentliche Recht und politische System, in: Der Weg der Schweiz zum modernen Bundesstaat: Historische Abhandlungen, Rüegger, Chur / Zurich 1998, p. 15 et seq.

rights (like economic freedom and an enhanced freedom of religion) as well as an upgrading of the Federal Supreme Court.

24 During the following 150 years the constitution was exposed to almost countless *partial revisions*, on average one every year! Many of these amendments added new items to the list of federal powers (for instance, the competence to unify civil and penal law and to regulate problems caused by economic and technological advances or due to increased social demands). Other reforms strengthened the democratic process, like the right of 50,000 citizens (raised in 1977 to 100,000) to propose partial revisions of the constitution (1891) or women's suffrage (introduced as late as 1971). Further noteworthy innovations concerned proportional representation in the National Council (1918), a shift in the economic system towards more governmental regulation after the Second World War (1947), the creation of the Canton of Jura (1978) and equal rights for men and women «in law and in fact» (1981). As a result of these frequent amendments the text of the constitution, which right from the beginning had lacked concise language and an appealing structure, looked evermore patchwork-like rendering it incomprehensible to ordinary citizens and unreliable as a support for those active in politics.

2. The Constitution of 1999

25 Beginning in 1965, there were numerous attempts to totally revise the constitution. After some failures it became apparent that substantial reform as regards the content would not meet with the necessary parliamentary approval nor survive a referendum. In this situation the Federal Assembly mandated the Federal Council to prepare a revision which should focus mainly on

2. The Constitution of 1999

formal aspects.[9] The principle objective was to completely update and improve the text without introducing basic innovations, in other words, to keep the fundamental law albeit phrased in modern understandable language, to eliminate sections of minor importance, bring the fundamental rights as developed by the practice of the Federal Supreme Court closer to the people, and group all this in one document with a clear system.

The Ministry of Justice headed by Federal Councillor ARNOLD KOLLER was entrusted with the drafting of a new constitution. In order to comply with the instructions given by parliament and at the same time keep the door wide open for later substantive reforms, the concept of *constitutional reform in a modular system («Verfassungsreform im Baukastensystem»)* was developed: following the implementation of an updated constitutional text, additional components, including substantial reforms, were to be inserted into the new structure at a later date after having undergone the procedure required for constitutional revision. Thus in June 1995 the government presented three reform packages:

1. the draft of an updated, concisely phrased and well arranged constitutional text without any intentional noteworthy innovations;
2. a package including a reform of the instruments of direct democracy, particularly initiative and referendum;
3. another package concerning the judicial system and constitutional jurisdiction.

Further reform packages concerning government, parliament, federal structure and revenue sharing were supposed to follow.

The Federal Council's proposals were exposed to broad consultation: apart from the cantons, political parties and associations, all

---

[9] BBl 1987 II 963.

citizens were invited to make suggestions, an opportunity widely utilised. Based on an appraisal of this consultation procedure, the government amended the texts and forwarded them to the Federal Assembly together with a comprehensive commentary which amounted to more than 600 pages.[10] The parliamentary debates took two years. On 18 December 1998, both chambers accepted the first package, i.e. the updated constitution. On 18 April 1999, the constitution attained the necessary majorities in a popular vote, the new basic law coming into force on 1 January 2000 – a well-shaped new bottle full of seasoned wine. Essentially, the constitution comprises principles and institutions which are the result of more than 150 years of constitutional development. Even innovations introduced during the parliamentary debate, for instance regarding cooperation between the federal and the cantonal authorities, the rights of parliament and the forms of laws and decrees, left the previous structures of government completely intact.

28 Substantial reforms, added later to the revised constitutional edifice as modules, concern the judiciary (2000) and direct democracy (2003) as well as task and revenue sharing between the federation and the cantons (2004).

3. Comparative Context

29 Like most countries, Switzerland embodies its basic legal rules concerning the organisation of government and citizens' rights in a *written constitution* which *overrides all other national law* and cannot be changed by ordinary legislation.[11] There are only few exceptions to this principle, the most famous being the United Kingdom where the sources of constitutional law are contained

---

[10] BBl 1997 I 1.
[11] The relation to international law will be discussed in n. 511 et seq.

in statutes, court decisions and constitutional conventions and parliament is – at least in theory – free to enact any law it likes.[12]

The enforcement of the constitution as superior paramount law, unchangeable by ordinary laws, is impaired by the obligation of the courts to follow federal statutes.[13] This contrasts with the concept of judicial review as developed by the famous Chief Justice JOHN MARSHALL more than 200 years ago,[14] and as practised in many countries with a fully developed constitutional jurisdiction.

Corresponding to its nature as superior law taking precedence over all other legal norms, constitutional norms are *enacted in a qualified procedure,* making them more rigid than ordinary legislation. This aspect is also in harmony with the customary model. But whereas parliamentary democracies are usually satisfied with a qualified majority or quorum in the legislative bodies deciding on constitutional amendments, in Switzerland revisions of the federal constitution are subject to a *mandatory referendum* and, as in Australia,[15] have to be passed by a «*double majority*», i.e. a majority of citizens taking part in the voting nationwide as well as a majority of those voting in a majority of the member-states. Ordinary laws on the other hand are only subject to an optional referendum, and – in case a referendum is required – have to be approved by a nationwide majority only, and not additionally in a majority of cantons as well.

In Switzerland, as in most countries, the entire federal constitutional law in its formal meaning (enacted as constitutional law and approved by a double majority) is contained in *one document,* whereas in Austria, in addition to the federal constitution, numerous constitutional provisions are isolated in ordinary laws

---

[12] Cf. ERIC BARENDT, An Introduction to Constitutional Law, Oxford University Press, Oxford 1998, p. 1 and 89 et seq.
[13] Art. 190 Const. Cf. n. 562.
[14] *Marbury v. Madison,* 5. U.S. (1 Cranch) 137 (1803).
[15] Cf. Art. 128 of the Australian Constitution.

Part I – Fundamentals

and international treaties, though they have been enacted as constitutional law and supersede ordinary legislation.

33 A constitution can prescribe explicitly that certain principles or rights regarded as the basis and foundation of the state may not be changed. The most famous example is Art. 79 par. 3 of the German Basic Law. Consequence of a tragic history, this norm provides that the protection of human dignity as well as the basic principles of state order and federalism are secure even against the constitution-making power. The Swiss constitution only prohibits the violation of peremptory norms of international law;[16] it does not bind constitutional amendments to any national barriers. The question of «inherent barriers», not expressly contained in the constitutional text, is sometimes discussed but lacks practical significance.

34 What should a constitution contain? Different answers to this question reflect various views on the function a constitution ought to fulfil; some constitutions are most communicative, others almost taciturn. The question was the subject of lively discussions in connection with the total revision of the Swiss constitution. From the beginning there was a consensus that a constitution should not be restricted to establishing governmental institutions, jurisdictions and processes, but ought to include a substantive values system, delimitating the fundamental principles governing the relationship between the individual and the state. A draft presented in 1977[17] adhered to the concept of an «open constitution», i.e. it left many options open to the legislative and partly open to the judiciary. This aroused a lot of criticism, especially as far as the sharing of competencies between the federation and the cantons was concerned. Consequently, those who drafted the constitution emphasised the demarcation of

---

[16] Art. 193 par. 4 and Art. 194 par. 2 Const.
[17] Verfassungsentwurf / Vorentwurf der Expertenkommission für die Vorbereitung einer Totalrevision der Bundesverfassung, Berne 1977.

powers, fixing the line of division between federal and cantonal tasks. In areas such as fundamental rights, a much higher degree of normative openness is unavoidable. At least in this area, the constitution is no «strait-jacket», but a «living organism».[18] Different opinions were voiced on the question to what extent there should be any room for stating general objectives which would give the political actors some guidance, but would not be directly enforceable in the courts. The view prevailed that although a constitution is primarily a legal document binding on all governmental powers, it should nevertheless make desirable objectives perceptible and formulate some guiding principles, without prejudicing unduly *how* the policy makers – who are responsible for allocating priorities and resources – implement them.[19]

4. Other Sources of Constitutional Law

In a wider sense constitutional law comprises not only those rules enacted in a qualified procedure and contained in a document called «the constitution». It also encompasses other important legal norms which regulate the organisation, tasks and proceedings of government bodies at the top level, as well as the citizens' relationship to the government. The main objective of the constitutional reform of 1999 was to ensure that all essential organisational and substantive rules in the above-mentioned sense were included in the new basic law, and that outdated or

35

---

[18] Justice LOUIS D. BRANDEIS, quoted in ALEXANDER BICKEL, The Least Dangerous Branch – The Supreme Court at the Bar of Politics, Bobbs-Merill Co., Indianapolis / New York 1962, p. 107. The European Court of Human Rights emphasises that the ECHR is a «living instrument» evolving through judicial interpretation; cf. LUZIUS WILDHABER, The European Court of Human Rights 1998–2006: History, Achievement, Reform, N.P. Engel, Kehl 2006, p. 39 et seq. and 66.

[19] Example: Art. 41 Const. regarding social goals; cf. n. 70.

dispensable provisions be removed. For this reason there is quite a lot of congruence between the constitution and the sources of constitutional law as a whole. Yet, three other sources deserve to be mentioned specifically:

A. International Law

36 International law supplements and partly superposes national law, given the country's web of contractual obligations towards other states, customary international law and commitments within international organisations.[20] In implementing fundamental rights the ECHR (European Convention on Human Rights) is of outstanding importance. Switzerland has also concluded a number of sectoral agreements with the European Community and its member-states.[21] In addition, many bilateral agreements regulate matters such as citizenship, domicile, neutrality, health care, energy supply, traffic, the economy and taxes. Such questions have in part a constitutional dimension.

37 In contrast to the dualist approach prevailing in the United Kingdom and in Scandinavian countries, in Switzerland, as in most continental European states, international law is part of the domestic legal order. When new obligations are created by treaty, they do not have to be «incorporated» into national law by legislation.

B. Statutory Law

38 Quite a number of statutes deal with matters of constitutional importance such as citizenship, the people's rights of co-determination and the federal authorities. The most significant are as follows:

---

[20] Cf. n. 79 et seq.
[21] Cf. n. 82.

- Federal Law 1952 on the acquisition and loss of Swiss citizenship (SR 141.0);
- Federal Law 1976 on political rights (SR 161.1);
- Federal Law 2002 on the Federal Assembly (SR 171.10);
- Federal Law 1997 on the Federal Government and the Federal Administration (SR 172.010);
- Federal Law 2005 on the Federal Supreme Court (SR 173.110).

Custom, i.e., practice which has been followed continuously and is recognized as being part of the law, is negligible as a source of Swiss constitutional law.

C. Case Law

The jurisprudence of the Federal Supreme Court has contributed much to the development of constitutional law, primarily in the area of fundamental rights. Under the Const. 1874 the court deduced from the guarantee of equality before the law a number of procedural principles such as the right to be heard in legal or administrative proceedings, the right to legal assistance for persons lacking the necessary means and the right to protection against arbitrariness. Furthermore, the court has derived, from judicial interpretation, implied fundamental rights such as personal liberty and the freedoms of opinion, language and assembly as well as a right to assistance when in need. This judge-made constitutional law was incorporated into the new constitution in 1999.[22] Even under the new constitution there is room for judicial interpretation to develop the text, especially when evolving the catalogue of fundamental rights. The jurisprudence of the European Court of Human Rights is also to be considered.

39

---

[22] Cf. Arts. 9, 10, 12, 16, 18, 23 and 29 Const.

5. Constitutional Interpretation

40 The idea that there can always only be one correct interpretation in establishing the meaning of a constitutional provision is outdated. Often no firm border-line can be drawn between making and applying the law. This is especially true of constitutional norms, due to their frequently high degree of abstraction. The open-endedness of many constitutional provisions defers important determinations to those who «interpret» the constitution, in Switzerland as elsewhere. When judges apply the constitution in a specific case, they sometimes create new law which will determine numerous future cases, but which was not extracted directly from the constitution. A look at abortion decisions by constitutional courts confirms this observation.[23] In Switzerland, *judge-made constitutional law* plays an eminent role as far as the development of fundamental rights, fair procedures and correct voting practices are concerned. In those domains where judicial review is excluded (such as foreign relations and economic policy on the federal level), the political players are the ultimate interpreters of the constitution.

41 The task of constitutional interpretation involves ascertaining the meaning of a constitutional provision when the text is either unclear or when it does not seem to correspond with its intended sense. Well established methods used by the courts in interpreting constitutional as well as statutory norms contribute to making the judicial process more rational and objective and hence to distinguishing judge-made law from purely political choices. Frequent reference to previous cases and to doctrine, combined with critical analysis, enhance the rationality of a decision. The overruling of precedents always requires stringent justification. The

---

[23] Cf. Roe v. Wade, 410 U.S. 113 (1973) and Planned Parenthood of Southeastern Pennsylvania v. Casey, 505 U.S. 833 (1992) with BVerfGE 39,1 and 88, 203.

5. Constitutional Interpretation

Federal Supreme Court applies various methods of interpretation side by side.

A. Verbal Analysis (wording)

Verbal analysis is the starting-point of all interpretation. It focuses on the wording, the literal sense and on common linguistic usage. Headings are part of the constitutional text and must therefore also be taken into consideration.

All federal laws, including the constitution, are published in each of the three official languages of the Confederation: German, French and Italian.[24] All wordings are equivalent. In cases of divergence between the three official texts the interpreter has to apply other established modes of analysis in order to determine which text corresponds with the real sense of the provision.[25]

B. Systematic Analysis

Systematic interpretation analyses a constitutional provision with respect to other constitutional norms and to the constitution's overall structure. As the articles of the new constitution are grouped in logical order, a systematic approach in interpreting norms may sometimes be helpful. Under the Const. 1874 a systematic analysis was usually of very limited value, as the old document was a patchwork of many more than a hundred amendments from different periods.

---

[24] Romansh is only an official language when communicating with persons of Romansh origin.
[25] Example: BGE 129 I 402 (2003) concerning exemption from punishment in the case of termination of pregnancy. The Court concluded that, based on a historical analysis, the French and Italian wordings of the Penal Code were decisive.

C. Historical Analysis (legislative intent)

45 Historical analysis focuses on either the intent of the framers (subjective historical analysis) or on the meaning which was generally attributed to the provision at the time of its enactment (objective historical analysis). In the United States, courts often invoke the «original understanding» or the «intent of the framers» when they interpret the constitution.

46 The subjective historical analysis is in harmony with the doctrine of separation of powers. But it is also confronted with the practical difficulty of determining who the framers were.[26] Constitutional amendments are drafted by experts within or outside the administration. They are exposed to consultation procedures, usually proposed by the Federal Council, and debated in parliamentary committees as well as in both chambers before finally being submitted to a compulsory referendum requiring a double majority (people and cantons). Thus many actors are involved.

47 Quite often the Federal Supreme Court places a good deal of emphasis on historical factors, sometimes combining the subjective with the objective approach. The intentions of those participating in the process of constitution-making are more likely to be respected if they have been expressed clearly and unequivocally in material preparatory to the constitutional amendments, have not been contested, and if, moreover, they are convergent with the ideas that prevailed at that time. The weight of historical analysis is stronger with regard to constitutional provisions that are relatively new.[27] It diminishes with the lapse of time, especially when the text leaves enough margin for taking into account evolving standards of justice and equity. By this means the Federal Su-

---

[26] Cf. RONALD DWORKIN, Law's Empire, Belknap Press, Cambridge Mass. 1986, p. 318 et seq.
[27] Cf. BGE 128 I 288, 292 (2002), right to a public court hearing (Art. 30 par. 3 Const.).

preme Court has extracted a number of specific procedural rules from the old equal rights clause.[28]

In interpreting the Constitution of 1999, the starting point is a relatively new text. But we have to keep in mind that the total revision was intended mainly to update and improve the text, thereby avoiding substantial innovations (which were left to later amendments) in an attempt to reach wide consensus.[29] As a consequence, interpretation of the new document often continues the practice and doctrines applied to the respective provisions of the Const. 1874. However, the new text and systematization have created a wide margin for reinterpretations.

D. Topical Analysis (contemporary understanding)

A topical analysis *(«zeitgemässe Auslegung»)*, often combined with a teleological interpretation, relies on a contemporary understanding of the wording and the circumstances prevailing when a provision is applied. The contrast to methods of historical analysis is apparent. An up-to-date interpretation is more comprehensible to the average citizen who often has no knowledge of preparatory materials. Besides, topical analysis conceives of the constitution as a living instrument, thus counteracting a petrification. This is of special importance in the field of human rights.[30] On the other hand, too dynamic an interpretation can weaken legal security and shift too much power from the legislative to the judicial branch which may be problematic in politically sensitive areas.

In 1990, the Federal Supreme Court applied the topical method when it ordered the Canton of Inner Appenzell in 1990 to extend

---

[28] Art. 4 par. 1 Const. 1874.
[29] Cf. n. 25.
[30] The European Court of Human Rights favours an «evolutive interpretation» of the ECHR as a «dynamic and living instrument».

the right to vote in cantonal matters to include women.[31] The terms «fellow countrymen» *(«Landsleute»)* and «Swiss» in the cantonal constitution of 1971 were given an interpretation which clearly exceeded the constituent's original understanding but which was in accordance with the contemporary perception that had been expressed in a federal constitutional amendment (introducing women's suffrage in federal matters) nineteen years earlier. Besides, all the other cantons had given full political rights to women. In Inner Appenzell such a reform could not be expected, as the *Landsgemeinde* (then an assembly of exclusively male citizens) had turned down women's suffrage time and again. In the fifties, however, the Federal Supreme Court had rejected a similar claim by women in Canton Vaud to interpret the term «tous les *Suisses*» in the cantonal constitution as including women *(«Suissesses»)*;[32] at that time judicial activism as practiced in the Appenzell case would have been inappropriate.

E. Teleological Analysis

51 A teleological interpretation searches for the purpose (*telos* in Greek) of a norm. The interpretation most conducive to achieving this purpose prevails. This method can be combined with an historical approach (what result did the legislator want to achieve?) or with a contemporary approach (when technical or social developments give the original intent a different dimension).

52 A practical instance concerning the Const. 1874 offers a good example of the latter case: the federal power to pass regulations concerning radio and television was deduced from Art. 36 par. 1 Const. 1874, which mentioned only «post and telegraph» as of concern to the central government. The purpose of the article,

---

[31] BGE 116 Ia 359, 379 (1990).
[32] BGE 83 I 173 (1957).

thus went the legal reasoning, was to enable federal legislation concerning all means of electronic news transmissions.[33]

F. Combination of Methods

There is *no hierarchy of interpretative methods*. All modes of analysis are taken into consideration and combined. In a specific case the interpreter has to decide which method or combination of methods is best suited to determining the real sense of a constitutional norm. The wording is quite often, but not always, decisive. Other modes of analysis can require a deviation from a text which seems clear.[34] In cases with far-reaching political implications a court will be more inclined to focus on the wording and the framer's intent, hence avoiding a topical approach; a satisfactory allocation of roles between legislators and judges should be achievable. Likewise, a court should not lose sight of the reasonableness and practical consequences of its decisions.

53

If various methods of interpreting statutes lead to different results and not all of them seem to be consistent with the constitution, an interpretation which is in line with the values of the constitution (constitutional interpretation) will suggest itself.[35] Similarly, the Federal Supreme Court uses a harmonising method of interpretation in the case of a conceivable conflict with international law: wherever possible, it will interpret Swiss domestic law in a way which conforms best with obligations under international

54

---

[33] This reasoning was only convincing as far as the technical aspects of transmission (and not the programming) were concerned. In 1984 the legislation on all aspects of radio and television was expressly transferred to the federation.

[34] Recent example: BGE 131 II 217, 221 (2005) concerning a norm in the Crime Victim's Assistance Law.

[35] Example: BGE 131 II 562, 567 (2005).

law. This approach is quite common in decisions concerning the ECHR. [36]

6. Basic Principles

55 Essentially, the Swiss constitutional order is based upon four basic principles: the rule of law, democracy, federalism and social justice. These principles are not phrased as such in norms enforceable in a court of law, but permeate the Swiss legal system, guide government action and underlie numerous constitutional and statutory norms that grant citizens' rights or allocate competencies.

A. Rule of Law

56 The concept of the «rule of law» as expounded by DICEY in his famous definition articulates three principles: the absolute supremacy and predominance of regular law as opposed to arbitrary power, the equal subjection of all to the ordinary law as administered by the law courts, and the protection of the citizen's freedoms by the ordinary law rather than by abstract constitutional declarations.[37] The German notion of «*Rechtsstaat*» referred to in Art. 5 Const., overlaps but is not entirely congruent with the Anglo-American understanding, in particular regarding the third element. «*Rechtsstaat*» includes both formal and substantive elements. The underlying goal is, as in the United Kingdom, to limit the power of the state in favour of individual liberty. This requires the predominance of a law that binds all state authority

---

[36] Example: BGE 123 IV 236, 248 et seq. (1997) concerning the protection of journalistic sources from being revealed.

[37] ALBERT VENN DICEY, Introduction to the Study of the Law of the Constitution, 10th ed., Macmillan Education, London 1959.

and implies a separation of powers crowned by an independent judiciary. With respect to substance, fundamental rights (guaranteed in a basic law and limiting also the legislator) are the essence of the «*Rechtsstaat*».

To a great extent the constitution fulfils the requirements of a state governed by the rule of law. Pursuant to Art. 5 par. 1 Const. all state activity is based on and limited by law. The obligation to respect international law is specially emphasised in Art. 5 par. 4 Const. A division (though not a strict separation) of powers lies at the basis of Title 5 Const. relating to the federal authorities. Title 2 Const. contains a comprehensive list of fundamental rights (substantive and procedural), while Art. 191c guarantees the independence of the judiciary. However, judicial review of federal laws is severely limited by Art. 190 Const. which obliges courts to apply federal statutes even when they conflict with the constitution.[38]

57

Art. 5 Const.   Rule of Law
(1) All state activity is based on and limited by law.
(2) State activity must be in the public interest and proportional to the goals pursued.
(3) Public authorities and private persons must act in good faith.
(4) The federation and the cantons shall respect international law.

B. Democracy

Democracy implies that all state power is based on the will of the people. In most modern democracies, in contrast with the Athenian «direct democracy» in antiquity, the principle of representation prevails, i.e., the popularly elected parliament and government are presumed to reflect the will of the people. By means of

58

---

[38] Cf. n. 562.

periodic elections citizens are entitled to confirm their choices or to demonstrate their disapproval and elect other representatives.

59 In Switzerland, the representative system is permeated with elements of direct popular participation. This is why Switzerland is often called a «referendum democracy» or a «semi-direct democracy».[39] Basically, the popularly elected parliament and the government are the primary decision-making institutions within the state. But, in addition, through referendum and initiative people can exercise direct influence on the creation of law, and can approve international treaties and other matters of substance. More than 50% of all referenda worldwide are conducted in Switzerland.

60 The contrast to the French plebiscite form of referendum[40] is striking: in France, the referendum is mainly a presidential instrument used to sidestep parliament and obtain the consent of the people directly. The popular vote is simultaneously a vote of confidence for or against a president and his government. In Switzerland, on the other hand, with the referendum and initiative the people possess their own means of affecting policies and are not restricted to giving their own view only when asked to do so. Besides, rejection of government policy in a referendum has no immediate personal consequences as the vote is primarily regarded as a factual issue, and is not linked to confidence in political leaders.

61 Despite the paramount importance of the democratic principle, it is not highlighted in a special article of the constitution in contradistinction to constitutions in adjoining countries.[41] Art. 51

---

[39] Some states in the United States, for example California, have also developed strong forms of semi-direct democracy.

[40] Art. 11 of the French Constitution.

[41] Cf. Art. 20 of the German Basic Law. In Austria, France and Italy the principle of democracy is stated in the first article of the respective constitutions.

Const. only obliges the cantons to adopt democratic constitutions. But the importance of democracy for decision-making is apparent from a number of constitutional provisions regarding political rights, initiative and referendum as well as Art. 148 par. 1 Const. which reads as follows: «Subject to the rights of the people and the cantons, the Federal Assembly is the highest authority of the Federation.»[42] Art. 190 Const. mentioned above as restricting constitutional jurisdiction, also indicates an overemphasis of the democratic principle even where the rule of law is at stake. In Swiss political life popular sovereignty is a frequently employed and sometimes mis-used catchword. There is a clear tendency to regard the will of the people, as expressed in the results of votes, as almost sacrosanct, even when its compatibility with international law appears to be questionable.

C. Federalism

In a comparative context the meaning of federalism requires some clarification. The German term «Föderalismus» is orientated towards a strengthening of the separate components of a state union, as opposed to centralism. In contrast, Anglo-American «federalism» is focused on an increase of central power within a federation. During the drafting of the U.S. Constitution of 1787, the federalists argued in favour of a strong national government, while the antifederalists under THOMAS JEFFERSON were hostile to such expansion and believed in decentralization. In discussions concerning the future of the European Union, «federalist» is quite often used to describe those who favour a stronger EU government. 62

The outlines of the term «federal state» are clearer, referring to a political system in which ultimate authority is distributed be- 63

---

[42] This differs from the conception of three «co-equal branches of government» in the U.S. Constitution.

tween a central government (powers of the federation) and state governments. A federal constitution divides the tasks of government between the two levels, providing the member-states with instruments of participation even in federal matters. Each individual state has its own constitution, organisation and area of responsibility. This particular political system fuses or synthesises elements of a confederacy and of a unitary state.[43]

64 As in the United States, Australia, Canada and Germany, Switzerland is equipped with all the main characteristics of a federal state:

– The constitution allocates the competencies between the federation (i.e. the central government) and the cantons. Within the boundaries of their jurisdiction, the cantons retain a very substantial autonomy. Policy-making on a cantonal level is governed by cantonal constitutional law.
– The cantons participate in decision-making at the federal level, first and foremost as indispensable organs for amending the federal constitution.
– The bicameral parliament, tailored on the U.S. senate model, is intended to stress the cantonal element in federal government.

65 In recent decades, a considerable *shift of competencies from the cantons to the federal level* has occurred. This tendency can also be observed in other federal states. In particular, legislation in economic and social policy, environmental protection and technology has been transferred to the federal level. Moreover, the increasing internationalisation of many public tasks often requires a unified approach.

---

[43] The fact that the constitution is labelled «Federal Constitution of the Swiss *Confederation*» (Bundesverfassung der Schweizerischen Eidgenossenschaft) as well as the proclamation in Art. 1 Const. that the Swiss people *and* the cantons form the Swiss *Confederation* (emphasis added) reminds us that the cantons were preexisting political entities.

The new constitution attaches much value to *cooperation between federal and cantonal authorities,* whereas the Const. 1874 was orientated more towards a separation of the respective areas of responsibility. 66

However, Swiss federalism (in the above-mentioned German meaning of *«Föderalismus»)* embodies more than the structural criteria of a federal state. It is the result of a prior history of conflict and its resolution in 1848 and an omnipresent element of Swiss politics, essential for national coherence in a multilingual and multicultural society with different religious creeds. 67

Federalism does not stop at the cantonal borders. Extensive communal autonomy coinciding with active citizen-participation in local matters can be regarded as a cornerstone of Swiss federalism. The three levels of government are manifestid in the triple citizenship: every Swiss has three citizenships – Swiss, cantonal and communal. 68

D. Social Justice

The preamble to the constitution declares inter alia that the strength of a people is measured by the well-being of its weakest members. Indeed, civil liberties, the rule of law, equality before the law and democratic processes are of dubious value for those who lack the adequate abilities and means to benefit from the respective rights. Therefore, the state has a duty to provide some form of welfare safety net. Of course there are many different conceptions as to the tightness of the net, depending on diverging political views of what social justice implies. 69

The constitution is reluctant to outline a model of social justice. Instead, it leaves the main responsibility in this field, and the assignment of priorities, to the democratically elected legislatures on the national and cantonal levels. Nevertheless, there are some important constitutional benchmarks. Art. 2 Const., describing 70 the aims of the «Swiss Confederation», includes the promotion of common welfare and equality of opportunity. Arts. 12 and 19 Const. even provide for two basic social rights: the right to assistance when in need and the right to free primary school education. Art. 41 Const. contains an impressive list of social goals which are intended as guidelines for legislators but do not grant citizens the accordant rights. Claims enforceable in courts derive from comprehensive legislation in social matters. Many competencies of the federation relate to social welfare, such as Arts. 111 and 112 Const. (social security and insurance for the elderly, dependents and the disabled), Art. 113 Const. (employee pension plans) or Art. 114 Const. (unemployment insurance). Art. 29 par. 3 Const. guaranteeing the right to legal aid for persons lacking the necessary means is both essential for implementing the rule of law and for achieving social justice.

E. Other Principles

71 Further principles may be regarded as basic and added to the preceding list. THOMAS FLEINER and his co-authors point out that next to democracy, federalism and the «Rechtsstaat», *neutrality* is one of the pillars of the Swiss constitutional system.[44] In this connection a distinction between neutrality as understood in *public international law* and neutrality as a *principle of Swiss foreign policy* seems necessary. At the Congress of Vienna in 1815, the European powers agreed to recognise Swiss neutrality permanently. Since then, this recognition has been reconfirmed several times. Neutrality in this international sense implies non-participation in wars between other states as well as the right to repel potential attackers («armed neutrality»). This notion of neutrality also underlies the V. and the XIII. Hague Conventions of 1907, stating

---

[44] THOMAS FLEINER / ALEXANDER MISIC / NICOLE TÖPPERWIEN, Swiss Constitutional Law, p. 27 et seq.

6. Basic Principles

the rights and duties of neutral powers in land and naval warfare.[45]

Neutrality is also a cornerstone of Swiss foreign policy, deeply engraved on the psyche of many Swiss, sometimes mythicized, and quite often exploited to oppose more active international cooperation, which, in turn, favours isolationism. The constitution enjoins parliament and government to safeguard «the external security, the independence and the neutrality of Switzerland».[46] This policy of neutrality has helped to save Switzerland from wars since the foundation of the federation in 1848, and has also helped to avoid or at least reduce conflict within its multilingual and multicultural population when armed conflicts ravaged surrounding countries. It is partly due to Switzerland's policy of neutrality, that many international institutions have their headquarters in Switzerland.[47]

When the iron curtain separating the West from the communist world was dismantled after the Cold War, the strict Swiss concept of neutrality had to be redefined. It no longer excludes the participation of the Swiss military in international peace-keeping missions or in military training exercises with other countries, and is compatible with membership of the United Nations.

RENÉ RHINOW and MARKUS SCHEFER include some further items on their list of basic principles: an economic order based on free competition, the principle of subsidiarity, sustainable development as well as integration into the international community and openness towards the world.[48]

---

[45] Cf. SR 0.515.21 and 0.515.22.
[46] Art. 173 par. 1 (a) and Art. 185 par. 1 Const.
[47] Examples: International Labour Organization (ILO), World Health Organization (WHO), World Trade Organization (WTO), all in Geneva; International Olympic Committee in Lausanne.
[48] RENÉ RHINOW / MARKUS SCHEFER, Schweizerisches Verfassungsrecht, p. 39 et seq.

75 *Sustainable development* is the subject of a special constitutional provision in a section concerning the environment and land planning:

> **Art. 73 Const.   Sustainable Development**
> The federation and the cantons shall strive to establish a durable equilibrium between nature and its capacity to renew itself, and its use by man.

76 Sustainable development reaches beyond the sphere of nature and the environment for it includes social and economic aspects. Development is sustainable when it covers present needs without impairing the future of generations to come. The constitution already mentions the responsibility towards future generations in the preamble, and, in Art. 2, lists sustainable development and the preservation of natural resources as one of the aims of the confederation (i.e. federation and cantons). The preservation of national resources is even a specific objective of foreign policy.[49]

7. Switzerland as Part of the International Community

77 In comparing the provisions relating to Switzerland's place in the international community in the Constitutions of 1874 and 1999, RENÉ RHINOW and MARKUS SCHEFER detect a fundamental change of paradigm from an «introverted nation state» to a modern state committed to international co-operation and respect for international law.[50]

---

[49] Art. 54 par. 2 Const.
[50] RENÉ RHINOW / MARKUS SCHEFER, Schweizerisches Verfassungsrecht, p. 696 et seq.

A. Constitutional Guidelines

The great importance that the framers of the new constitution 78
attributed to international obligations and cooperation with the rest of the world is apparent in a number of constitutional provisions. The preamble expresses the will to strengthen independence and peace «in solidarity with and openness towards the world». According to Art. 2 par. 4 Const. the confederation is committed to a just and peaceful international order. The federation and the cantons must respect international law.[51] Peremptory norms of international law are even a barrier to changing the constitution.[52] The catalogue of fundamental rights reflects the influence of international conventions, in particular the ECHR and the jurisprudence of the European Court of Human Rights. The formulation of social goals in Art. 41 Const. was inspired by the U.N. Covenant on Economic, Social and Cultural Rights.

B. Switzerland and Europe

Conspicuous by its absence is any constitutional norm concern- 79
ing Switzerland's relations with the rest of Europe.[53] Although Switzerland is not a member of the European Union, the intense involvment in agreements and policies on a European level would certainly have justified some mention in the basic law. Yet, any such reference might have severely diminished the chance of the constitution being accepted as a whole in the subsequent referendum required for constitutional revision, as the issue of Switzerland's future role in relation to the European Un-

---

[51] Art. 5 par. 4 Const.
[52] Art. 193 par. 4 and Art. 194 par. 2 Const.
[53] Constitutions of some neighbouring countries contain detailed provisions relating to the EU, for instance Art. 23 of the German Basic Law, Art. 88-1 to 88-5 of the French Constitution and Art. 23a to 23f of the Austrian Constitution.

ion is highly controversial. Many Swiss regard accession to the EU as a threat to Swiss identity, in particular Switzerland's direct democracy and federalism. Certain right of centre parties such as the Swiss People's Party (*Schweizerische Volkspartei*) have been known to exploit these fears.

80 The European Union and Europe are not the same. Switzerland lies in the centre of Europe and has played an active role in promoting the rule of law, human rights and other common values on the European level. Milestones on this road include the accession to the *Council of Europe* in 1963 and the ratification of the *European Convention on Human Rights* in 1974.[54] LUZIUS WILDHABER, a Swiss national, even presided over the European Court of Human Rights from 1998 to 2006. Switzerland has also been an active participant in the *Organisation for Security and Cooperation in Europe* (formerly the Conference on Security and Cooperation in Europe), a valuable instrument of European peace policy, since its first meeting in Helsinki in the year 1973.

81 In the field of foreign trade, the establishment of the *European Free Trade Association (EFTA)* in 1960 and an agreement with the European Community of 22 July 1972, gave Switzerland the opportunity to benefit from some advantages of European economic cooperation. Once some of the members of EFTA had joined the EU, all that remained were Iceland, Norway, Switzerland and Liechtenstein. These countries were willing to participate in the common market, but were not prepared to assume the full responsibilities of EU membership. In May 1992 they signed the *European Economic Area (EEA)* treaty. It implied structural partnership with the EU and acceptance of the «acquis communautaire», i.e. the body of EU law accumulated so far in the fields of the «four freedoms» (of movement of goods, per-

---

[54] Both steps occurred with a considerable delay due to concerns of maintaining neutrality, and to incompatibilities which had to be eliminated between the national legal order and the ECHR.

sons, services and capital). Parliament approved the agreement creating the EEA which then had to be submitted to a mandatory referendum. On 6 December 1992 after a vigorous campaign, the voters, with an unusually high turnout of 78.3%, rejected the EEA. Only 50.3% of those who voted said «No», but the additional requirement of a majority in the cantons was far from achieved. In the French-speaking part of Switzerland over 70% voted «Yes», but in the German-speaking part of Switzerland only two cantons (Basle-City and Basle-Land) accepted the EEA. This division between language communities, often called *«Röschtigraben»*,[55] is not unusual in matters concerning international cooperation and openness towards the world. But, as a more detailed analysis showed, there were similar divisions between cities and rural areas as well as between social groups.

Since the rejection of the agreement on the EEA, Switzerland has been aiming to secure access to the EU market through the negotiation of *sectoral agreements with the European Community and its member-states.* Seven such agreements (dubbed «Bilaterals I») were concluded in 1999 and, after the positive outcome of an optional referendum, entered into force on 1 June 2002. They concern the free movement of persons, air and land transport, scientific and technological co-operation, public procurement, trade in agricultural products and mutual recognition of conformity assessment.[56] In a second round («Bilaterals II»), negotiations on further sectoral agreements were completed in 2004. Bilaterals II cover the following sectors: taxation of savings, fight against fraud, cooperation in the fields of border controls, police, asylum and migration («Schengen / Dublin»), as well as cooperation in the European Environmental Agency, in the media programme and in future programmes in the field of education, moreover,

82

---

[55] Trench (Graben) separating those who eat a typical Swiss German potato dish called «Röschti» or «Rösti» from the francophone parts of Switzerland where fondue is more popular.

[56] BBl 1999, 6489 et seq.

statistical collaboration, trade in processed agricultural products and avoidance of double taxation of retired EU officials.[57] At the same time, the existing agreement on free movement of persons was adapted to allow for the accession of the ten new member-states. By means of referenda, voters voted in favour of the agreement on Schengen / Dublin and in favour of the extension of the agreement on the free movement of persons (5 June 2005 and 25 September 2005, respectively). On 8 February 2009 the Swiss decided with a clear majority of 59.6% of those who voted, to continue the agreement with the EU and its member-states on the free movement of persons for an unlimited period, and to authorise the Federal Council to ratify the protocol extending the named agreement to Bulgaria and Romania.

83 The passage of the «Schengen / Dublin» accords is particularly significant for the policy of working towards closer cooperation with the EU. Since the implementation of these accords, systematic border controls between Switzerland and its EU neighbours have been replaced by more effective and institutionalised cooperation with the EU on matters relating to fighting crime, as well as immigration and asylum.

84 The Swiss government had already applied for full membership of the EU in May 1992.[58] It is reasonable to conclude that this premature step led voters who had rejected membership of the EU to say «No» to the EEA a few months later. As a result of the negative referendum on the EEA and the clear rejection of a popular initiative calling for immediate negotiations for EU membership in March 2001, the issue of full membership, although formally still pending, is on ice for the foreseeable future.

85 Membership of the EU would have far-reaching consequences for the Swiss constitutional order and affect some basic constitu-

[57] BBl 2004, 5965 et seq.
[58] BBl 1992 III 1185 et seq.

tional principles. The cession of essential competencies to supranational bodies would not only restrict the powers of parliament and government (as is the case for other member-states), but, in addition, would limit the scope of popular initiatives and referenda at both the federal and cantonal levels. The idea of having to accept regulations and directives from Brussels, issued in procedures regarded as bureaucratic and of dubious democratic legitimacy, is not popular among many Swiss citizens who are accustomed to vote and have the last word on, as they perceive it, all important political matters.

On the other hand, membership would give Switzerland a chance to take an active part in the shaping of Community law, at least through its representatives in Brussels. However, as a small country Switzerland cannot be interested in a democratisation of decision-making procedures in Brussels, because small countries are better represented (in relation to their population) in executive bodies like the Council of Ministers and the Commission than in the European Parliament. 86

In order to limit the disadvantages of «going it alone», Switzerland can hardly refrain from harmonising legislation with European standards in many areas (making it «Europe-compatible»). In fact, Switzerland is already highly integrated into the European economy. Nevertheless, it is inevitable that EU membership would mean a significant shift of power from parliament to government which could cause specific problems in view of Switzerland's non-parliamentary system of government. In all likelihood, basic governmental reform would have to be undertaken to enable the Federal Council to cope with the additional tasks in Brussels and, at the same time, introduce new mechanisms of co-operation with parliament and the cantons in matters of European policy-making. In addition, the Federal Supreme Court would have to be given the power to implement Community law even when it contradicted federal legislation. 87

Part I – Fundamentals

C. Membership in the United Nations and other Global Organisations

88 Switzerland seems to be the only country that joined the *United Nations* on the basis of a popular vote. The first attempt failed when Swiss voters rejected membership by a margin of 3-to-1 in 1986. After the Cold War the strategic situation with regard to external security, however, completely changed and the concept of armed neutrality needed to be adapted. This paved the way for a popular initiative calling for Switzerland to accede to the U.N. This was endorsed by both parliament and government. In a close vote on 3 March 2002 the people and the cantons supported full membership of the U.N. Since September 2002, Switzerland has been a full member of the U.N. Prior to that, Switzerland had already participated in some of the U.N.'s specialised institutions and, in accordance with U.N. Security Council Resolutions, repeatedly applied U.N. economic sanctions.

89 Most important for Switzerland in regard to the world economy has been its participation in the *World Trade Organisation (WTO)* since 1 January 1995.[59] Already in 1959 Switzerland joined the General Agreement on Tariffs and Trade (GATT), the forerunner of the WTO.

90 Switzerland also participates in the *International Monetary Fund (IMF)*, an organisation that oversees the global financial system and offers financial and technical assistance. Furthermore, Switzerland works together with the *World Bank* to finance projects and deliver programs to combat poverty in the developing world.

---

[59] SR 0.632.20.

Part II – Federation, Cantons and Communes

1. Three Levels of Government: Overview

A. Federal Diversity

Switzerland is a relatively small, multilingual country with an area of 41 285 square kilometres (= 15 940 square miles) and a population of about 7.6 million.[1] State functions are divided among three levels of government: federal, cantonal and municipal.

91

The federation is composed of *26 cantons* and over *2,700 communes*. Even the latter enjoy a high degree of autonomy, varying from canton to canton. The deep-rooted concept of small self-governing entities, the result of age-long development, gives the Swiss federal system a uniquely «bottom-up» character, quite unlike the situation in countries with a powerful central bureaucracy and weak regional structures such as France or Italy.

92

The cantons and communes vary significantly in size and population. The Canton of Grisons is 191 times larger than the smallest canton, Basle-City. The city of Zurich (capital of the Canton of Zurich) has over 360,000 inhabitants, whereas the population of eight of the cantons (Uri, Obwalden and Nidwalden, Glarus, Schaffhausen, Outer Appenzell and Inner Appenzell, Jura) is not even 80,000. In each of five of the cantons (Berne, Fribourg, Grisons, Aargau and Vaud) there are over 200 communes, some of

93

---

[1] For comparison: The State of California is more than ten times the size of Switzerland and has over 33 million inhabitants. Even two of the sixteen German member-states (Bavaria and Lower Saxony) are larger and three of them (Bavaria, Baden-Württemberg and North Rhine Westfalia) have a considerably higher population.

which have a population of less than 100! The number of communes, however, is declining as a result of amalgamation.

94 Art. 2 par. 2 Const. includes promotion of the cultural diversity of the country among its public aims. The finely meshed federal structure reflects Switzerland's *cultural and linguistic diversity*. The four *national languages* are German, French, Italian and Romansh (Art. 6 Const.). The cantons designate their own official languages.[2] 63.7% of the population speak German as its main language, 20.4% French, 6.4% Italian and only 0.5% Romansh; about 9% have other languages as their mother tongues (about 20% of the population are foreign nationals).[3] What German speaking Swiss actually speak in private life is «Schwyzerdütsch» (or Swiss German) within which there are a large number of dialects almost incomprehensible to most Germans. The situation is even more confusing with regard to Romansh (or Rhateo-Romanic). There are basically five Romansh idioms: Sursilvan, Sutsilvan, Surmiran, Putér and Vallader. The creation of a common written form of Romansh (Rumantsch Grischun), used in official texts in the Grisons since 1997, may be an invaluable contribution to the struggle of Romansh for ethnic survival, though it is almost as artificial as Esperanto.

B. The Federation

95 Pursuant to Art. 1 Const. the «*Schweizerische Eidgenossenschaft*» is composed of the Swiss people and the 26 cantons. «Eidgenossenschaft» literally means «a cooperative based on oath». In the other national languages the term confederation is used.[4] The

---

[2] In the case of the Grisons these are German, Italian and Romansh.

[3] For exact and updated information consult the homepage of the Swiss Federal Statistical Office www.statistik.admin.ch.

[4] French: Confédération Suisse; Italian: Confederazione Svizzera; Romansh: Confederaziun Svizra. The official abbreviation «CH» (for in-

term *federation* though is more accurate from a legal viewpoint. For, as we have seen, Switzerland emerged from a confederation (Staatenbund) to a federal state (Bundesstaat) as early as 1848.[5]

The Swiss Federation possesses all the features of statehood: a *state populace*, a *state territory* and *state authority*. As Art. 1 Const. sets out, the Swiss people as a whole (not only the cantons) are a constitutive element of the federation, unlike the legal situation in a confederacy of sovereign states. The Swiss territory corresponds to the sum of the cantons' territories. Consequently, all territory within Switzerland is also territory of a canton thus creating a dual territorial jurisdiction. In contrast to some other federal states, there is no exclusively federal territory directly subordinated to the federal government (like the District of Columbia and the national parks in the United States or the Australian Capital Territory). The cantons retain public authority in accordance with the constitutional framework of their powers, which means that cantonal competencies can be reduced only by amending the federal constitution.

96

C. Cantons

> **Art. 1 Const.   Swiss Confederation**
> The Swiss People and the Cantons of Zurich, Berne, Lucerne, Uri, Schwyz, Obwalden and Nidwalden, Glarus, Zug, Fribourg, Solothurn, Basle-City and Basle-Land, Schaffhausen, Outer Appenzell and Inner Appenzell, St. Gall, Grisons, Aargau, Thurgau, Ticino, Vaud, Valais, Neuchâtel, Geneva, and Jura form the Swiss Confederation.

---

stance on vehicle number plates) derives from the Latin «Confoederatio Helvetica» and avoids having to favour one of the national languages.

[5]   Cf. n. 20.

Part II – Federation, Cantons and Communes

97 The order in which the cantons are enumerated is an historic reference without legal significance. The three first mentioned cantons (Zurich, Berne, Lucerne) were the Directorate Cantons (Vororte) under the Confederate Treaty of 1815. Subsequently, the cantons are named in the chronological order of their joining the old Confederacy. In 1848, when the cantons ceded part of their sovereignty to the new Federation, the list did not include the last mentioned Canton of Jura which was formerly a part of Berne and did not receive the status of a canton until 1978.[6]

98 Six cantons have only half of a cantonal vote in connection with mandatory referendums («Kantone mit halber Standesstimme»)[7] and only one seat in the Council of States.[8] The reason for this legal phenomenon is that the cantons in question, sometimes still referred to as «half-cantons» (though the new constitution intentionally avoids such a term), are the product of divisions of former «full cantons» into two parts which occurred before Switzerland became a federal state in 1848.[9] Apart from the regulations concerning mandatory referendums and the Council of States, all cantons are *equal* from a legal viewpoint. They have the same competencies as well as the same duties and obligations among one another and in relation to the federation.

99 Cantonal constitutions regularly describe the canton as a state, republic or even as a sovereign state, although cantonal powers depend upon the distribution of competencies in the federal constitution. Cantonal constitutions need federal approval, and foreign relations are almost entirely a federal matter. Art. 3 Const.

---

[6] Cf. n. 111.
[7] Art. 142 par. 4 in conjunction with Art. 140 par. 1 Const.
[8] Art. 150 par. 2 Const.
[9] The reasons for separating Unterwalden into Obwalden and Nidwalden were mainly geographical. In the case of Basle a dispute between the City of Basle and the countryside led to the division in Basle-City and Basle-Land, whereas in Appenzell religious conflicts caused the split into the protestant Outer Appenzell and the catholic Inner Appenzell.

obviously respects cantonal sensitivities, but is somewhat contradictory in declaring that the cantons are «sovereign insofar as their sovereignty is not limited by the federal constitution». However, the question whether the cantons are states or even sovereign states is hardly of any legal or practical significance. At any rate, the cantons have many attributes of statehood: their own populace, territory and legal personality, a great number of powers in important and politically sensitive areas, and their own constitution and governmental structure. It suffices to conclude that the cantons enjoy a far-reaching autonomy in regulating their own affairs, that they levy taxes and, in addition, even participate in decision-making at the federal level.

Their *autonomy* is apparent from a number of constitutional provisions which outline the relationship between the federation and the cantons:[10] the cantons define which tasks they shall accomplish within the framework of their powers (Art. 43). They adopt their own constitutions (Art. 51) which, apart from cantonal areas of responsibility and their financing, regulate the composition and functions of the basic cantonal institutions (parliament, government and courts), acquisition of cantonal citizenship, the degree and means of direct participation of citizens in cantonal decision-making, fundamental rights in addition to those guaranteed in the federal constitution and the territorial organisation within the canton. In the implementation of federal law, the federation must leave the cantons as much latitude as possible and take their particularities into account (Art. 46 par. 3). Art. 44 et seq. puts great emphasis on federal comity and on the *cooperation between the federation and the cantons*, treating them almost as equal partners. The main purpose of a very substantial constitutional reform approved by popular vote in November 2004, was to strengthen cantonal autonomy by, inter alia, introducing a system of task and revenue sharing

100

---

[10] Arts. 42 to 53 Const.

which provides the cantons with the sources of revenue necessary to accomplish their duties. At the same time this contributes to the equality of the cantons not only in law, but also in fact, by reducing differences in financial capacity.

101 In a comparative context the centralist components of Swiss federalism may be qualified as relatively weak in comparison with quite a number of other federal states, for instance Austria, where the «Länder» are severely limited in their organisational autonomy and all courts are federal courts.[11]

102 The cantons participate in federal decision-making.

> **Art. 45 Const. Participation in Federal Decision-making**
>
> (1) In accordance with the provisions of the federal constitution the cantons participate in the decision-making process at the federal level, in particular in federal legislation.
> (2) The federation shall inform the cantons in a timely manner and comprehensively of its plans; it shall consult them if their interests are affected.

These rights to participate can be grouped as follows:

103 1. When a *mandatory referendum* is required, a majority of cantons (respectively a majority of those voting in at least twelve cantons) has to approve the proposal in addition to a majority of citizens nationwide; whereby the six «half-cantons» have one half of a cantonal vote (Art. 142 Const.). This procedure applies to *all constitutional amendments* as well as to the *most important decisions of foreign policy* like joining the United Nations or the European Union (Art. 140 par. 1 Const.). Up until now a constitutional amendment has been approved by the majority of citizens eight times but has failed to clear the

---

[11] Arts. 82 and 95 et seq. of the Austrian Constitution.

additional hurdle of approval by a majority of cantons.[12] Only three times has a proposal favoured by more than half of the cantons failed to gain the support of a majority of electors nationwide.[13] The accession to the U.N. in 2002 was approved by 54.6% of those casting their vote nationwide, but only attained the absolute minimum of twelve cantonal votes. The requirement of a double majority works in favour of minorities, namely in small, rural and mostly conservative cantons. A voter in the Canton of Uri has the same power to block a constitutional amendment or a treaty submitted to the mandatory referendum as 36 electors in the Canton of Zurich![14]

2. The cantons can also influence the *legislative process* and *decision-making in the Federal Assembly*. Pursuant to Art. 160 par. 1 Const., every canton has the right to submit *initiatives to the federal parliament*. Moreover, the cantons have to be consulted in a preparatory phase on important bills, international treaties and other projects with major implications (Art. 147 Const.). The bicameral system of parliament, modelled on the U.S. system, guarantees every canton an (almost) *equal representation in the Council of States:* 20 cantons elect two members each while the six «half-cantons» each have one seat (Art. 150 Const.).[15] At the request of eight cantons, *federal*

104

---

[12] This happened twice on 12 June 1994. The two proposals turned down intended to give the federation certain powers in cultural matters and to ease the naturalisation of young foreigners who grew up in Switzerland.

[13] Most recent example: on 24 November 2002, a popular initiative directed against so-called «abuse of the right of asylum» was narrowly approved by 12½ cantons, but rejected by 50.1% of those voting.

[14] A certain disadvantage for populous member-states with large urban areas in the constitutional revision process is not a Swiss peculiarity. According to Art. V of the U.S. Constitution an amendment has to be ratified by three-fourths of the states.

[15] In a legal sense the members of the Council of States are not agents of «their» canton; cf. n. 270.

statutes and certain *international treaties* have to be submitted to an *optional referendum* (Art. 141 Const.). This has happened only once in Swiss constitutional history when 11 cantons opposed a federal taxation bill.[16]

D. Communes

105 The new constitution dedicates a special section, composed of one article only, to the communes:

> **Art. 50 Const.**
> (1) Communal autonomy is guaranteed in accordance with cantonal law.
> (2) In its activities, the federation shall take into account the possible consequences for the communes.
> (3) In so doing, it shall consider the special situation of cities, agglomerations and mountainous areas.

106 Communal autonomy had already been protected by the Federal Supreme Court as a constitutional right of the communes long before it was written into the federal constitution. Long-standing Federal Supreme Court practice regards communes as autonomous in areas where cantonal law leaves them a «relatively important decision-making power».[17] Art. 50 par. 1 Const. clarifies, in line with this practice, that the *cantons* determine the scope of autonomy at the communal level. This scope varies from canton to canton; generally, autonomy is greater in German-speaking cantons and in trilingual Grisons than in the francophone part of Switzerland. Within the cantonal parameters, the communes organise their structures of decision-making in municipal charters. In most communes municipal assemblies, made up of all citizens

---

[16] The referendum was a success. Two thirds of those voting rejected the bill on 16 May 2004.
[17] BGE 128 I 8, Arosa (2002).

entitled to vote, decide on the most important local matters. Typically, communal matters include local police, zoning and building regulations, public utilities and the implementation of primary and pre-primary education. All communes levy taxes which, together with the annual budget, need the approval of the citizens, who also decide whether or not to accept the annual accounts. In a relatively small number of communes (especially in francophone cantons and in cities) such tasks are performed by a municipal parliament. Communal autonomy permits democratic decisions at the level most affected. Communes are also regarded as a training ground for future careers in cantonal and federal politics.[18]

Apart from the political communes *(«politische Gemeinden», «Einwohnergemeinden»)* exercising general powers and comprising all inhabitants entitled to vote, many cantons have specialised organisations dealing with educational, religious or other matters. These organisations do not have to correspond territorially with the political communes, and membership can be limited, for instance to a certain confession in parishes deciding on ecclesiastical affairs. In most cantons Protestants and Catholics are organised in corporations under public law with democratic structures of decision-making on the communal as well as cantonal level.[19]

107

Quite a number of cantons additionally divide their territory into *districts* covering a number of communes. These are usually, except in the Grisons and in the Canton Schwyz, purely administrative units and not – like the communes – legal entities with powers of self-government.

108

---

[18] For detailed information see THOMAS FLEINER / ALEXANDER MISIC / NICOLE TÖPPERWIEN, Swiss Constitutional Law, p. 134 ff.

[19] This sometimes leads to vehement clashes between Catholic Church communities and the Holy See, for instance when the Catholic Synod of the Canton of Zurich opposed the authoritarian course of a bishop (he was later transferred to the Principality of Liechtenstein) and cut contributions to diocesan funds in 1995.

2. Federal Guarantees

109 The federal constitution guarantees the existence and territory of the cantons and their constitutional order.

A. Existence and Territory of the Cantons

110 Art. 1 Const. enumerates all the cantons.[20] Art. 53 Const. guarantees their existence and their territory and provides for procedures in case of changes relating to these safeguards. These guarantees are the basis of the Swiss federal state. They command respect by the central government and cantons alike.

Art. 53 Const.   Existence and Territory of the Cantons

(1) The federation shall protect the existence and the territory of the cantons.

(2) Modifications relating to the number or status of the cantons are subject to the consent of the relevant electorate and of the cantons concerned and have to be accepted by the people and the cantons.

(3) Modifications of the territory of a canton are subject to the consent of the relevant electorate and of the cantons concerned, and have to be approved by the Federal Assembly in a federal decree.

(4) Inter-cantonal boundary adjustments may be agreed upon by treaty between the cantons concerned.

---

111 In the Const. 1874 there were no provisions on how to proceed in the event of modifications relating to the number or status of cantons. This caused problems of a constitutional dimension perceived in connection with endeavours to reunite the Cantons of Basle-City and Basle-Land, and would become most apparent during the controversies that eventually led to the *creation of the Canton of Jura* in 1978. Art. 53 Const. anchors principles and

---

[20] Cf. n. 97.

2. Federal Guarantees

rules developed on a case-by-case basis. Art. 53 par. 2 Const. is a direct consequence of lessons learnt from the Jura crisis: at the Congress of Vienna (1814/15), the Jura districts[21] (which had belonged to the Prince-Bishopric of Basle for about 800 years) were given to Canton Berne as compensation for the loss of former subject territories in other cantons (Vaud and Aargau). While the residents of the southern districts of the Jura, who were mostly Protestant like the Bernese, welcomed the decision, the mainly Catholic northern districts rejected it. A strong separatist movement (which had been latent for a long time) re-emerged and troubled Swiss politics from 1947 onwards, leading to violent confrontations in the sixties. A cascade of plebiscites fixing the borderlines of a new Canton of Jura were organised in the seventies. The first of these took place in the Canton of Berne, then in all Jura districts, and afterwards in the three southern districts that had opted to remain within the Canton of Berne, as well as in the communes which hat voted on different borderlines to the majority of their district. The new Canton of Jura now comprised of the three northern districts and some adjoining communes. A constitutional convention, elected by the people of the future canton, drafted a cantonal constitution which was subsequently approved in a popular vote. The Canton of Jura was added to the Swiss federal landscape with nationwide approval by the people and the cantons in a mandatory referendum held on 24 September 1978.

Art. 53 Const. distinguishes between three different cases relating to modifications to the existence, status and territory of the cantons:

1. The modification may concern the *number of cantons* or their *status* (Art. 53 par. 2 Const.).[22] The consent of the relevant

112

---

[21] Districts are administrative units; cf. n. 108.
[22] The status is only mentioned explicitly in the French text. The status of a canton is modified when two cantons with half a cantonal voice and only one seat in the Council of States (cf. n. 98) are amalgamated to one

electorate, i.e. those with domicile in the territories concerned, is a prerequisite. This is in line with the general rule that political rights shall be exercised at the place of domicile (Art. 39 par. 2 Const.). As the Jura case demonstrates, a number of plebiscites may be necessary. In any event, the electorate of the cantons concerned has to agree. Finally, the Swiss electorate and the electorate in a majority of cantons must sanction the modification – a procedure which always necessitates constitutional amendments.[23]

113 2. A modification can leave the existence and status of all cantons intact but modify *cantonal territory* (Art. 53 par. 3 Const.). In this case too, the relevant electorate in the territory concerned and the cantons involved have to agree. Such modifications no longer require the acceptance in a mandatory nationwide referendum, as was the case under the old constitution.[24] Instead, any change of territory needs the approval of the Federal Assembly in the form of a federal decree which is subject to an optional referendum pursuant to Art. 163 par. 2 Const.

114 3. Mere *adjustments of cantonal boundaries* (Art. 53 par. 4 Const.) can be effected by treaty agreement between the cantons concerned. Boundary adjustments with neighbouring countries are not specifically mentioned in the constitution. They are a federal matter, decided in consultation with the canton concerned and the approval of the Federal Assembly.[25]

---

regular canton or when such cantons are elevated to the status of separate «full» cantons. In the case of Basle-City and Basle-Land both options have been discussed.

[23] Apart from Art. 1, the provision concerning the composition of the Council of States (Art. 150) would be affected. Modifying the status of a canton would also affect the required majority for referenda submitted to the people and the cantons (Art. 142 par. 4).

[24] Example: change of the commune Vellerat from Canton Berne to Canton Jura in 1996.

[25] Cf. Art. 54, 55 and 166 par. 2 Const.

B. Cantonal Constitutions

Most constitutions of federal states establish certain standards with which the constitutions of their member-states have to comply. They aim to secure a certain degree of compatibility between the governmental systems and basic principles, and to prevent violations of federal law. In return, the federation will protect the constitutional order of its components against external or domestic assaults. The U.S. Constitution confines itself to guaranteeing to every state a republican form of government.[26] The German Basic Law is more specific, requiring among other things that the constitutions of the «Länder» must conform to the principles of republican, democratic and social government based on the rule of law, as set out in the Basic Law.[27]

As we have seen, the cantons enjoy a very high degree of autonomy.[28] Yet, in exercising their constitution-making power, they have to respect important standards set by the federal constitution, and they have to submit their constitutions to the Federal Assembly for approval.

Art. 51 Const.   Cantonal Constitutions

(1) Every canton shall adopt a democratic constitution. The constitution must be approved by the people, and must be subject to revision if a majority of the electorate so requires.

(2) Cantonal constitutions must be guaranteed by the federation. The federation shall grant this guarantee provided there are no provisions contrary to federal law.

Basically, the content of a cantonal constitution has to be in accord with two requirements: compliance with federal law and adherence to democracy (as specifically understood in the Swiss context).

---

[26] Art. IV section 4 U.S.Constitution.
[27] Art. 28 par. 1 German Basic Law.
[28] Cf. n. 100.

117 *Compliance with federal law* (Art. 51 par. 2 [2]) means that the constitution has to be consistent with federal law on all levels, including statutory law and ordinances. As international law is part of the domestic legal order,[29] federal law also includes international treaties ratified by Switzerland such as the ECHR or the U.N. Covenant on Civil and Political Rights (CCPR).

118 The requirement of a *democratic constitution* (Art. 51 par. 1 [1] presupposes a cantonal parliament elected by the people in universal, equal, free, direct and secret elections. In addition, it calls for a division of powers between parliament, government and judiciary, since an all-powerful parliament would hardly be in line with the essential prerequisites of a modern democracy. While the federal constitution contents itself with a system of representative democracy in the cantons for ordinary legislation, it goes a step further with regard to passing and amending constitutional norms: par. 1 (2) of the article cited above requires a *mandatory constitutional referendum* («must be approved by the people») and a *popular initiative in constitutional matters* if a majority of the electorate so requires. All cantons are content with a much lower number of signatures for constitutional initiatives. Furthermore, the cantons also introduced the need for referenda and popular initiatives for ordinary legislation.

119 For every adoption and reform of their constitution the cantons are obliged to obtain *federal approval* (Art. 51 par. 2 [1]). It is the task of the Federal Assembly to «guarantee» cantonal constitutions (Art. 172 par. 2 Const.). This competency is noteworthy as the approval is not primarily a discretionary decision, but rather one that has to be based on a review of the compatibility of cantonal norms with federal law and with democracy as outlined in Art. 51 Const. – a task better suited to judicial review. The desirability and expediency of the provisions submitted for approval is not a relevant criterion. The Federal Supreme Court treats par-

---

[29] Cf. n. 37.

liamentary competency as a sort of special jurisdiction as it regards itself bound by parliamentary approval, i.e. it refuses to review the conformity with superior law, unless the latter has been modified since the Federal Assembly's decision.[30]

It is rare for the Federal Assembly to refuse to approve cantonal 120 constitutional amendments. The most famous instance concerned an article in the brand-new constitution of the Canton of Jura. The article in question claimed to re-unite the southern districts, which had opted to remain within Canton Berne, with Canton Jura «after an orderly separation in accordance with federal law and the law of the canton concerned». The federal parliament agreed with the federal government that such a provision contradicted the federal guarantee of cantonal territory and the (then unwritten) principle of federal comity.[31] This interpretation is not easy to defend from a purely legal point of view, as the legality of a modification of territory was reserved. In refusing to approve this provision, it is likely that the federal authorities took political considerations into account to avoid jeopardising the consensus eventually reached after the protracted Jura crisis, and immediately prior to a nationwide referendum on the creation of Canton Jura.

C. Protection of the Constitutional Order in the Cantons

Art. 52 Const. empowers the federation to protect the constitu- 121 tional order of the cantons, and to intervene if the public order of a canton is disrupted or threatened and cannot be restored by the canton alone or with the help of other cantons. Federal interventions to safeguard the inner security within a canton have scarcity value. Since 1848, there have been only ten such cases,

---

[30] As in the case of women's right to vote in Inner Appenzell, cf. n. 50.
[31] BBl 1977 II 273 et seq., 1977 III 256.

the last one occurring in the thirties in Geneva. Good collaboration between the cantons and their police forces, if necessary complemented with the support of federal resources, have made such interventions unnecessary. Art. 58 par. 2 sentence 2 Const., in conjunction with Art. 83 of the Federal Military Law[32], permits the deployment of army units to support cantonal (and federal) authorities should they have to deal with serious threats to internal security or cope with other exceptional circumstances. In anticipation of events which could seriously threaten security and require the assignment of large numbers of police, such as the World Economic Forum in Davos or European football championships, preventive measures coordinated with other cantons and the federal authorities are more effective than intervention after the fact.

3. Distribution of Competencies

A. Methods of Allotment in a Comparative View

122 Theoretically, there are three possible ways to distribute power between the federation and the member-states in a federal constitution:

1. enumerate the competencies of the federation and of the member-states;
2. list the competencies given to the federation, while the states retain all residual power;
3. list the competencies of the member-states, leaving the residual power to the federation.

123 The first model is bound to cause gaps in the federal system: every time a new task calling for statutory regulation comes up,

---

[32] Of February 3, 1995; SR 510.10.

for instance in response to new technologies such as IVF treatment, neither the federation nor the states would be competent to act until a constitutional amendment had clarified the situation. This complication could be avoided by giving one of the two entities residual power. The third model (residual power of the federation) is sometimes regarded as too centralist, as newly arising tasks automatically go to the federation.[33] Therefore, the second variant, *enumerating all federal competencies and leaving the residual power to the states*, is the predominant method applied in federal states.[34] This scheme was already being advocated in the eighteenth century by JAMES MADISON in the *Federalist Papers*.[35]

Whereas the U.S. Constitution enumerates most federal powers in Art. I section 8 relating to the powers of Congress, modern federal constitutions distinguish between the horizontal and the vertical separation of powers. This is achieved by drawing a demarcation line between federal competencies and powers available to the states in special chapters.[36]

124

Central government can embrace the right to legislate in a given area *and* execute laws, or simply exercise the right to legislate. Under U.S. constitutional law the execution of federal laws is basically the concern of federal authorities, while state administrations implement state law (or participate voluntarily in the execution of federal law). In European federal states on the other

125

---

[33] This model has been realized in Canada. Cf. Section 91 et seq. of the Canadian Constitution Act 1867.

[34] Examples: U.S. Constitution Amendment X; Arts. 106 to 108 Australian Constitution; Arts. 30 and 70 par. 1 German Basic Law; Art. 15 par. 1 Austrian Constitution.

[35] *Federalist Papers*, No. 45: «The powers delegated by the proposed Constitution to the federal government are few and defined. Those which are to remain in the state governments are numerous and indefinite.»

[36] Cf. as an example, the German Basic Law, VII: Legislative Power of the Federation; VIII: Execution of Federal Laws and Federal Administration; VIIIa: Joint Tasks.

Part II – Federation, Cantons and Communes

hand, the implementation of federal law is predominantly delegated to the member-states (so called *executive federalism*). The German Basic Law differentiates between three modes of executing federal law: i) execution by the «Länder» as matters of their own concern, which is the rule, ii) execution by the «Länder» as agents of the federation and iii) direct federal administration.[37]

126 The *scope* of federal competency to legislate can be *comprehensive* or *limited*. In the former, the federation is authorised to regulate all matters pertaining to a specific area, such as civil or criminal law. In the second case, the competency is only *partial*, for instance if the power to tax is limited to specific taxes such as the value-added tax. Finally, competency may be restricted in such a way that the federation can only establish a *framework* or *guidelines* in a skeletal law.[38]

127 A further distinction focuses on the *effect* a federal power has *on the jurisdiction of the member-states*. In the case of *exclusive* federal competency member-states lose their jurisdiction at the moment the federal power is established in the constitution, unless federal law explicitly makes a reservation.[39] As a rule, federal competencies are not exclusive but *concurrent*, i.e. they have a subsequent derogating effect only. Art. 72 par. 1 of the German Basic Law expresses this legal situation succinctly:

> «On matters within the concurrent legislative powers the Länder have authority to legislate as long as, and to the extent that, the federation does not make use of its legislative power.»

In many situations this legal construct prevents anarchy: for instance, if the power to enact penal law is transferred to the fed-

---

[37] Art. 83 et seq. German Basic Law.

[38] Example: Art. 75 German Basic Law gives the federation the right to enact general rules in a number of areas like higher education or the status of the press and films.

[39] Cf. Art. 71 and 73 of the German Basic Law; the list includes matters like foreign affairs, defence, currency, and air traffic.

eration, state penal codes remain in force unless and until they have been replaced by a federal code (this took 43 years in Switzerland!). Otherwise, state penal codes could not be amended and criminal offences which occurred in the interim could not be prosecuted.

It is also possible that the federation and the member-states act simultaneously and independently from each other in a given area of responsibility, for instance, when both are authorised to run universities; here federal competency is *parallel*.

B. Swiss Method of Assigning Tasks

The Swiss Constitution, like most constitutions in federal states, *enumerates the federal competencies,* while the *cantons retain all residual power.*

> **Art. 42 Const. Tasks of the Federation**
> The federation shall accomplish the tasks which are attributed to it by the constitution.

Originally, this article contained a second paragraph stating that the federation «shall assume the tasks that require uniform regulation». A constitutional reform in 2004 replaced this provision with the following: «The federation assumes only those tasks that either exceed the capacity of the cantons or require uniform regulation» (Art. 43a par. 1 Const.). The purpose of these norms was to emphasise that the establishment of new federal competencies and the use of existing ones ought to be in line with the *principle of subsidiarity,* anchored in a new Art. 5(a) Const. These provisions were by no means intended to open up federal competencies not based on a *specific authorisation* in the constitution. In the absence of such assignment, the task remains within the residual power of the cantons.

130 Sometimes cantonal competencies are explicitly mentioned in order to clarify or to modify the scope of residual cantonal power, for instance, when the constitution delegates the implementation of federal legislation to the cantons, as in the case of environmental protection.[40]

131 In enumerating federal tasks the Swiss constitution avoids blanket clauses.[41] The duties assigned to the federation are circumscribed rather precisely, normally referring to a *specific subject* like civil defence (Art. 61), protection of forests (Art. 77), national highways (Art. 83), banking and insurance (Art. 98), or to a *field of law*, such as civil law (Art. 122). The competency may also focus on a *complex problem* of public concern that affects different areas of law, as in the case of protection of the environment (Art. 74). Art. 2 Const., which states public aims in a very general way, is not a basis for deducing a federal power. The same applies to the social goals listed in art. 41 Const. Both norms formulate guidelines which the federation *and* the cantons must strive to comply with.

132 The assignment of competencies in the constitution is *complete* and *conclusive*. However, this does not exclude the interpretation of provisions relating to federal powers in such a way as to lead to the subsumption of a novel task under an already existing norm.[42] Where this is not justifiable, the matter falls within residual cantonal jurisdiction. Federal statutory norms in such cases can only be enacted following transferral of the relevant cantonal competency to the federation. This requires constitutional amendment which, in turn, has to be approved by a double majority, i.e. by the citizens nationwide and in more than

---

[40] Art. 74 par. 3 Const. Without such a proviso it is up to the federal legislator to designate the entity responsible for implementing the law.

[41] Unlike the power of the U.S. Congress to «provide for ... the general welfare of the United States» in Art. I section 8 par. 1 U.S. Constitution.

[42] Cf. an example in n. 52.

3. Distribution of Competencies

half of the cantons.[43] Even the consensus of all cantons to transfer a power to the federation cannot replace constitutional revision.

The preceding comments may give the impression that cantonal 133 and federal powers constitute two domains completely separate from each other. This would not be correct. Art. 44 Const. emphasises that the federation and the cantons must collaborate and support each other in the fulfilment of their tasks, owing each other mutual respect and support. Federal authorities have to keep the cantons informed of their plans and consult with them every time cantonal interests are affected (Art. 45 par. 2 Const.).

The *scope of a federal power* emanates from the text and interpretation 134 of the constitutional provision in question. The formulations used are not always consistent: a *comprehensive competency to legislate* is expressed in different ways: by calling a subject a «federal matter»,[44] by stating that the federation «shall legislate»,[45] or that the federation «shall ensure»,[46] or even by stating that the federation «shall take measures».[47] Such powers to legislate regularly include the competency to determine whether the cantons or federal agencies must implement the law, unless the constitution reserves this function for the cantons.[48]

Partial competencies are widespread with regard to taxation. The 135 bulk of direct taxes is levied by the cantons and the communes. The federation is confined to raising those taxes specified in the constitution, i.e. a direct tax on a severely limited percentage of

---

[43] Cf. n. 103.
[44] Art. 60 par. 1 Const. (organisation, instruction and equipment of the army).
[45] Art. 74 par. 1 Const. (protection of the environment).
[46] Art. 104 Const. (agriculture).
[47] Art. 100 par. 1 (economic development policy).
[48] Cf. n. 130.

the income of individuals and the net profit, capital and reserves of legal entities (Art. 128 Const.), a value added tax (Art. 130 Const.), special consumption taxes (Art. 131 Const.), and stamp and withholding taxes (Art. 132 Const.). Even in the area of public health the federation has merely fragmentary powers, restricted to specific issues like the fight against contagious, widespread, or other diseases which are particularly dangerous to humans and animals (Art. 118 Const.).

136 In some areas federal competencies are restricted to passing a *skeletal law*, leaving the cantons enough latitude for detailed regulations tailored to their special needs. In order to signalise such a competency, the constitution uses the phrase «the federation shall lay down principles».[49]

137 Finally, the constitution sometimes authorises the federation to «support» or «encourage» efforts in areas for which the cantons are primarily responsible, for instance the protection of nature and cultural heritage (Art. 78 par. 3 Const.). This includes the power to determine the modalities of distributing federal funds which is of enormous practical significance in, for instance, research carried out at cantonal universities.[50]

138 As far as the *effect on the jurisdiction of the cantons* is concerned, almost all federal powers belong to the category of *concurrent competencies*. This means that cantonal laws in their respective fields remain applicable and can even be amended by the cantonal legislature as long as, and to the extent that, the federation has not made use of its legislative powers. The federal lawmaker can postpone legislation or decide to regulate only some questions in the relevant area. In this case the cantons remain competent to regulate those matters not covered by federal rules. To

---

[49] Art. 129 par. 1 (harmonisation of taxes).
[50] Cf. Federal Law on Research of October 7, 1983 (SR 420.1), based on Arts. 63a and 64 Const.

make matters clearer, a federal law may expressly delegate rule-making power to the cantons. It is also admissible to establish a federal order and at the same time to allow additional or even divergent cantonal rules when complete unification does not seem appropriate.[51]

In exceptional cases, federal competencies are *exclusive*. In these areas there is, from the outset, no room for cantonal regulations. Sometimes the exclusiveness is unambiguous, for instance when Art. 99 par. 1 Const. states that the federation «alone» shall have the right to mint coins and to issue bank notes. However, the inference of an exclusive power can also be a matter of interpretation: pursuant to Art. 133 Const., legislation on customs duties is a federal matter. The exclusiveness of this competency follows not from the wording, but from a historical and teleological interpretation, as the abolishment of customs duties between the cantons was an essential attribute of the federal state created in 1848.

139

Parallel competencies, enabling the simultaneous and independent exercise of power by the federation and the cantons, do exist, for instance in the field of direct taxation, although federal power is limited to a percentage of the income, net profits and capital.[52] Another example concerns universities: the federation operates two renowned institutes of technology *(Eidgenössische Technische Hochschulen, ETH)* in Zurich and Lausanne, based on Art. 63a par. 1 Const. Parallel to these two institutions there are a number

140

---

[51] Examples: federal penal and civil codes contain comprehensive regulations. Yet Art. 335 par. 2 of the Penal Code (SR 311.0) reserves cantonal norms on contraventions (i.e. minor criminal offenses) as far as they are not covered by federal law. The Code of Obligations (SR 220) sets forth, inter alia, extensive regulations on civil liability which are even applicable to cantonal civil servants. Art. 61, on the other hand, reserves divergent cantonal rules.

[52] Cf. n. 135.

Part II – Federation, Cantons and Communes

of cantonal universities with overlapping activities in teaching and research.

141 Sometimes the constitution combines the allocation of a power to the federation with *principles that shall determine the legislation*. An illustrative example is Art. 112 Const. pertaining to social insurance for the elderly, dependents, and the disabled: The insurance is obligatory. Pensions must cover basic living expenses appropriately and be adjusted to the effects of inflation. The maximum pension is limited to twice the amount of the minimum pension. Further detailed guidelines concern the financing of the insurance.

142 As far as the *implementation* of statutory federal law by the judiciary and the administration is concerned, the constitution rarely assigns it to either the federation or the cantons. In practice, the most important allocation in favour of the cantons concerns the administration of justice in the fields of civil and criminal law, whereby an appeal to the Federal Supreme Court can still be filed against the judgments of cantonal courts of last resort.[53] In the absence of such a proviso it is up to the federal lawmaker to assign law enforcement responsibilities. As a rule, cantons are entrusted with executing federal law, a power they often delegate to the communes. To take a simple example: A municipal authority, elected by the communal electorate, issues a building permit. In so doing it not only applies cantonal and communal building and zoning laws, but even federal norms on protection of the environment, water resources and forests. Only a few tasks within the sphere of federal competencies, such as foreign relations, customs clearance, postal and rail services, are directly administered by federal office-holders. A model of growing importance, successfully tested for decades in areas like higher education, the protection of employees, zoning, or building and maintaining national highways, involves both federal and cantonal agencies

---

[53] Arts. 122 par. 2, 123 par. 2 and 189 Const.

in administrating the law. A new provision, passed in November 2004, paves the way for a promising co-operation:

> **Art. 46 al. 2 Const.**
> The federation and the cantons may agree that the cantons achieve certain goals in implementing federal law, and execute programs, assisted with federal funds, to that end.

C. Competencies of the Federation: Overview

Title 3 of the constitution concerning «Federation, Cantons, and 143 Communes» contains three chapters: 1. Relationship between the Federation and the Cantons; 2. Powers; 3. Finances. Most federal competencies are to be found in Chapter 2 (Art. 54–125) and in Chapter 3 (Art. 126–135). A number of provisions in other parts of the constitution also enumerate federal powers.[54]

Art. 54 et seq. Const. list diverse subject matters, beginning with 144 relations with foreign countries. The rather intricate constitutional situation in this field deserves more detailed comment. Other areas of responsibility, some of which have already been mentioned, will be referred to briefly in order to illustrate the different means of allocating competencies.

Foreign affairs are a federal matter (Art. 54 par. 1 Const.). This in- 145 cludes the power of the federation to conclude *international treaties*. Formerly, scholars could not agree on whether or not the federal treaty-making power included any treaty, whatever its subject-matter, even if it fell within the domain of cantonal powers, such as questions concerning cantonal taxes, schools or police power. Many years ago, LUZIUS WILDHABER discussed this con-

---

[54] Examples: Art. 38 (acquisition and loss of citizenship, fragmentary federal competency); Art. 39 (exercise of political rights in federal matters). Title 5 (Federal Authorities) includes federal rule-making powers with regard to the organisation and procedures of federal authorities.

troversy in detail in a comparative study.[55] Writers advocating a so-called «federalist» interpretation argued that the federation had the power to conclude treaties only with respect to matters which were within its competency such as customs administration, civil and criminal law. The «centralists» countered that the power to conduct foreign affairs had to be regarded as an independent substantive source of federal power including matters otherwise within cantonal jurisdiction. The latter viewpoint prevailed and has since become long-standing practice. Thus, the federation has concluded a number of treaties in areas such as the prevention of double taxation, legal assistance or the enforcement of foreign judgments. However, the federal authorities are obliged to take into consideration the powers of the cantons and to protect their interests (Art. 54 al. 3 Const.). The new constitution emphasises the right of cantons to participate in decisions concerning foreign affairs:

Art. 55 Const. Cantonal Participation in Foreign Policy Decisions
(1) The cantons participate in the preparation of foreign policy decisions affecting their competencies or their essential interests.
(2) The federation must inform the cantons in time and comprehensively, and consult with them.
(3) The responses of the cantons must be given particular weight when their powers are affected. In these areas, the cantons will participate in international negotiations as appropriate.

146 Such safeguards are commendable in view of the growing impact of international treaties on domestic law which threaten to undermine the equilibrium essential in a federal state. However, cantonal participation in foreign policy is not unproblematic from a democratic point of view, as it is usually performed by the

---

[55] LUZIUS WILDHABER, Treaty-Making Power and Constitution, Helbing & Lichtenhahn, Basle 1971, p. 310 et seq.

3. Distribution of Competencies

executive and is not necessarily based on decisions made by cantonal parliaments or the electorate.

Within the scope of their powers cantons may also conclude treaties with foreign countries (Art. 56 Const.). As the federation has concurrent competency, cantonal treaties are only permitted in matters not covered by federal treaties. Furthermore, the cantons have to inform the federation before concluding a treaty, and may deal directly only with lower ranking foreign authorities;[56] in other cases, the proceedings are to be conducted by the federation acting on their behalf. Pursuant to international law, the federation also bears responsibility for the implementation of such treaties. Treaties concluded by cantons usually concern relations with immediate neighbours. Cross-border cooperation between adjacent border areas has led to a number of treaties and even to the establishment of special institutions. An interesting example is the association called *Regio Basilensis* in the «three countries' corner» stretching across a number of northern Swiss cantons (Basle-City, Basle-Land, Aargau, Solothurn and Jura) as well as French and German territory (Alsace and Baden-Württemberg).[57]

147

In the area of *security, national and civil defence*[58] the responsibilities of both the federation and the cantons are involved. Both shall provide, within the framework of their respective powers, for the security of the country and the protection of the people. Roughly speaking, the army is federal, and the police cantonal. Legislation on *military matters,* and the organisation, training and equipment of the army, is a federal matter. The army's main

148

---

[56] I.e. below the *central* government. Direct contacts with the governments of German or Austrian «*Länder*» are quite frequent.

[57] This association, founded in 1963, initiated intensive co-operation resulting in a number of important cross-border projects such as the EuroAirport Basle / Mulhouse / Freiburg and a rapid rail-transit system.

[58] Arts. 57–61 Const.

tasks, as outlined in the constitution, are to prevent war, maintain peace, defend the country and protect its population, support civil authorities in their efforts to repel serious threats to internal security, or to master other exceptional situations. Moreover, the constitution formulates principles that are the basis of statutory regulations: every Swiss male must render military service, although statutory law also provides for an alternative form of service. In principle, the army is organised as militia, not as a professional army. Legislation on *civil defence* is also a federal competency. Its purpose is to protect persons and property against the consequences of armed conflicts and to intervene in catastrophes and emergencies. To a great extent responsbility for its implementation rests with the cantons. Traditonally the *police* has always been a cantonal domain. However, the federation plays a leading role in preserving external and internal security and in fighting serious crimes like money laundering. The Federal Public Prosecutor investigates and prosecutes specific criminal offences directed against the state or the general public, such as espionage, crimes caused by the use of explosives, assaults on federal officials or counterfeiting money.

149 The responsibility for *education, research, and culture*[59] lies mainly with the cantons. Education and culture as well as the relationship between church and state have always been regarded as cantonal domains. However, a constitutional revision in 2006 emphasised the duty of the cantons and the federation to co-operate and coordinate their efforts to achieve high quality education in Switzerland, including permeability between vocational training and studies at the tertiary level. The constitution obliges the cantons to provide sufficient, compulsory and free primary education under state direction or supervision. The cantons must also ensure an adequate education for handicapped children and young people up to the age of 20. The federation can establish

---

[59] Arts. 61a–72 Const.

principles to harmonise certain questions such as the duration of compulsory education. Furthermore, the federation can legislate on professional education. In the field of university education, for example, a new Art. 63a Const. contains detailed provisions which provide for contractual agreements, common institutions and federal competency to regulate certain other aspects. Since 1973 the federation has had the power to encourage scientific research and to make its support conditional upon taking co-ordinative measures and meeting other requirements. In addition to the two institutes of technology (ETH),[60] the federation also supports a sports school and promotes sport education. Culture and language are predominantly cantonal matters, but the federation is authorised to support cultural activities of national interest and to nurture languages.

A section entitled *environment and land use planning*[61] assigns comprehensive legislative competency to the federation in the following areas: the protection of human beings and their natural environment against harmful effects and nuisance; topographic surveys; water protection and the securing of sufficient residual water; protection of plant and animal life (particularly endangered species), and the treatment of animals. With regard to land use planning and the protection of forests, fishery and hunting, the federation has the power to pass 'skeleton' laws only. Zoning and building law is predominantly a cantonal matter within certain principles established by federal legislation. The federation may also support cantonal efforts towards the protection of the landscape and cultural heritage. Even where detailed federal regulations exist, implementation is almost entirely left to the cantons.[62]

150

---

[60] Cf. n. 140.
[61] Arts. 73–80 Const.
[62] Cf. the example in n. 142.

Part II – Federation, Cantons and Communes

151 The federation may, in the interests of the country, or of a large part of it, build and operate *public works* or promote their realisation; this power has considerable practical impact in connection with the federation's various obligations concerning *traffic*.[63] Thus, the federation has to ensure the construction and maintenance of a network of national highways and legislate on rail and road traffic, cable cars, navigation, aviation and activities in outer space. The section dedicated to traffic deals with the duties to be imposed on heavy goods traffic and excise on motor fuel as well as the use of national highways. It also contains detailed directives about the protection of alpine regions from transit traffic by limiting drastically border-to-border transit on the roads.[64] The federation may even lay down principles regarding a network of paths and trails.

152 Competencies in the field of *energy and communication* are outlined in a further section.[65] Concerning energy, the federation has comprehensive power to regulate nuclear energy, the transport and supply of energy, including pipelines for transporting liquid or gaseous fuels, and the consumption of energy by fixed installations, vehicles, and appliances. Moreover, the federation may establish principles for the use of domestic and renewable energy and the economical and efficient use of energy. Measures concerning the use of energy in buildings are primarily a cantonal matter. Within their respective powers, the federation and the cantons have a constitutional obligation to work towards a sufficient, reliable and efficient energy supply compatible with the protection of the environment, and the economical and rational use of energy. With regard to communications, the constitution declares postal and telecommunication services a federal matter, and gives the federation comprehensive power to legislate on ra-

---

[63] Arts. 81–88 Const.
[64] This provision is the result of a popular initiative, approved in a referendum in 1994, now Art. 84 Const.
[65] Arts. 89–93 Const.

dio, television and other forms of telecommunication. The classification of a matter as federal not only includes the competency to delegate implementation to the cantons, but also to private entities. While extensive privatisation has occurred with regard to telecommunications, efforts to liberalise the energy market have so far failed; a law with this objective was rejected by popular vote in 2002.

The allotment of competencies relating to the *economy*[66] is bound up with the question of economic freedom, guaranteed in Art. 27 Const., and the conditions under which this fundamental right may be limited.[67]

153

As long as a measure is regarded as *compatible with the principle of economic freedom*, i.e. with the essence of a free market economy, the federation has comprehensive but concurrent competency to legislate on the exercise of remunerative private economic activities. Cantons will only lose their jurisdiction to the extent that such an activity is governed by federal law. There are countless cantonal laws (and sometimes even municipal regulations) affecting a wide range of professions and business activities, such as mountain guides, private detectives, marriage brokers, beauticians, dental technicians, chiropractors, physiotherapists, realtors, hotel and restaurant businesses, cinemas, or the opening hours of shops. Only recently was admission to the practise of law standardised under federal law.[68] There is also federal regulation concerning the necessary professional qualifications for physicians, dentists, veterinarians and pharmacists.[69] The constitu-

154

---

[66] Arts. 94–107 Const.
[67] Cf. n. 438 et seq.
[68] Bundesgesetz über die Freizügigkeit der Anwältinnen und Anwälte = Federal Law on the Vocational Mobility of Lawyers of 23 June 2000 (SR 935.61).
[69] Bundesgesetz über die universitären Medizinalberufe = Federal Law on Medical Professions requiring University Training of 23 June 2006 (SR 811.11).

Part II – Federation, Cantons and Communes

tion directs the federation to provide for a unified Swiss economic area, guaranteeing that persons with a university education, or a federal, cantonal or cantonally approved education certificate may exercise their professions throughout Switzerland.[70]

155 *Deviations from the principle of economic freedom*, in particular measures aimed at restraining competition, are allowed only if provided for in the federal constitution, or if based on cantonal monopolies (Art. 94 par. 4 Const.). Where the constitution admits such a deviation, the power to regulate is a federal and not a cantonal matter. The constitution explicitly assigns the following areas to federal legislation (sometimes permitting a departure from the principle of economic freedom): combatting economically or socially damaging effects of competition; consumer protection; banking, the stock exchanges and private insurance; monetary economic policy; foreign trade; supply of essential goods and services to meet military or other severe threats; structural policy to support economically threatened regions, branches or professions; agriculture; the production, importation, refining and sale of spirits; gambling and lotteries; weapons and military equipment.

156 The provisions concerning *housing, work, social security and health*[71] demonstrate how the scope of power given to the federation as well as the constitutional guidelines imposed on the legislator may vary. We have already mentioned the provisions pertaining to social security and social insurance for the elderly, dependents and disabled, to employee pension plans and to unemployment insurance.[72] In all these matters the allocation of comprehensive legislative power to the federation is combined with the formulation of a whole catalogue of principles deter-

---

[70] Sectoral agreements with the European Community and its member-states (cf. n. 82) have extended labour mobility further.
[71] Arts. 108–120 Const.
[72] Cf. n. 70 and n. 141.

3. Distribution of Competencies

mining the content of statutory law. The same applies to medically assisted procreation and human genetic engineering. Less detailed directions concern medical transplants, genetic engineering in the non-human field, regulations against abuses in landlord and tenant relationships, family allowances and maternity insurance, as well as health and accident insurance. As far as health and labour are concerned, the federation has only fragmentary powers restricted to specific issues.[73] With regard to the construction and ownership of housing, federal competency is by and large restricted to supporting relevant measures. In the case of assistance to persons in need, the constitution states the principle that they must be assisted by the canton in which they are domiciled, but does give the federation the power to provide for exceptions.

Legislation on foreigners entering, residing in and leaving the country, and on the granting of asylum are federal matters.[74] 157

The chapter on powers concludes with a section embracing *civil and criminal law;* as well as *weights and measures.*[75] As in other European federal states, but in contrast to the United States, legislation in the fields of civil and criminal law is a federal matter. These competencies were assigned to the federation as early as 1898. Cantonal statutory law continued to be valid until the national government made use of its legislative power by enacting three codes which have had a tremendous impact on legal life: the Civil Code dates from 1907, the Code of Obligations followed in 1911 and, thirty years later, the Penal Code eventually materialised. On the other hand, unlike the situation in Ger- 158

---

[73] As to health, cf. n. 135. Concerning labour, aspects pertaining to civil law are governed entirely by federal law; in addition, the federation may legislate on aspects of public labour law as specified in Art. 110 Const.

[74] Art. 121 Const. In September 2006 the Swiss electorate approved a new law on foreigners and a far-reaching revision of the law on asylum.

[75] Arts. 122–125 Const.

Part II – Federation, Cantons and Communes

many, up until now civil and criminal procedures have been governed by 26 different cantonal rules of procedure, supplemented by some federal provisions connected with specific federal tasks, such as the procedures to be followed before the Federal Supreme Court. Substantial reform concerning the judiciary, accepted by the people and the cantons in 2000, assigned comprehensive powers to the federation to regulate civil and criminal procedures.[76] Organisation of the judiciary and the administration of justice in civil and criminal law (as far as the cantonal level is concerned) remain in the cantonal domain, as is the execution of penal sentences. Legislation on weights and measures is a federal matter.

159 The power to tax is dealt with in a separate chapter concerning *finances*.[77] The federation is confined to raising a number of taxes which are enumerated in the constitution.[78] In addition to taxes, the federation may also impose duties on heavy goods traffic, the use of national highways and motor fuel.[79] Most taxes are levied by the cantons and communes. Individuals are taxed at their place of residence, companies at the place where they are registered or carry out their business activities. Apart from individual income taxes and corporate taxes, the cantons may introduce additional taxes (except the indirect taxes assigned to the federation), for instance on real estate transfers, inheritance and gifts, or motor vehicles. The tax burden for individuals and business enterprises differs greatly from canton to canton, and even within a canton among communes – much more so than in any other

---

[76] The Federal Council presented draft laws including detailed commentary in BBl 2006, p. 1085 et seq., and p. 7221 et seq. These bills have to clear parliamentary scrutiny and possible referenda, and will not come into effect before the year 2010.
[77] Arts. 126–135 Const.
[78] Cf. n. 135.
[79] Arts. 85 and 86 Const.

federal state.[80] Intense competition at cantonal and municipal levels to attract affluent taxpayers and prosperous companies, in conjunction with the citizens' involvement in deciding on the tax rates, contributes to keeping taxes in Switerzland lower than in most European countries. However, at the same time, it can also create injustice. One of the reasons for the constitutional reform of 2004 concerning *task and revenue sharing* was to alleviate some of the negative effects of fiscal federalism.

A newly adopted Art. 135 Const. on *equalisation of finances and burdens* combines two equalising measures: an equalisation of financial resources to diminish the differences in financial capacity between the cantons and to secure for every canton a minimal endowment. The funds for this measure are to be raised by the wealthier cantons and the federation. The aim is that every canton must dispose of at least 85% of the Swiss average per capita after equalisation. In addition, the equalisation of burdens is destined to alleviate extra costs incurred by certain cantons due to their topography and geographic location (for instance mountainous cantons with heavy north-south traffic like Ticino and Uri), or owing to socio-demographic factors (such as cantons with a greater proportion of old and low-income people in areas of high population density).

160

---

[80] In 2006 the tax burden (based on an overall index and including communal taxes) was 137.8% of the Swiss average in the Canton of Uri and only 52.4% in the Canton of Zug; *Neue Zürcher Zeitung* Nr. 149, 30 June 2007, p. 19.

4. Primacy of Federal Law

161 Many federal states explicitly lay down in their constitutions that federal law overrides state law.[81] This precedence presupposes that the federal legislator has acted within the competencies attributed to the federation. If not, a federal statute encroaching on state law would have no effect. In Switzerland the situtation is slightly more complicated as we are going to see.

162 Art. 49 par. 1 Const. asserts that federal law takes precedence over contrary cantonal law. International law shares this primacy, provided that it is self-executing.[82] Any legal rule emanating from a federal authority overrides conflicting cantonal law, regardless of the latter's hierarchical level. Thus, an ordinance issued by the federal government precedes a cantonal law enacted by the cantonal parliament and subjected to a referendum. A cantonal statute may violate fundamental rights guaranteed by the federal constitution or the ECHR, affect a federal power or be inconsistent with a norm in a federal law or ordinance. Conflicts are most likely to occur when a problem touches both cantonal and federal powers and the extent of a federal regulation is not quite clear, for instance whether a cantonal regulation on opening hours for shops or paid public holidays is compatible with federal legislation protecting employees. A number of disputes which the courts have had to decide concerned the relationship between federal civil law and cantonal public law, for instance whether cantonal police regulations affecting professions and business activities were compatible with federal civil law. Pursuant to the practice of the Federal Supreme Court, such norms are

---

[81] Cf. the «supremacy clause» in Art. VI par. 2 of the U.S.Constitution, or Art. 31 German Basic Law. In the EU, community law enjoys primacy in relation to national law since the judgment in Costa v. ENEL of the Court of Justice of the European Community in 1964.

[82] Due to the monistic system, international law is part of the domestic legal order (cf. n. 37).

valid under the cumulative conditions that they are justified by a public interest; that federal civil law leaves room for such a regulation; and that the norms do not contradict the meaning and spirit of federal civil law.

As a rule, the federal legislator takes care not to interfere with the residual power retained by the cantons. The federal administration regularly examines whether a bill the government wants to submit to parliament is within federal competencies. If in doubt, the question may be debated in parliamentary committees or even in a plenary session. Sometimes external constitutional experts are consulted. If, in spite of such precautions, a statute emerges which does conflict with the constitutional division of powers thus impinging upon the powers of the cantons, this statute is still factually valid, despite its apparent unconstitutionality. This extraordinary result is a consequence of Art. 190 Const. which obliges the Federal Supreme Court and other authorities to apply federal statutes irrespective of their conformity with the constitution.[83]

While cantonal statutes which conflict with federal law are regarded as null and void, and are therefore to be disregarded by courts and other bodies entrusted with judiciary functions, individual decisions based on such a statute are as a rule not invalid until they have been formally quashed. Otherwise, legal certainty would be seriously compromised. The primacy of federal law is qualified as a *constitutional right* which citizens can invoke when they challenge cantonal legislation.

---

[83] Cf. n. 562 et seq.

Part II – Federation, Cantons and Communes

5. Federal Supervision and Federal Coercion

165 Art. 49 par. 2 Const. directs the federation to ensure that the cantons respect federal law. Federal supervision varies in intensity, depending on the nature of a cantonal activity:
- If the federation has delegated a task to the cantons, as is the case with the execution of most federal statutes, the federation has to ensure that the statute is correctly implemented.
- With respect to matters largely belonging to the residual power of the cantons, such as primary education, public health, police and zoning, federal supervision is designed to prevent the cantons from violating federal law. In these areas the cantons enjoy extensive autonomous decision-making which strictly limits federal supervision to questions of legality, and excludes control over discretionary decisions.

166 Supervision may be directed at legal norms or their application. Federal supervision is basically assigned to the federal government.[84] Yet judgments of cantonal courts can only be set aside by higher courts through legal proceedings. The Federal Law on the Federal Supreme Court grants certain federal agencies the right to appeal to the Federal Supreme Court against cantonal acts that could violate federal law in their field of responsibility.[85]

167 Various supervisory means are to be considered:
- objections in a particular case;
- annulment of decisions that violate federal law;
- directives to all cantons as to how to implement federal legislation;

---

[84] Art. 182 par. 2 and Art. 186 par. 4 Const. A delegation to federal departments or administrative units subordinated to them is possible, Art. 177 par. 3 Const.

[85] Art. 89 par. 2 (a) BGG.

5. Federal Supervision and Federal Coercion

- statutory obligation to produce periodic reports;
- inspections;
- obligation to have cantonal statutes or ordinances approved by a federal agency.

These means will almost always suffice to ensure the observance of federal law. *Coercive measures* will only very rarely have to be taken, but no federal state can do without them as a last resort. When a German «*Land*» fails to comply with obligations of a federal character, the Federal Government may, with the consent of the Bundesrat (i.e. the upper house of parliament through which the «*Länder*» participate in federal legislation and administration), take the necessary compulsory measures.[86] The U.S. Constitution does not specifically mention federal coercion but seems to imply it; in practice, for example, coercive measures against the states were unavoidable in order to implement school desegregation.[87] In Switzerland, the constitutional basis for federal coercion is contained in provisions describing the powers of the Federal Assembly and the Federal Council.[88]

168

Coercive measures must respect the principle of *proportionality* and thus not exceed the degree of constraint necessary to implement a federal obligation. Some federal laws provide for *execution by substitution*, giving federal authorities the power to act instead of the cantons. To take an example: pursuant to Art. 37 of the Federal Law on Land Use Planning of 22 June 1979[89], the Federal Council may (when in spite of admonitions a canton has refused to take the necessary measures) temporarily establish specific

169

---

[86] Art. 37 German Basic Law.
[87] Cf. Brown v. Board of Education of Topeca (Brown II), 349 U.S. 294 (1955). In 1957, President Eisenhower dispatched troops to enforce the enrollment of black children at an all-white high school in Little Rock, Arkansas.
[88] Arts. 173 par. 1 (e), 182 par. 2 and. 186 par. 4 Const.
[89] SR 700.

zones to be kept free from building in order to protect imminently endangered areas of special importance for agriculture or for protection of the landscape. An extension by substitution is even regarded as admissible without an explicit legal basis. Other coercive measures include *curbing subsidies* when a canton has violated a specific obligation for which federal funds have been granted. Theoretically even *military intervention* would be possible. In practice, federal coercion or even the threat to take such measures hardly occurs. Military force has never had to be applied.[90]

6. Intercantonal Treaties

170 That cantons interact collectively to solve common problems has a long tradition in Switzerland. Due to the small size and population of Swiss cantons, intensive cooperation is even more indispensable than in other federal states. Moreover, the increasing complexity and high cost of many cantonal tasks have enhanced the necessity for close cooperation between the cantons. More recently, models have emerged that include the participation of federal authorities.

171 The most important legal instrument to achieve such cooperation is the intercantonal treaty. An intercantonal treaty is roughly parallel to an interstate compact as known in the United States. Thanks to such treaties, the more centralist solution of attributing a new power to the federation can sometimes be avoided, especially when most or even all cantons participate.

---

[90] Federal interventions aimed at restoring the public order in a canton (cf. n. 121) are intended to support the cantonal authorities and not to coerce cantons that disregard federal obligations.

6. Intercantonal Treaties

Intercantonal treaties in the legal sense are agreements between two or more cantons concerning a matter pertaining to their (residual or delegated) powers. They are governed by public law and are to be distinguished from contracts under private law (as in the case of a sales contract or a tenancy agreement relating to cantonal property).[91] They *precede cantonal law* and can cover the creation or application of law as well as the administration of justice.

The constitution dedicates two separate provisions to intercantonal treaties.

> **Art. 48 Const.   Intercantonal Treaties**
> (1) The cantons may conclude treaties, and may create common organisations and institutions. In particular, they may jointly perform tasks of regional significance.
> (2) The federation may participate within the limits of its powers.
> (3) Intercantonal treaties may not be contrary to federal law or federal interests, nor to the rights of other cantons. The federation must be notified of such treaties.
> (4) By means of an intercantonal treaty, cantons may empower intercantonal bodies to enact legal rules implementing a treaty, provided that the treaty:
>   a. has been approved by the same procedure that applies to legislation;
>   b. determines the contents of such rules in its main aspects.
> (5) The cantons shall observe intercantonal law.

Art. 48a Const., inserted in the year 2004, introduced the possibility of declaring an intercantonal treaty to be generally applicable, and of obliging cantons to join the treaty as far as certain matters which the constitution lists conclusively are concerned.

---

[91] However, an intercantonal treaty can create a company under private law with the goal of fulfilling a public task, as in the case of the treaty creating the Northeastern Swiss Electricity Supply Company (*Nordostschweizerische Kraftwerke AG*) in 1914.

Part II – Federation, Cantons and Communes

This innovation, introduced in the framework of the new model of task and revenue sharing between the federation and the cantons, was very controversial. The modalities are regulated in the Federal Law on the Equalisation of Finances and Burdens (Bundesgesetz über Finanzen- und Lastenausgleich) of 3 October 2003.[92] Pursuant to Art. 14 of this law, the *declaration of general application* requires the proposal of at least 18 cantons and a decision by the Federal Assembly subject to an optional referendum. The hurdles for obliging a canton to join an intercantonal treaty are lower: Art. 15 contents itself with the application of at least 12 cantons already participating plus a federal decree not subject to referendum.

175 Intercantonal treaties have to respect the limits on cantonal competencies. They may concern residual cantonal power, as in the case of primary education, or delegated competencies, namely with respect to implementing statutory federal law. It is not possible to create a new federal power in a treaty, as this would amount to an evasion of the procedure prescribed for amending the federal constitution.[93] Where the federation and the cantons have parallel powers, as in higher education, an intercantonal treaty including *federal participation* may be useful. Intercantonal treaties embracing *foreign contracting parties* are of growing importance for cross-border cooperation.[94]

176 Treaties establishing a special union within the federation – like the defence alliance (*Sonderbund*) of 1845 – are excluded, as they would be contrary to the rights of other cantons, federal interests and the principle of comity laid down in art. 44 Const.

177 The procedure for *accession to an intercantonal treaty* is governed by cantonal constitutional law. In particular, cantons decide

---

[92] SR 613.2.
[93] Cf. n. 506.
[94] Cf. an example in n. 147.

whether accession is to be subject to a mandatory or an optional referendum, or whether it may be decided conclusively by parliament. The anwer to this question often depends on the legal impact of the treaty.

Whereas pursuant to Art. 7 par. 2 Const. 1874 the federation had to approve intercantonal treaties, Art. 48 par. 3 sentence 2 Const. only requires that the federation be *notified*. Yet, if the Federal Council or a canton raises an objection, it is up to the Federal Assembly to decide whether to approve the treaty.[95] 178

Some treaties settle a specific problem, like the adjustment of cantonal boundaries, the administration of a penal institution with occupants from various cantons, or police operations on motorways. Others unify legal rules for the participating cantons. An illustrative example of the latter are treaties granting legal assistance in enforcing final judgments and administrative decisions emanating from bodies of other cantons. Quite a number of treaties create *common bodies*, for instance to administer an educational establishment funded by the contracting cantons. Such bodies can even be endowed with the power to legislate (Art. 48 par. 4 Const.). 179

The growing tendency to utilise intercantonal treaties for lawmaking purposes tends to strengthen federalism, as such unification of legal rules concentrates power in the hands of the cantons, thus preventing the transferral of power to the national level. On the other hand, intercantonal law-making runs the risk of weakening democracy, as the main impetus in generating such rules – that have to be negotiated with other contracting cantons – shifts even more from parliaments to governments and administrators. The possibility of empowering intercantonal bodies to enact legal rules would aggravate this concern. 180

---

[95] Art. 172 par. 3 and Art. 186 par. 3 Const. The same rules apply to treaties between cantons and foreign countries.

181 Apart from intercantonal treaties, there are manifold *other varieties of federative cooperation:* In many important areas such as education, health care or finances, the heads of cantonal departments (corresponding to ministries) meet regularly to exchange views and coordinate measures. Sometimes a representative of the federal government will join them. Thus the Conference of Cantonal Ministers of Education coordinates matters of educational policy like common teaching aids, instruction in information technology or foreign languages in primary education.[96] The conditions of admission to cantonal universities and to the two federal institutes of technology (ETH) are coordinated between the Conference of Cantonal Ministers of Education and the Federal Council. The question of prioritising heart surgery and other high-tech medical niches in distinct geographical areas and research centres, is a concern of the Conference of Cantonal Ministers of Health.

182 The *Conference of Cantonal Governments* (*Konferenz der kantonalen Regierungen, KdK*), created in 1993, provides a platform for intercantonal cooperation and lobbies most effectively for cantonal interests in the federal decision-making process.[97]

---

[96] The question whether English or a second national language ought to be taught first was the subject of lively debate which eventually led to a recommendation in favour of English.

[97] A certain parallel to the Council of State Governments established in the United States as early as 1933, is noteworthy, and not quite accidental as some of the founders of the KdK were aware of the American institution.

Part III – Citizenship and Political Rights

1. Swiss Citizenship

A. Main Features

Citizenship is a *legal status* closely linked to the identity of a person. Every Swiss has (at least) *three citizenships:* Swiss, cantonal and communal (Art. 37 par. 1 Const.). The acquisition or loss of Swiss citizenship thus necessarily means the acquisition or loss of at least one cantonal and one communal citizenship.[1]

Various *rights and duties* ensue from Swiss citizenship: political rights;[2] diplomatic protection abroad; the right to establish a domicile anywhere within the country, and to leave or to enter Switzerland (Art. 24 Const.); the right not to be expelled from the country and not to be involuntarily extradited to a foreign authority (Art. 25 par. 1 Const.); Swiss men have a duty to render military service (Art. 59 par. 1 Const.); serving in a foreign army is prohibited. Within narrow limits, the cantons and communes may state further legal consequences tied to cantonal or communal citizenship, such as the right of cantonal citizens living abroad to take part in cantonal and municipal elections, or the right to participate in municipal assets linked to the citizenship of the respective commune. However, as a general rule, no Swiss enjoys a privilege or suffers prejudice due to his or her cantonal or communal citizenship.[3]

The right of citizenship is either *acquired by law*, in other words acquired automatically when certain legally defined prerequisites are fulfilled, or by an official decree called *naturalisation*. A com-

183

184

185

---

[1] It is possible to be a citizen of several cantons and communes.
[2] Cf. n. 212 et seq.
[3] Art. 37 par. 2 (1) Const.

parison of legal systems worldwide shows that there are basically two different models of obtaining citizenship by law: a child either becomes a citizen of a parent's country at birth (*ius sanguinis* = right of blood), or a citizen of the country where it is born (*ius soli* = right of the soil). The two systems may be combined. *Ius soli*, sometimes modified by the imposition of additional requirements, is common in immigration countries that wanted to increase their own citizenry, for instance on the American continent and in Australia. *Ius sanguinis* is still the predominant means of passing on citizenship in most continental European countries. Switzerland too adheres to the *principle of ius sanguinis:* the acquisition of citizenship by law is based on ancestry; an additional point of reference is adoption.

186 Besides *ius sanguinis*, there are some more principles underlying Swiss legislation on citizenship, such as *integration into Swiss society as a prerequisite for naturalisation, avoidance of statelessness* (with the consequence that only dual citizens can be deprived of their Swiss citizenship), and (though with significant exceptions) a *tendency to extend Swiss citizenship to all members of the same family.*

B. Distribution of Competencies

> **Art. 38 Const.   Acquisition and Loss of Citizenship**
> (1) The federation shall regulate the acquisition and loss of citizenship through descent, marriage and adoption. Moreover, it shall regulate the loss of citizenship on other grounds, and the reinstatement of citizenship.
> (2) It shall establish minimum requirements for the naturalisation of foreigners by the cantons, and grant naturalisation permits.
> (3) It shall facilitate the naturalisation of stateless children.

187 The *naturalisation* of foreigners has traditionally been regarded as a cantonal domain. Within the framework of cantonal law, communes regularly play a dominant role in conferring Swiss

citizenship on foreigners. Nevertheless, the federation establishes minimum requirements, and ensures that nobody is naturalised without a permit issued by a federal authority (Art. 38 par. 2 Const.). The federation also has the responsibility of facilitating the naturalisation of stateless children (Art. 38 par. 3 Const.).

As far as the *acquisition of citizenship by law* as well as the *loss of citizenship* are concerned, the federation has a comprehensive power to legislate. Moreover, the federation may establish special procedures for *facilitated naturalisation* tied to marriage or descent (particularly when a foreigner is married to a Swiss citizen), or when someone's Swiss citizenship is to be reestablished. Unfortunately, various attempts to give the federation the power to facilitate the naturalisation of young foreigners who grew up in Switzerland could not obtain the double majority required for constitutional amendment.[4]

With regard to the acquisition of cantonal and communal citizenships in the case of marriage, Art. 161 of the Civil Code states that a wife acquires her husband's citizenship without losing the citizenzhips she held while single. In all other cases, the Federal Law on the Acquisition and Loss of Swiss Citizenship[5] is pertinent. In addition, all cantons have established rules regarding the acquisition of cantonal and communal citizenship.

C. Acquisition of Citizenship by Law

The following persons acquire Swiss citizenship automatically *at birth* (Art. 1 BüG): a child whose parents are married, if at least one of the parents is Swiss; the child of a Swiss mother who is not married to the child's father; and the minor foreign child of a

---

[4] The respective mandatory referenda were in 1983, 1994, and 2004.
[5] Of 29 September 1952, SR 141.0; abbreviation: BüG (Bürgerrechtsgesetz).

Swiss father in case of a subsequent recognition of paternity. Together with Swiss citizenship these children also attain the Swiss parent's cantonal and communal citizenships.[6] As a result cantonal and communal citizenships are passed on from generation to generation, even if the descendants live elsewhere and have lost all ties to «their» canton or commune. If a minor foreign child is *adopted* it thereby acquires the citizenships of the adopting parent (Art. 7 BüG; Art. 267 [a] Civil Code).

D. Ordinary Naturalisation

191 Naturalisation is the process by which Swiss citizenship is conferred upon an alien on application. Next to ordinary naturalisation there is a special procedure for facilitated naturalisation and for the reinstatement of citizenship. As a rule, the applicants' minor children are included in naturalisation (Art. 33 BüG); minors over the age of sixteen only if they consent (Art. 34 BüG.)

192 Naturalisation that has been obtained surreptitiously by false declarations or concealment of essential facts can be nullified (Art. 41 BüG).

193 *Ordinary naturalisation* involves the federal, cantonal as well as municipal authorities, and sometimes even the communal electorate. The Federal Office for Migration examines whether the general requirements for naturalisation have been fulfilled. These include *residence* in Switzerland for twelve years, three of which in the last five years before applying for Swiss citizenship. The time spent in Switzerland between the ages of ten and twenty counts double (Art. 15 par. 1 and 2 BüG). If foreign spouses or registered gay couples apply for citizenship jointly and one of the applicants has been living in Switzerland for at least twelve years,

---

[6] If the parents are married, the father's citizenships are decisive; Art. 4 par. 2 BüG.

the necessary time of residence is reduced for the other applicant (Art. 15 pars. 3–6 BüG). Moreover, Art. 14 BüG requires the applicant's *suitability* to become a Swiss citizen, in particular that he or she be integrated into the Swiss community, and be accustomed to Swiss traditions and the Swiss way of life. In addition, the applicant will be expected to respect the Swiss legal order and not to endanger Switzerland's internal or external security. The federal office regularly charges cantonal authorities with ascertaining the facts (which has on occasion been carried out by the police somewhat indelicately). If all the conditions have been satisfied, the Federal Office for Migration will grant a naturalisation permit. Such an authorisation is a *prerequisite of validity* for the subsequent naturalisation at cantonal and communal level, but does not accord any right to be naturalised.

Cantonal and municipal law regulate the procedures and the criteria for obtaining cantonal and communal citizenship.[7] In addition to the minimum standards established by federal law, the cantons regularly require a minimum time of residence in the canton and the commune, as well as knowledge of one of the canton's official languages. The applicant's suitability and degree of integration are judged in a more local context. The procedures involve both cantonal and municipal authorities.

194

Until recently, in many communes the power to confer citizenship on foreigners (assuming federal authorisation) was held by the municipal electorate which decided in either a convened assembly or by secret ballot. That prejudices on the grounds of an applicant's origin or race could influence or even determine the outcome of the vote seems obvious. Thus, in a popular referendum in the municipality of Emmen (Canton Lucerne) in March

195

---

[7] Such regulations may also pertain to Swiss citizens who already have the citizenship of a different canton. In the text the focus is on *foreigners* applying for Swiss citizenship. They normally have to meet stricter requirements and undergo more cumbersome procedures.

Part III – Citizenship and Political Rights

2000, the electorate approved of all four applications submitted by Italian citizens but declined all sixteen applications submitted by persons from the former Yugoslavia. Similar events occurred elsewhere. Numerous Swiss, especially in rural areas, are inclined to regard votes concerning the naturalisation of foreigners as a purely political act that may be exercised arbitrarily, like the casting of a vote at an election. Not so the Federal Supreme Court. In two landmark cases decided in July 2003, the Court declared that secret ballots on the naturalisation of foreigners violated the federal constitution.[8] The Court argued as follows: when the electorate decides on the application of an individual it performs a state activity which is based on and limited by the law (Art. 5 par. 1 Const.) and, as such, must respect fundamental rights (Art. 35 par. 2 Const.). In this context, the *prohibition of discrimination* (Art. 8 par. 2 Const.) and the *right to be heard* (Art. 29 par. 2 Const.) are of special relevance. The right to be heard includes an obligation on the part of the relevant authority to give reasons for negative decisions touching upon an applicant's legal status. Decisions based on secret ballots inherently lack justification. Yet the Federal Supreme Court did not rule out the possibility of letting the electorate decide on naturalisations all together. In a subsequent judgment it demonstrated that a justifiable decision can be reached in a communal assembly, provided that the discussions and voting are conducted properly.[9]

196 The summarised court judgments gave rise to heated political debate. A popular initiative, which demanded that the electorate of every commune determine in the municipal charter the organ responsible for conferring communal citizenship, and that this decision be final, only just gathered the necessary 100,000 signa-

---

[8] BGE 129 I 217 (2003), Emmen; 129 I 232 (2003), Swiss Popular Party.
[9] BGE 130 I 140 (2004), Canton Schwyz.

tures.[10] In June 2008, this initiative was overwhelmingly rejected by the voters nationwide and by all but one canton.

The new case law has certainly made a contribution to the rule of law. It encouraged some cantons and many communes to shift decisions concerning naturalisation from the electorate to elected bodies that decide after a thorough evaluation of the relevant files. This development is in line with the insight that naturalisations are not purely political acts but are primarily individual decisions guided and limited by legal rules. 197

E. Facilitated Naturalisation and Reinstatement of Citizenship

Simplified naturalisation is granted by the Federal Office for Migration to an applicant who satisfies the requirements stated in the federal law and whose suitability is not in doubt. The canton concerned is consulted, but has no veto power. The main factor giving access to facilitated naturalisation is *marriage*.[11] The spouse of a Swiss man or woman can obtain Swiss citizenship (including the spouse's cantonal and communal citizenships) after three years of having lived together as a married couple when he or she has resided in Switzerland for a total of five years and at least the last year before filing the application (Art. 27 BüG). If a married couple has lived together abroad for six years, the foreign spouse can obtain Swiss citizenship if he or she has close connections with Switzerland (Art. 28 BüG). 198

The reinstatement of Swiss citizenship is also regulated exclusively by federal law, and follows the same procedure as facili- 199

---

[10] Only 100,038 signatures were valid; BBl 2006, 8954.
[11] Under a patriarchal regulation in force until the end of 1991, a foreign woman (but not a man) obtained Swiss citizenship automatically when she married a Swiss citizen.

tated naturalisation. Such reinstatement is possible for former Swiss citizens who lost their citizenship by law and omitted to declare that they wished to maintain it for justifiable reasons (Art. 21 BüG).[12] Furthermore, persons who have voluntarily given up their Swiss citizenship can apply for a reinstatement after having resided in Switzerland for one year (Art. 23 BüG). In both cases, the applicant has to demonstrate, among other things, close ties to Switzerland (Art. 18 BüG).

F. Loss of Citizenship

200 Swiss citizenship can be lost either automatically when legally defined situations arise (loss by law), or by official decree. The most important case of *loss by law* concerns Swiss citizens who were born and have lived abroad. They automatically lose their citizenship at the age of 22, but under two conditions only: if they are a national of another country and, in addition, they have not declared to a Swiss authority (for instance a Swiss embassy) that they want to maintain their Swiss citizenship (Art. 10 BüG).

201 The concern to avoid statelessness also prevails in two other cases where Swiss citizenship is lost by law: when the link of parentage to the person who transferred Swiss citizenship is severed (Art. 8 BüG), or when a Swiss minor is adopted by a foreigner (Art. 8a BüG). The loss only occurs if the child already possesses or acquires another citizenzhip.

202 The law provides for *loss by decree* when a Swiss citizen born and living abroad, and having dual citizenship requests to have his citizenship revoked (Art. 42 BüG). In addition, the deprivation of Swiss citizenship is possible against citizens holding double citizenship who have seriously violated the interests and reputation of Switzerland (Art. 48 BüG), for instance in cases of espionage.

---

[12] Cf. n. 200.

In practice, the provision concerning deprivation of citizenship is of no significance. On the other hand, naturalisations obtained through fraudulent behaviour can, based on Art. 41 BüG, be nullified.[13]

2. Legal Status of Aliens

Foreigners account for over 20% of the Swiss population, not including asylum seekers. More than half the residents without a Swiss passport have either been living in Switzerland for more than fifteen years or were born here. 26.5% of the children born in Switzerland in 2004 were foreign nationals. The foreign population is young: for every 100 foreigners of working age, there are only 9 of retirement age (compared with 30 among Swiss). More than half of the foreign citizens living in Switzerland are nationals from one of the following countries: Italy, Germany, Serbia Montenegro, or Portugal.[14] That Switzerland has a considerably higher percentage of foreign residents than any of the member states of the EU (except Luxembourg), is due not only to its geographic location in the centre of Europe, but also to the comparatively restrictive Swiss naturalisation policies.

The main difference between the legal status of Swiss citizens and that of foreign nationals concerns their *political rights*. At the federal level, political rights are granted to Swiss citizens only.[15] However, the cantons may accord the right to vote and other political rights in cantonal and communal matters to non-Swiss citizens. Eight cantons have introduced such regulations, whereby they require that the foreigner has resided in Switzerland for a

---

[13] Cf. n. 192.
[14] Cf. Swiss Federal Statistics Office, Statistical Data on Switzerland 2006, p. 5. For an update and more details, see www.statistik.admin.ch.
[15] Cf. n. 216.

certain period of time. The Canton of Jura, for example, grants foreigners the right to vote at cantonal and communal level and to be elected to municipal parliaments after ten years domicile in the canton. The cantons Neuchâtel, Vaud, Fribourg and Geneva allow foreigners to take part in communal elections, and to sign initiatives and requests for a referendum at this level. Three cantons, Outer Appenzell, Basle-City and the Grisons, provide that the communes can accord voting rights to foreigners.

205 *Fundamental rights*, on the other hand, are not tied to citizenship. Thus, not only Swiss citizens, but foreign nationals and stateless persons alike are protected by the fundamental rights guaranteed in the constitution. As an exception, Art. 24 Const. restricts the freedom of domicile to Swiss citizens.

206 The Federal Supreme Court decided that a popular initiative launched in the city of Zurich demanding the preferential treatment of Swiss citizens violated the federal constitution. It thereby emphasised the importance of equal protection and the prohibition of discrimination, as contained in Art. 9 Const., for all human beings irrespective of their nationality.[16]

207 Foreigners even enjoy those fundamental rights that are essential for the functioning of a democracy and thus closely linked to political rights: freedom of opinion and information; freedom of the media; freedom of assembly, and freedom of association. Nevertheless, the political activities of aliens are subject to more stringent limitations.

208 The Federal Law on Foreigners (Bundesgesetz über Ausländerinnen und Ausländer) of 16 December 2005 regulates the entry to, residence in and departure from the country by foreigners and their families, and lists a number of measures intended to achieve the integration of foreign nationals into the Swiss community. The main aims of this legislation are to limit the number

---

[16] BGE 129 I 392 (2003).

2. Legal Status of Aliens

of foreigners residing in Switzerland in order to avoid an excessive proportion of non-Swiss nationals, and to protect the security and economic interests of the country. However, foreign labour has greatly contributed to Swiss prosperity.

Finding the right balance between openness towards the world and national self-interest has proved to be particularly fraught, especially in view of widespread fear within the Swiss population (quite often exploited in political debates and election campaigns) of being threatened by a flood of aliens taking away jobs, enhancing the crime rate, causing problems at state schools, and undermining Swiss culture and traditions. Swiss authorities have to take such concerns even more seriously than their counterparts in other countries, as the Swiss electorate can permanently interfere with policies adopted by government and parlament: either by preventing laws voted by parliament from becoming effective (legislative referendum), or by bringing its own proposals for constitutional amendments (popular initiative) to a direct vote of the people. Since 1970, several initiatives backed by right-wing parties aimed at restricting the number of foreigners to a certain percentage of the resident population have been defeated at the polls. However, the fact that many citizens vote in favour of such initiatives[17] has indirectly influenced legislation. In order to prevent popular initiatives hostile to foreigners from succeeding (and to take the wind out of the sails of political parties trying to capitalise on such sentiments), the goveernment has the tendency to propose, and parliament to pass, relatively strict legislation concerning aliens and asylum seekers. 209

Foreigners need special authorisation to reside in Switzerland for more than three months, or if they intend to be gainfully em- 210

---

[17] For instance, in September 2000 an initiative seeking a strict limitation of aliens to 18% of the resident population was supported by 36.3% of those voting. In November 2002, a popular initiative directed against the «abuse of the right of asylum» was supported by 49.9%.

ployed in Switzerland. The work permit and residency permit are normally combined in a single authorisation. There are several types of authorisations. The most common are the temporary residency permit, limited in time and requiring renewal, and the permenanent residency permit issued after several years of residence. The permanent residency permit confers roughly the same rights and duties which Swiss citizens enjoy, except political rights and the duty to render military service.

211 The Federal Law on Foreigners has very limited application as far as citizens from EU- and EFTA member states are concerned. For them, the Agreement on the Free Movement of Persons, concluded in June 1999 with the European Community and its member-states,[18] and the corresponding EFTA provisions, confer priority. The consequence is, as some critics have remarked, that there are two classes of foreigners in Swiss law: those from EU- and EFTA member-states who enjoy a relatively privileged status, and those from the rest of the world.

3. Right to Vote

A. In General

212 Art. 34 par. 1 Const. guarantees «the political rights». Political rights allow citizens to take part in the conduct of public affairs. In a comparative context, the scope of political rights varies greatly.

213 In *representative democracies*, such as the United States or the Federal Republic of Germany, the people exercise governmental power on the federal level indirectly only through freely chosen representatives elected periodically on the basis of universal and

---

[18] Cf. n. 82.

equal suffrage. The people themselves do not decide on legislative or other substantial issues. In Switzerland, on the other hand, the tools of initiative and referendum *integrate the people into the legislative process*. Together with parliament they constitute the legislator. Therefore, Switzerland is sometimes called a *semi-direct democracy*, i.e. a mixture between pure direct democracy[19] and representative democracy. As a rule, the government and the popularly elected parliament make the decisions. Yet, through referenda and popular initiatives, the people can directly exercise influence on many substantial issues and can subject them to popular vote.

Thus, on the Swiss federal level, the right to vote includes participation in elections to the National Council;[20] the right to launch and sign popular initiatives and referenda in federal matters, and the right to take part in ballots on federal issues such as constitutional amendments, federal statutes, or international treaties. At the cantonal and communal levels, the right to vote is even more comprehensive. 214

The exercise of political rights is regulated partly by federal law and partly by cantonal law, whereby the following standards set by the federal constitution have to be respected: 215

---

[19] Like in New England town meetings, Swiss «Landsgemeinden», or municipal voters' assemblies in various countries.
[20] Cantonal law determines how the members of the Council of States are elected; cf. n. 271.

> **Art. 39 Const. Exercise of Political Rights**
> (1) The federation regulates the exercise of political rights in federal matters; the cantons regulate the exercise of these rights in cantonal and communal matters.
> (2) Political rights are exercised at the domicile. Federation and cantons may stipulate exceptions.
> (3) No person exercises political rights in more than one canton.
> (4) A canton may provide that persons who newly establish residence in the canton exercise political rights in cantonal and communal matters only after a waiting period of no more than three months.

B. Prerequisites in Federal Matters

216 The requirements for exercising political rights in federal matters are set down in Art. 136 par. 1 Const. The Federal Law on Political Rights[21] contains additional provisions. Political rights in federal matters are accorded to all Swiss citizens over the age of 18 not placed under guardianship by reason of mental illness (Art. 136 par. 1 Const.). The last mentioned condition excludes persons who lack the capacity to make reasoned judgments on political issues. Women's suffrage in federal matters was introduced as late as 1971. In 1991 the voting age was reduced from 20 to 18; there is some discussion as to whether to reduce the age to 16. Formerly, the right to vote was contingent on residency in Switzerland. Since 1992 however, Swiss nationals living abroad are allowed to participate in the political process at the federal level without having to be in the country at the time.

---

[21] Of 17 December 1976, SR 161.1; abbreviation: BPR (Bundesgesetz über die politischen Rechte). The political rights of Swiss citizens living abroad are regulated in a special statute (Federal Law on Political Rights of Nonresident Swiss [Bundesgesetz über die politischen Rechte der Auslandschweizer], of 19 December 1975, SR 161.5).

Political rights are normally exercised at the individual's domi- 217
cile. The traditional form of voting by placing the ballot paper in
a ballot box at a polling station is being replaced increasingly by
postal voting, whereby voters send their ballot papers to the relevant
polling authority in the commune where they reside. In
some places voters are allowed to vote with the aid of special
electronic voting systems; such electronic voting pilot schemes
are currently being tested. Swiss citizens living abroad can exercise
their right to vote either personally at their commune of origin
or former Swiss domicile, or by mail from abroad.

In order to ensure that only persons entitled to vote exercise their 218
political rights, and that political rights are not exercised at more
than one place (Art. 39 par. 3 Const.), every commune is obliged
to keep a voting register listing all persons residing in their commune
who are permitted to vote (Art. 4 BPR). Swiss citizens living
abroad who wish to vote by mail are entered in the register of
the relevant commune. Prior to each opportunity to vote all citizens
who are registered are automatically provided by their
communes with ballot papers and information brochures. The
voting register is also the source for determining whether those
who have signed popular initiatives or requests for a referendum
are entitled to vote.

C. Prerequisites in Cantonal and Communal Matters

The cantons determine to whom and to what extent they want to 219
confer political rights at the cantonal and communal levels. Apart
from the above-mentioned limits set down in Art. 39 Const., the
cantons have to respect the requirements of a democratic constitution
(Art. 51 par. 1 Const.),[22] as well as fundamental rights

---

[22] Cf. n. 118.

such as equality before the law (Art. 8 Const.), and protection against arbitrariness (Art. 9 Const.). It is no longer admissible to exclude persons from political rights based on their sex. But it is up to the cantons to decide whether and to what extent foreigners are to be given political rights.[23] Within their sphere, the cantons may also fix the voting age independently of the federation. Thus, in May 2007, the «Landsgemeinde» of the Canton of Glarus reduced the voting age from 18 to 16. Gender quota with regard to the composition of popularly elected cantonal bodies are regarded by the Federal Supreme Court as a violation of the guarantee of free and unaltered expression of the citizens' will at the polls.[24]

220 Cantonal and communal parliaments are elected regularly by proportional representation, i.e. political parties are allocated seats in proportion to the number of votes they receive. Proportional representation does not exclude the setting of electoral districts. However, according to recent Federal Supreme Court practice, electoral districts have to be large enough to ensure that any party receiving at least 10% of the votes will obtain a seat in the legislative assembly.[25]

---

[23] Cf. n. 204.

[24] Formerly an unwritten right derived from the 1874 Const., now formally set forth in Art. 34 par. 2 Const. Cf. BGE 123 I 152 (1997), Popular Initiative Solothurn, confirmed in BGE 125 I 21 (1999), Popular Initiative Uri.

[25] BGE 131 I 74 (2005), Parliament Aargau. This jurisprudence still leaves cantonal and communal legislators more discretion than their colleagues in the United States under the Supreme Court's 'one man, one vote' practice initiated in Reynolds v. Sims, 377 U.S. 533 (1964) for both houses of state legislatures, and Wesberry v. Sanders, 376 U.S. 1 (1964) for congressional districts.

4. Instruments of Direct Democracy: Overview

A. Definitions

The main instruments of direct democracy are the referendum 221 and the popular initiative. The *referendum* allows the citizens entitled to vote to prevent any constitutional amendment, statute, treaty, or parliamentary decision regarding a concrete issue from entering into force (suspensive referendum), or to repeal such an act in full or in part (abrogate referendum). In Switzerland the referendum normally has a suspensive effect, whereas the Italian legislative referendum is abrogate.[26]

When the popular referendum occurs automatically under the 222 provisions of the constitution, the vote is referred to as a *mandatory referendum*. An *optional referendum*, in contrast, has to be requested. It can be triggered by a predetermined number of citizens entitled to vote, by lower self-governing units such as member-states in a federation, or by parliament. If only a parliamentary majority can demand that the matter be referred to the people, the referendum loses its characteristic as a means of control and opposition, because the direct participation of the electorate depends on the will of the ruling majority.[27]

The French Constitution of the Fifth Republic provides for a spe- 223 cial form of *plebiscite triggered by the head of state* enabling him to override parliament: according to Art. 11 of the French Constitution, the President of the Republic may call a vote on any government bill (even if not yet approved by parliament!) dealing with the organisation of public authorities or touching on impor-

---

[26] Pursuant to Art. 75 of the Italian Constitution either 500,000 citizens entitled to vote or five Regional Assemblies can request a ballot on the abrogation of statutory provisions.

[27] This is the case in Austria with regard to the legislative referendum. See Art. 43 of the Austrian Constitution.

101

tant foreign affairs. The popular vote, should this proposal be rejected, is regarded simultaneously as a vote of no confidence in the president.[28]

224 *Popular initiatives* make it possible for a predetermined number of voters to demand a change in the law or in areas of public administration such as building a hospital or a new road. If parliament rejects the initiative, the electors themselves decide on the issue, and their vote is binding. Citizens can thus bring their own proposals to a direct vote by the people. A well informed American observer of Swiss democracy put it shortly and to the point: «While the referendum offers the people an important veto on the acts of the legislature, the initiative allows them to force issues or ideas onto the agenda that the political elites might prefer to ignore.»[29]

225 Other tools of direct democracy are *expanded election rights* that extend well beyond the right to merely elect parliament every few years including, for instance, popular elections of executive bodies, members of administrative agencies, or judges. In the United States some states and municipalities practice the right of *recall*. Recall allows a specified number of electors to demand a vote to remove elected officials from office before their term has expired. In the event that a majority votes in favour of such a request, new elections must be conducted immediately. In Switzerland, some cantonal constitutions include a right of recall; however, it has hardly any practical significance. Referenda and popular initiatives are more effective tools for citizens to voice their dissatisfaction.

---

[28] In April 1969, President Charles de Gaulle immediately resigned from office after the electorate's rejection of a proposed reform of the senate and of regional structures.

[29] GREGORY A. FOSSEDAL, Direct Democracy in Switzerland, 2nd ed., Transaction Publishers, New Brunswick (USA) / London 2006, p. 90.

B. Federal Level

The introduction of referendum and initiative at the federal level 226
occurred gradually. The first federal constitution, enacted when
the Swiss federation was created in 1848, provided for direct citizen participation in *constitutional* matters only with a *mandatory
referendum* for all amendments to the constitution, and a *popular
initiative for total revision of the constitution*. A constitutional referendum allowing the people to vote on an amendment approved
either by parliament or a constitutional convention, is nothing
unusual in a comparative context.[30] On the other hand, a popular
initiative regarding the national constitution has scarcity value.

The Constitution of 1874 introduced an *optional referendum for* 227
ordinary legislation. This reform had a substantial impact on the
political system as a whole. The fact that 50,000 (originally
30,000) citizens can challenge laws passed by parliament and request that a popular ballot be held, forces government and parliament to draft proposals that can pass a referendum. For this
reason, the legislative process is a continuous search for political
compromise. The legislative referendum is one of the main factors contributing to a «*concordance democracy*» or a «*consensus-oriented democracy*», as Switzerland is quite often referred to. The
Swiss model contrasts with a typical parliamentary democracy. It
can be characterised as a political system where the power of
governing is shared among a wide range of political parties and
interest groups, which are in turn controlled on specific issues by
the people.

---

[30] Respective provisions for a constitutional referendum can be found in the constitutions of the following countries, to name but a few: Australia (Art. 128), Austria (Art. 44 par. 3), Denmark (§ 88), France (Art. 89), Italy (Art. 138), Japan (Art. 96), as well as some member-states in Germany and the United States. Sometimes, as in France and Italy, approval by a qualified majority in parliament can replace a popular vote.

228 Another most important step towards more direct democracy has been the *popular initiative for partial revision of the constitution*, created in 1891. Here, a number of citizens entitled to vote (currently 100,000) can bring about a popular vote on an amendment they want to introduce to the constitution. While a referendum gives the citizens veto power and is therefore often compared to a brake, a popular initiative is more like an accelerator pedal as it puts new issues on the political agenda and forces politicians to react.

229 A *referendum regarding international treaties* was introduced in 1921 and extended in 1977 and 2003. In the event of proposed entry into organisations for collective security or supranational communities like the European Union the referendum is mandatory and, as for constitutional amendments, requires the double majority (of the cantons and of citizens nationwide). In other cases as specified in the constitution, a referendum is optional. The treaty referendum gives those who oppose closer international or European cooperation formidable blocking leverage.

230 Other expansions of direct democracy rejected by popular votes include the popular election of the Federal Council, a fiscal referendum, administrative referenda challenging decisions in controversial areas (such as national road construction, nuclear power plants, armaments) and a mandatory referendum for entering into negotiations to join the European Union.

The instruments of direct democracy at the federal level will be discussed in more detail in Part VI.

C. Cantonal Level

231 At the cantonal level the tools of direct democracy are even more extensive. In all cantons the executive is directly elected by the people. In some cantons the people even elect judges, public prosecutors and certain civil servants. The popular initiative is not restricted to constitutional amendments but covers ordinary

legislation as well. Quite often the legislative referendum is mandatory, i.e. occurs automatically after parliament has passed a law. Decisions concerning expenditure exceeding certain limits are regularly subject to a (mandatory or optional) referendum. Some cantons also subject other important decisions on specific issues such as the location of a nuclear power plant or the issuance of licences for hydroelectric power plants, to a referendum.

Two rural cantons, Glarus and Inner Appenzell, still practise the *Landsgemeinde*, one of the oldest forms of direct democracy: once a year, on a Sunday, citizens eligible to vote meet in the open air to decide on the most important cantonal matters including constitutional amendments and legislation. Everyone can debate a question and submit a proposal. Voting is accomplished by show of hands. As a rule the votes are not counted but estimated.

Direct democracy is most developed at the communal level. Many communes have voters' meetings throughout the year to discuss and decide on local matters.

5. Freedom of Decision as the Essence of Political Rights

Political rights imply that all citizens entitled to vote can reach and express their decisions free of state pressure or undue interference. This precondition of a democracy ought to be enforced by an independent judiciary. The Swiss constitution guarantees this freedom of decision and perceives political rights as fundamental rights actionable even before the Federal Supreme Court:

> **Art. 34 Const.   Political Rights**
> (1) The political rights are guaranteed.
> (2) The guarantee of political rights protects the free formation of opinion and the unaltered expression of the voter's will.

Part III – Citizenship and Political Rights

235 The phrasing in Section 2 of this article is in line with jurisprudence developed under the old constitution. Thus the Federal Supreme Court intervenes when public authorities have interfered with up-coming ballots by means of incorrect information or excessive propaganda. On the other hand, the common practice of delivering an information brochure together with the ballot papers is admissible and even desirable as long as the information is factual and neutral.[31]

236 While the fundamental principle of anonymous voting has unlimited validity at federal level, it is not ensured by the forms of democracy practised in the «Landsgemeinde» and in communal voters' meetings. However, while the Federal Supreme Court has criticised certain deficiencies in the «Landsgemeinde», it has not put the constitutionality of this venerable institution, sometimes even regarded as an exemplary emanation of collective self-government, into question.[32]

237 Popular initiatives, as well as governmental proposals submitted to the people, have to respect the principle of the unity of subject matter, i.e. they may not comprise several proposals which have no interrelationship; otherwise, an unaltered expression of the voter's will would not be possible.[33]

---

[31] Summary of the court practice in BGE 130 I 290 (2004), Zurich Bar Association.

[32] BGE 121 I 138 (1995), Outer Appenzell. Nonetheless, the Landsgemeinde was abolished in Outer Appenzell two years later.

[33] Good summary of court practice in BGE 129 I 366 (2003), concerning a constitutional amendment in the Canton of Zurich. For partial revisions of the federal constitution the principle of the unity of the subject matter is guaranteed in Art. 194 par. 2 Const.; cf. n. 502.

Part IV – Parliament, Government and the Judiciary

1. System of Government in a Comparative Context

Most modern democracies have either a parliamentary, a presidential or a semi-presidential system of government. This distinction focuses on the relationship between the executive branch of government and parliament. The Swiss political system differs in many respects from both the parliamentary and the presidential forms of government. Nor can it be adequately described as a combined form such as the semi-presidential model. 238

A. Parliamentary System

The parliamentary system prevails in Europe and in countries that formerly belonged to the British Empire such as Canada, Australia and India. Japan and Israel, too, have such political regimes. The parliamentary system is distinguished by the following characteristics: the Prime Minister and his government are dependent on the support of the parliament and can be removed from office by a vote of no confidence. The Head of State (either elected or a hereditary monarch) is a symbol of national identity transcending partisan rivalries. As a rule, he or she entrusts the majority leader with the formation of a government. Countries with a proportional electoral system tend to produce election results in which no single party obtains a majority of seats; hence, a coalition between two or more parties is inevitable, with the leader of the strongest party becoming Prime Minister or the equivalent. On the Prime Minister's advice, the Head of State dissolves parliament. The underlying premise of the parliamentary 239 system is that the parliament constitutes the government. As a consequence, parliamentary elections tend to be elections between party leaders and their political programs. There is no clear-cut division of powers between the legislative and the executive branches of government. Since parliament and government are closely linked, it is mainly up to the parliamentary opposition to control governmental action. The permanently visible and active opposition parties offer the electorate an alternative for the next election. Obviously, party discipline tends to be strong under this system.

240 A great variety of organisational patterns, all belonging to the parliamentary type of government, exists. In the German Federal Republic, for instance, the Federal Chancellor is elected by the Lower House of Parliament (Bundestag) and can only be removed by the Head of State (Bundespräsident) after a motion by the Federal Chancellor for a vote of confidence fails in the Bundestag.[1] However, the Bundestag can only express its lack of confidence in the Federal Chancellor by simultaneously electing a successor.[2] In Italy, the government has to retain the trust of a majority of members from both the Lower House (Camera dei Deputati) and the Senate.[3]

B. Presidential System

241 The presidential system was first established in the United States in 1787. Later on, it was adopted by a number of countries, primarily in Latin America, but also in Africa and Asia. The most characteristic feature of the presidential system is that the legislative and the executive branches are – institutionally and person-

---

[1] Art. 63 and 68 German Basic Law.
[2] Art. 67 German Basic Law (*constructive* vote of no confidence).
[3] Art. 94 Italian Const.

ally – completely separate from one another.[4] Both branches obtain their legitimacy independently through popular elections. The President is both Head of State and head of government. In the United States he is elected indirectly by the People through an electoral college for a fixed term of four years. Congress cannot remove him from office by a vote of no confidence.[5] On the other hand, the President possesses no right to dissolve Congress. Members of Congress quite often cross party lines when voting on a given issue; this has no serious consequences with regard to the stability of government.

The strong concentration of power in the President and his administration is only in line with public interest when this power is held in check by the other branches of government. In the United States an intricate system of checks and balances between Congress, the President and the Supreme Court keeps the three «coequal branches of government» in equilibrium. In addition, a highly developed democratic culture and a strong sense of federalism work against authoritarianism. Some other countries which implemented presidential systems have been less successful. Experiences made in Chile and Argentina demonstrate the dangers of slipping into presidential dictatorship. This is particularly so when the military exerts a strong influence and the position of parliament and the political parties opposing the regime is tenuous.

---

[4] With the minor exception of the Vice President presiding over the U.S. Senate.
[5] The impeachment power is restricted to «high crimes and misdemeanours» (Art. II Section 4 U.S. Const.) and has nothing in common with the purely political instrument of a vote of no confidence under parliamentary systems.

C. Semi-Presidential System

243 The semi-presidential system combines elements of the presidential and the parliamentary systems. France, Finland, Russia and some other states of the former Soviet Union are among the countries with this type of system. In France, General de Gaulle and other architects of the Fifth Republic (founded 1958) wanted to attain higher governmental stability by strengthening the presidency at the expense of parliamentary power.

244 In contrast to the parliamentary model, the President is elected by the people for a fixed term of five years and cannot therefore be removed from office by a parliamentary vote of no confidence. Furthermore, he has wide-ranging executive functions. Nevertheless, his executive power is shared with a cabinet under a Prime Minister, who, although appointed by the President, is responsible to the legislature and, as under a parliamentary system, must resign should he lose parliamentary support. In most countries with this model, the power of the presidency dominates the legislative branch, in particular in relation to foreign policy. However, a system of checks and balances (which can result in bitter controversies within the executive branch) exists in periods during which a President does not belong to the main political party, thus forcing him to name a Prime Minister who will be acceptable to that majority.[6]

D. Swiss System: Overview

245 Unlike either the presidential or the parliamentary system, all important decisions of the Swiss executive branch are taken by a

---

[6] Such a constellation is called *cohabitation* in the French Republic. It has occurred three times: from 1986–1988 (President Mitterand / Prime Minister Chirac), from 1993–1995 (Mitterand / Balladur) and again from 1997–2002 (Chirac / Jospin).

multi-party collegiate body of seven equal members collectively referred to as the Federal Council. The chair of this body, the Federal President, is essentially the «first among peers» (primus inter pares) and is rotated annually. The President's role is restricted to chairing meetings and representing the government. There is no official Head of State, not even for ceremonial occasions.

The Federal Council is elected by parliament for a fixed period of four years. In contrast to a parliamentary system, federal councillors are not members of parliament, and neither the government as a whole nor its individual members can be removed from office by a vote of no confidence before the term expires. This also applies to members of parliament as the government lacks the power to dissolve parliament.

In large measure the Swiss political system is shaped by the citizens' participatory rights. By means of referenda and initiatives the people can assume the role of opposition, whereby this opposition is focused not on politicians and their respective parties, but on specific issues. The referendum has an extraordinarily preventive effect as it forces government and parliament to draft proposals which are based on a wide consensus hence reducing the risk of being defeated by a popular vote. This promotes compromise and is the feature of the Swiss method of political decision-making quite often referred to as «concordance democracy».[7] The difference between the Swiss system and the perpetual competition between majority and opposition parties in parliamentary democracies such as Great Britain or Germany seems evident. Nevertheless, concordance does not always produce the best results. It has to be borne in mind that a consensus-orientated democracy as practiced in Switzerland not only complicates but sometimes even obstructs decisions, and that the constant threat of a referendum weakens the system's ability to

---

[7] Cf. n. 227.

Part IV – Parliament, Government and the Judiciary

respond to challenges quickly. An attentive and sympathetic foreign observer of Swiss history and politics put it in a nutshell:

> «The system shuns conflict and hence very unwillingly takes hard decisions, and never quickly ... Switzerland seems to go nowhere, its system turns on heavy slow wheels which somehow never quite engage.»[8]

248 The referendum also impacts on the composition of the government: the more the larger political parties are represented in the Federal Council, the smaller is the risk that government and legislature are severely hampered by frequent interference by the populace. However, even parties represented in government quite often make use of the referendum and the popular initiative to achieve their goals, or at least to propagate their programmes.

249 A division of powers at federal level underlies Title 5 of the Swiss Constitution. Under the heading «Federal Authorities» it contains general provisions followed by separate sections on the Federal Assembly (parliament), the Federal Council (government) and the Federal Supreme Court. The offices are mutually exclusive (incompatibility). No member of any one of these institutions can belong to any one of the other bodies at the same time (Art. 144 par. 1 Const.). However, as far as the tasks to be performed are concerned, the separation of the executive from the legislative branch is not as strict as in the United States. The bulk of proposals for new legislation come from the government which regularly attends meetings of the two houses of parliament and its committees. The new constitution expresses the notion of co-operation between the legislative and executive branches in governing the country, for instance in shaping foreign policy (Art. 166 par. 1 Const.) and in planning state activities (Art. 173 par. 1 [g] Const.).

---

[8] JONATHAN STEINBERG, Why Switzerland?, 2nd ed., Cambridge University Press, Cambridge 1996, p. 127.

The checks and balances tend to overemphasise democratic val- 250
ues; most of them involve checks by the people (referendum and
initiative) and by parliament (election of federal councillors and
federal judges by both houses of parliament in joint session).
Constitutional jurisdiction is severely limited.[9]

A most noteworthy feature in a comparative context is that Swiss 251
members of parliament are only part-time parliamentarians (the
so-called *militia system*). They take on public office alongside their
professions, even though they normally have to devote a great
deal of time to parliamentary business. As it is quite difficult to
combine certain professional activities with a moderately compensated mandate, the composition of parliament reflects only
partly that of the population at large. For instance, compared to
physicians or owners of small businesses, lawyers, teachers and
functionaries of large associations promoting specific interests
are well represented. Furthermore, the rather poor allocation of
resources for parliamentary staff and technical support widens
the gap between the legislators and the executive branch as far as
the potential to base decisions on expert knowledge and thorough examination of files is concerned.

2. Bicameral Parliament

A. In General

In a bicameral parliament some or all of its tasks are accom- 252
plished by two chambers working together. In federations the bicameral system is intended to strengthen the influence of the
member-states at the national level. Even some unitary states,
such as Spain and Italy, have a second chamber of parliament in
order to provide some sort of territorial representation.

---

[9] Cf. n. 561 et seq.

253 In the United States and in Switzerland, both chambers are elected by the people, and they possess equal power in the legislative process. As in the U.S. Senate, the Swiss Council of States consists of two delegates from each canton.

254 The German Basic Law provides us with a model that differs in its entirety from the American and Swiss models: the *Bundesrat*, through which the member-states (*Länder*) participate in federal legislation, consists of members of the *Länder* governments appointed by them.[10] All laws that affect the interests of the member-states (about 70%) have to be approved by the *Bundesrat*; as for the rest, the Upper House has a suspensive veto only which can be overruled by the *Bundestag*.[11] The principle of equal state representation is modified by giving the *Länder* between three and six votes in the *Bundesrat*, depending on the size of their respective population.[12]

255 It is no coincidence that the Swiss and the American bicameral system have so much in common. As already mentioned, the Swiss Federal Assembly was modeled on the U.S. Congress.[13] As in the United States, this marked the transition from a confederation to a federal state and was seen as a compromise between an assembly of delegates from various states and a centralised representation of the people, thus preventing highly populated member-states dominating less populous member-states. This reflects the idea that parliament is based on two fundamental constitutional values: democracy and federalism.

---

[10] Art. 51 German Basic Law. That the German Upper House has the same denomination as the Swiss government is rather confusing, and even more so the fact that the official title of the German head of government is *Bundeskanzler* (Federal Chancellor), whereas the Swiss «Bundeskanzler» is in charge of the government's staff office.

[11] Art. 77 German Basic Law.

[12] Art. 51 par. 2 German Basic Law.

[13] Cf. n. 20.

2. Bicameral Parliament

B. In Switzerland

The Swiss *National Council* (*Nationalrat*) represents the overall population. Each canton forms an electoral constituency. The 200 seats are distributed among the cantons in proportion to their population. The *Council of States* (*Ständerat*) consists of 46 cantonal delegates, two from each canton, whereby the six «half-cantons»[14] have only one representative each.   256

Whereas elections to the National Council are governed by federal law, the cantons determine the electoral body, the mode of election and the term of office of their respective state councillors.   257

Both councils are *equal* and have *identical powers*, not only in the field of legislation, but also with regard to federal spending and the supervision of other branches of government. No chamber can claim a priority in debating or deciding any matter. This question is agreed upon by the two chamber presidents and, if agreement cannot be reached, by drawing lots. Both chambers have their own standing committees and deliberate separately. Decisions of the Federal Assembly require the approval of both chambers (Art. 156 Const.). If decisions differ, business goes back and forth between the two councils until all differences have been eliminated. If differences remain despite threefold examination by each council, a conciliation committee attempts to hammer out a compromise which is then submitted to a final vote in each chamber.   258

The principle that both chambers are equal and that decisions require the approval of the National Council as well as the Council of States, applies neither to elections nor to some other matters which have to be decided but where a deadlock would be intolerable. Such matters are assigned to the *United Federal As-*   259

---

[14] This term is explained in n. 98.

sembly (Vereinigte Bundesversammlung) which consists of all members of both councils under the chairmanship of the president of the National Council. This body deliberates jointly to hold elections and to decide on applications for pardons and disputes between the highest federal authorities (Art. 157 Const.). The most important elections concern the members of the Federal Council, federal judges and, in the case of war, the Commander-in-Chief of the armed forces who is called «*the* General» (Art. 168 Const.). Given its larger size, within the United Federal Assembly the National Council has preponderance as decisions are taken by the majority of those voting.

3. The National Council

A. Composition

260 Pursuant to Art. 149 Const., the National Council is composed of 200 *representatives of the people*. The seats are distributed among the cantons in proportion to their resident population, i.e. including foreigners and other persons who do not have the right to vote in federal matters. Each canton (or «half-canton») is entitled to at least one seat. The Federal Council fixes the distribution of the seats based on the latest population census. At present,[15] six cantons have one seat only, namely Uri, Obwalden, Nidwalden, Glarus, Outer Appenzell and Inner Appenzell. The majority of seats go to Zurich (34), Berne (26) and Vaud (18).

B. Eligibility and Incompatibilities

261 All Swiss citizens over the age of 18 who have not been placed under guardianship by reason of mental illness are eligible for

---

[15] Based on an ordinance of 2 July 2002 (SR 161.12).

membership in the National Council (Art. 143 in conjunction with Art. 136 Const.). Domicile in Switzerland at the time of the election is not required.

Members of the National Council may not simultaneously belong to the Council of States, the Federal Council or the Federal Supreme Court (Art. 144 par. 1 Const.). Statutory law sets out further incompatibilities. 262

C. Mode of Election

The members of the National Council are elected directly by the people according to the system of *proportional representation* whereby each canton forms an electoral district (Art. 149 par. 2 and 3 Const.). Proportional representation means that political parties are allocated seats in proportion to the number of votes received. The majority vote, which had been in existence since the foundation of the federal state in 1848, resulted in the Liberal Party dominating parliament and government while the smaller parties were grossly underrepresented. When in 1918 a General Strike brought the country to the verge of civil war, the Socialist Party lacked any parliamentary real power. In the same year, the people and the cantons approved a popular initiative demanding proportional representation. Among other effects, this enabled the growing labour movement to find more adequate representation in the federal authorities, thus contributing to conflict resolution within the prevailing constitutional order. 263

However, the impact of the proportional representation system is seriously curtailed by the rule that each canton forms a separate electoral constituency. Switzerland is thus divided into 26 such constituencies. Only in the seven cantons with at least nine seats can a political party attaining 10% of the vote be allocated a seat; in other cantons these parties come away empty-handed. In addi- 264 tion, in the six cantons with only one seat the vote necessarily has to follow the majority rule.

265 Federal elections are regulated by the Federal Law on Political Rights.[16] Those who are entitled to vote in their respective electoral constituency (i.e. canton) may submit a *candidate proposal* which may contain as many candidates as the number of mandates to be filled (Art. 22 par. 1 BPR). In order to avoid any confusion, each proposal must have its own title or designation (Art. 23 BPR), quite often but not necessarily the name of a political party. Each candidate proposal must be backed by between 100 and 400 voters, the quorum of signatures necessary depending on the number of seats allotted to the canton in question (Art. 24 BPR). Swiss citizens may run for a seat in a canton where they do not have domicile and therefore do not have the right to vote. But the same name may not appear on more than one candidate proposal. The candidate proposals are examined and, if necessary, corrected by the canton in question (Art. 29 BPR). Once candidate proposals have undergone this checking procedure they are called *ballot lists* (Art. 30 BPR). Allied or linked lists are admissible; they are treated as a single list when it comes to the allocation of seats (Art. 31 and 42 BPR). This instrument is widely utilised, for instance in order to improve the smaller parties' prospects of obtaining a seat.

266 The *election* is run by the cantons under the supervision of the Federal Chancellery. The voters are provided with all the lists in their constituency, including a blank list. Every voter puts one of these official lists in the ballot box or sends it to the relevant municipal polling authority. He or she can alter a list by striking out names, voting twice for the same candidate (cumulation) or replacing a candidate from one list with a candidate from another list (panachage). It is also possible to take the blank list

---

[16] Of 17 December 1976, SR 161.1; abbreviation: BPR (Bundesgesetz über die politischen Rechte).

and insert a title (party designation) as well as the names of as many candidates as there are vacant seats from any official ballot list.

The *determination of the election result* consists of two phases. In a first step, the number of seats every party receives is determined in proportion to the percentage of votes cast in their favour. A vote for a candidate counts as a vote for the candidate's political party (Art. 39 [c] BPR). If, to take an example, in a district with ten seats the voter has crossed out two names on the List of Party A and replaced them with two candidates from Party B, then Party A only gets eight party votes, losing two to Party B. If a list contains less names than the number of seats assigned to the electoral district, the «empty» lines are treated as votes for the party indicated in the title of the ballot list. The second step which determines who has been elected is considerably less complicated. Those candidates who have obtained the highest number of votes on «their» ballot list are elected (Art. 43 BPR). Those who are not elected may, in the event of a vacancy, act as substitutes, in the order of the votes they received. 267

D. Term of Office

Elections to the National Council are held once every four years. After the expiration of this fixed election period a new election takes place. 268

Following the last elections, held in October 2007, more than a dozen political parties are represented in the National Council. The five strongest parties occupy 190 of the 200 seats. 269

4. The Council of States

270 The Council of States constitutes the federal element in the Swiss bicameral parliamentary system. However, unlike the German Upper House, the Swiss *Ständerat* is not a «representation» of the member-states in a strictly legal sense. As with the members of the National Council, the State Councillors vote «without instructions» (Art. 161 par. 1 Const.). In law, they are subject only to their conscience when they vote. In fact, however, councillors have certain commitments to the political party they belong to and, to a lesser degree, to «their» canton. As the council's composition mirrors rather evenly the various regions and, in particular, cultural and linguistic minorities, Council of States' debates are usually more conciliatory and party conflicts less polarised than in the National Council. Quite often, legal issues are discussed more carefully and objectively.

Art. 150 Const. Composition and Election of the Council of States

(1) The Council of States consists of 46 delegates of the cantons.
(2) The Cantons of Obwalden, Nidwalden, Basle-City, Basle-Land, Outer Appenzell and Inner Appenzell elect one delegate each, the other cantons elect two delegates.
(3) The elections are governed by cantonal law.

---

271 The cantons determine the electoral body and the mode of election. Whereas formerly some cantons entrusted the elections to their parliaments, nowadays all councillors are elected by the people. Except in the Canton of Jura where a proportional system is applied, all other cantons elect their deputies by a majority voting system. As a rule, a candidate must receive an absolute majority of the votes in order to be elected in the first round; in the second round a simple majority suffices.

272 Even the right to take part in the elections, the eligibility of the candidate and the term of office are regulated by cantonal law.

Thus cantons may allow non-Swiss citizens to take part in the elections, or preclude re-election after a certain period of office. They may even introduce further incompatibilities in addition to those set forth in Art. 144 Const,[17] for instance, by stating that members of the cantonal government or administration may not serve on the Council of States. In most but not all cantons, state councillors are elected at the same time the elections to the National Council take place, also for a term of four years.

5. Parliament at Work: Organisation, Procedures and Powers

Apart from the constitution, the most important source of law relating to parliament is the Law on the Federal Assembly.[18] 273

A. Institutional Framework

Both Councils elect from among their members a president, a 274 first vice-president and a second vice-president for a term of one year only; re-election for the following year is excluded (Art. 152 Const.). As a rule, the first vice-president becomes president the following year which ensures some degree of continuity. The main tasks of the *presidency* consist of setting the agenda, chairing the meetings of the respective chambers and their multi-party steering committees, and representing the councils on ceremonial occasions.

Each council appoints *committees* from among its members 275 (Art. 153 par. 1 Const.). These committees prepare all items of

---

[17] Cf. n. 249.
[18] Enacted 13 December 2002, SR 171.10; abbreviation: ParlG (Parlamentsgesetz).

business before they are debated in full session, and formulate recommendations. Statutory law can even entrust them with decision-making powers that are not of a legislative nature (Art. 153 par. 3 Const.). Each chamber has twelve standing committees with the same mandates: finance; parliamentary supervision; foreign affairs; science, education and culture; social security and health; the environment, land use planning and energy; defense; transport and communications; economic affairs and taxes; political institutions; legal affairs; public buildings. In addition, in the fields of finances and parliamentary supervision there are so called delegations consisting of members of the respective committees of both councils. Furthermore, there are the committees of the United Federal Assembly.[19]

276 In order to clarify «events of great import» the Federal Assembly can set up a special investigative committee composed of members of both chambers (Art. 163 ParlG). Such committees are appointed very rarely, for example, where there have been serious indications of gross maladministration at top executive level. For instance, in 1990 the activities of the military intelligence service were scrutinised by such a special committee which led, among other things, to the dissolution of secret extraordinary intelligence agencies that had no legal basis.

277 The influence of these committees on parliamentary decision-making can hardly be over-stated, especially where sustainable compromises have to be found. This is for a number of reasons: all important political parties are represented in the committees; the parties aim to delegate persons who have special competence in the subject matter covered by a given committee; committees have specific rights to obtain information, consult documents and conduct inquiries (Art. 153 par. 4 Const.; Art. 150 et seq. ParlG) and, last but not least, fruitful issue-related debates are

---

[19] Like the Judicial Committee; cf. n. 330.

more likely in closed committee meetings with a limited number of participants than in plenary sessions open to the public.

Important preliminary discussions concerning the business of the two councils and their committees occur in *parliamentary factions*. Such factions are composed of deputies of the same party, which is the general rule, or of several parties sharing similar political views. At least five national councillors or five councillors of state are needed to form a faction (Art. 154 Const.; Art. 61 par. 3 ParlG). The factions are parliamentary organs. They are entitled to appoint representatives to all parliamentary committees, and their secretariats are granted subsidies. 278

The Federal Assembly and its organs benefit from *parliamentary services*, headed by a secretary general. In addition, they may call on the services of the federal administration (Art. 155 Const.), although they are separate from the federal administration. Parliamentary services organise parliamentary sessions and committee meetings and provide invaluable support in many fields, for instance, the interpretation of parliamentary law, information and documentation, internet support, public relations, and – most important in a multi-lingual country – translations from and into the three official languages. 279

B. Meetings

Although the National Council and the Council of States deliberate and decide separately,[20] their sessions are held at the same time. They meet regularly, usually for three weeks in spring, summer, autumn and winter. One fourth of the members of a council or the federal government itself may request that the chambers be called to an extraordinary session (Art. 151 par. 2 Const.). 280

---

[20] Cf. n. 258.

Part IV – Parliament, Government and the Judiciary

281 Members of parliament have a range of instruments at their disposal. They can submit *initiatives* containing a draft bill or proposing in general terms that a text be drafted (Art. 160 par. 1 Const.; Art. 107 et seq. ParlG). They can question the government by means of an *interpellation* or an *ordinary question* (Art. 125 ParlG).[21] Finally, by means of a so-called *postulate*, parliament can call on the government to determine whether new legislation or other measures would be appropriate (Art. 123 ParlG). With the approval of a *motion* in both chambers, the government can be obliged to present a specific draft bill or decree or compelled to take appropriate measures (Art. 120 ParlG).

282 The sessions of both houses are *public*, although legislation may provide for exceptions (Art. 158 Const.). Committee meetings on the other hand are secret.

283 Deputies (as well as members of government) are not liable for their statements in parliament and before parliamentary organs (Art. 162 par. 1 Const.). In this respect, the constitution provides for *absolute immunity.*[22]

284 The chambers' deliberations are valid only if a majority of their members is present (Art. 159 par. 1 Const.). In practice, this *quorum* is required for the casting of votes only, not for debates. *Decisions* are taken by the majority of those voting. However, in certain cases such as a declaration that a federal act is urgent,[23] a majority of all the members of the respective councils (i.e. 101 National Councillors or 24 Councillors of State) is necessary (Art. 159 par. 2 and 3 Const.). As parliamentary decisions require

---

[21] A question is replied to in writing. An interpellation paves the way for a debate on the response received.

[22] By way of contrast, the deputies enjoy *relative immunity* for criminal offences connected with their political office. In such cases prosecution is permitted upon authorisation of both chambers; Art. 17 par. 1 ParlG.

[23] Cf. n. 526.

the approval of both chambers, business quite often goes back and forth between the two chambers.[24]

C. Powers

The overriding significance of the democratic principle in the Swiss constitution is reflected not only in the numerous elements of direct popular participation, but also in the extensive powers of parliament. However, as deputies have to balance their parliamentary work with their professional careers,[25] and as, moreover, the electorate directly influences political decision-making by means of referendum and popular initiative, the Swiss parliament wields less power than the actual text of the constitution suggests.

In accordance with Art. 148 par. 1 Const., the Federal Assembly is «the highest authority of the Federation», even though «subject to the rights of the people and the cantons». However, this provision is not an open-ended ticket to erode the division of powers underlying the constitution. The Federal Assembly's competencies are grouped neatly in a special section comprising Arts. 163 to 173 Const. Statutory law may assign parliament further tasks and powers (Art. 173 par. 3 Const.).

By and large the main tasks of the Swiss parliament correspond to those of parliaments in other countries. These tasks include *legislation, finances* and *control* of the other branches of government.

The two chambers debate and decide on constitutional amendments, federal laws and decrees, and they approve international treaties. In these areas, however, parliament is not the ultimate arbitrator, as amendments to the constitution, federal laws and

---

[24] Cf. n. 258.
[25] Cf. n. 251.

important treaties are subject to referendum (mandatory or optional).[26]

289 Over the years the increasing impact of *foreign policy* on the legal order has prompted the drafters of the constitution to strengthen the status of parliament in this area. Apart from approving treaties, the Federal Assembly participates in shaping foreign policy and supervises foreign relations (Art. 166 Const.). The parliamentary committees for foreign affairs serve as an important link to the government in such matters. Parliament and government have parallel competencies in safeguarding the external security, independence and neutrality of Switzerland (Art. 173 par. 1 [a]; Art. 185 par. 1 Const.).

290 The most important decisions with regard to *federal finances* are made by the Federal Assembly. Parliament decides on federal spending, adopts the budget (which the government presents) and approves the federal accounts (Art. 167 Const.). Taxes which the constitution empowers the federation to impose are determined by federal laws and are therefore, in contrast to the budget, subject to a legislative referendum. Art. 126 Const. sets some limits on the budget: expenditures and receipts are to be balanced. The maximum amount of total expenditure is based on the estimated revenue after taking into account the economic situation. Exceptional financial needs may justify exceeding the limits but must be approved by the majority of the members of each chamber. Such excess expenditure has to be compensated for in the subsequent years.

291 In the first session following National Council elections, the United Federal Assembly, i.e. both chambers in a joint session, *elect* the members of the Federal Council, the Federal Chancellor,

---

[26] The procedures for amending the constitution, enacting laws and concluding treaties will be dealt with in Part VI.

5. Parliament at Work: Organisation, Procedures and Powers

and the judges of the Federal Supreme Court and other federal courts (Art. 168 Const.; Art. 130 et seq. ParlG).

Parliamentary control of the federal government and administration, the federal courts and other bodies entrusted with federal tasks constitutes an important means of checks and balances, but does not include the power to abrogate administrative acts or judicial decisions. In order to distinguish this sort of control from hierarchical surveillance, Art. 169 Const. uses the term «supervisory control» (*Oberaufsicht*). As far as the courts are concerned, parliamentary supervision requires prudent restraint in order to avoid jeopardising the independence of the judiciary (Art. 191c Const.) – the cornerstone of a constitutional system based on the rule of law. In particular, parliament must not interfere with pending lawsuits. 292

Other tasks of the Federal Assembly are of a *judicial nature*. For example, assigning the following functions concerning the competencies of the Swiss parliament: 293

– *approval of cantonal constitutions* after a review of their compatibility with federal law (Art. 172 par. 2 in conjunction with Art. 51 Const.);[27]
– decisions on the validity of popular initiatives (Art. 173 par. 1 [f] Const.);[28]
– decisions on jurisdictional conflicts between the highest federal authorities (Art. 173 par. 1 (i) Const.).[29]

Other modern democracies assign similar functions to the judiciary.

---

[27] Cf. n. 119 et seq.
[28] In Italy, to take an example, the Constitutional Court decides on the constitutionality of an abrogative referendum; Art. 2 legge costituzionale 11 marzo 1953, p. 1.
[29] In Germany, such disputes are settled by the Constitutional Court; Art. 93 par. 1 (1) German Basic Law.

294 Based on statutory law, parliament has the power to decide on certain *individual acts* which the legislator regards as particularly sensitive, for instance approval of authorisation for a nuclear power plant.

6. The Federal Council

> **Art. 174 Const. Federal Council**
> The Federal Council is the highest governing and executive authority of the Federation.

295 This provision highlights the dual function of the Swiss federal government: to govern and to administer. The order of the words is intentional: governing in a collegiate body has priority over the task of heading a specific ministry (or «department»). In practice, however, many members of the government tend to be absorbed primarily with administering their departments.

A. Composition

296 The Federal Council consists of *seven members*. This number has remained unchanged since 1848 when Switzerland was created as a federal state. An increase has been discussed repeatedly. Popular initiatives demanding such an increase combined with the popular election of the federal councillors were defeated in 1900 and 1942. The popular election of federal councillors would give the Federal Council the same democratic legitimacy as the Federal Assembly and hence weaken parliament. In addition, the desirability of having various language groups and regions represented in the federal government would probably necessitate some sort of quota system or the establishment of electoral districts. These may be reasons why the members of the

federal government, as opposed to their counterparts at the cantonal level, have no direct mandate from the people, but are elected by parliament.

All members of the Federal Council are equal. The chairman, called the Federal President, changes every year, and many Swiss (not to mention foreign observers) are often unaware of just who happens to be the Federal President at any particular time.

The Federal Council meets for one ordinary session every week; further meetings can be and often are convened at short notice. The meetings are not public. Four members constitute a quorum. Decisions are taken by a majority.[30]

The Federal Chancellor, who heads the *Federal Chancellery*, and the two Vice-Chancellors attend Federal Council meetings. The Federal Chancellery is the highest staff unit of the executive branch (Art. 179 Const.). It prepares the Federal Council meetings. Further tasks include legislative planning, language services, information and communication, data protection, edition of the federal gazette and other official publications, and – every four years – organizing elections to the National Council.

B. Election

The members of the Federal Council are elected for a term of four years from among Swiss citizens eligible to be elected to the National Council (Art. 175 par. 3 Const.). Before the term of office expires, removal by a parliamentary vote of no confidence or by popular recall or impeachment is not possible. The term of office is renewable. Councillors who stand for re-election are normally re-elected; only four exceptions to this have occurred since 1848 (in 1854, 1872, 2003 and 2007).

---

[30] In practice, a majority position usually emerges from the opinions expressed in the discussion, thus making voting unnecessary.

301 Formerly, no two members living in the same canton could be elected. This provision was replaced in 1999. Art. 175 par. 4 Const. stipulates that the various regions and language communities be appropriately represented. The Federal Council regularly includes at least two and often three members from the minority non-German speaking regions. Since the 2007 elections, three of the seven members are women.[31]

302 Members of the Federal Council may not simultaneously be members of one of the chambers of parliament or of the Federal Supreme Court. Nor may they hold any federal or cantonal office, or exercise any other gainful occupation (Art. 144 Const.).

303 The members of the Federal Council are *elected by the United Federal Assembly*, i.e. in a joint session of both chambers of parliament, following each full renewal of the National Council (Art. 175 par. 2 in conjunction with Art. 168 Const.). Election procedures are governed by the Federal Law on the Federal Assembly (Art. 130–134 ParlG). Voting is secret. The seats are filled separately and in turn, beginning with the incumbents running for re-election in the order of their seniority in office. This implies that seven separate elections are held, with the result that the deputies of each party act cautiously for fear of negative responses from the other factions. Attempts to alter this rather peculiar system of composing a government have hitherto failed.

304 To be elected, an absolute majority of the votes (i.e. over 50% of the valid votes) is required. In the first two rounds of voting the name of any person who fulfils the eligibility requirements can be written on the ballot paper. From the third ballot on, only candidates who received at least ten votes in the previous round are eligible; those who receive the least number of votes in a ballot are excluded from the next ballot.

---

[31] The first woman elected to the Federal Council was Elisabeth Kopp from the Liberal Party in 1984.

6. The Federal Council

From 1959 to 2003 the Federal Assembly allocated Federal Council seats to the most important political parties according to an informal «*magic formula*»: i.e. corresponding to their share of votes, the Social Democrats (SP), the Liberals (FDP) and the Christian Democrats (CVP) each had two seats, and the Swiss People's Party (SVP) had one.

In the 2003 elections the SVP emerged as the strongest party in parliament while the CVP ranked fourth. This prompted parliament to re-adjust the «magic formula» by not re-electing Ruth Metzler of the CVP, replacing her instead with Christoph Blocher of the SVP. Four years later the Assembly chose not to re-elect Blocher but to put another SVP politician, Eveline Widmer-Schlumpf, in his place. Although the SVP had again achieved the best results in the prior National Council elections and its parliamentary representatives had unanimously proposed Blocher's re-election, a parliament majority rejected the candidate for personal reasons. Blocher had apparently found it difficult to adjust to the collegiate system of a multi-party government. In addition, his party, the SVP, had conducted the electoral campaign for the National Council in such a way as to suggest that voters could only choose between Blocher as the preserver of Swiss values, and disorder. Other political parties did not appreciate such a personality cult.

That parliament chooses candidates other than those supported by their parties occurs time and again. But not to re-elect a federal councillor from a party that was «entitled» to the respective seat was most unusual and caused some controversy within the SVP culminating in the fragmentation of the party and the demise of the «magic formula».

C. Collegiate Principle and Administrative Units

> **Art. 177 Const. Principle of Collective Authority and Division into Departments**
>
> (1) The Federal Government takes its decisions as a collective body.
> (2) The preparation and implementation of the affairs of the Federal Council are distributed among its members according to Departments.
> (3) Decisions on certain matters can be entrusted to Departments or other units subordinated to them, provided that the right of appeal is guaranteed.

308 At the federal level as in the cantons, the government consists of several equal peers representing different political views taking all important decisions as a collegiate body either unanimously or by a majority. This hinders the concentration of power in any one member and at the same time contributes to decisions being based on a broad political consensus. Councillors are expected to support the majority decisions publicly, without expressing their possibly dissenting opinion. From a contemporary comparative perspective, this system is exceptional.[32]

309 Both the *President of the Federation* and the Vice President are elected by the United Federal Assembly from among the members of the Federal Council for a term of one year only (Art. 176 Const.). The presidency rotates among the members in order of seniority, whereby new members have to wait until they have served under their seniors. The President's main functions are to chair the meetings of the council and to perform special ceremonial duties.

310 Apart from its governing function, the Federal Council directs the federal administration (Art. 178 Const.). Each councillor heads

---

[32] A comparison may be made with the five member *Directoire* under the French Constitution of 1795.

one of the seven *Departments*, which are: the Federal Department of Foreign Affairs; the Federal Department of Home Affairs; the Federal Department of Justice and Police; the Federal Department of Defence, Civil Protection and Sports; the Federal Department of Finance; the Federal Department of Economic Affairs and the Federal Department of Environment, Transport, Energy and Communications. The members of the Federal Council decide among themselves who will head which department, whereby the more senior members have first choice. The capability to head a specific department appears to be secondary.

The Federal Law on the Organisation of Government and Administration[33] is the most relevant statute concerning the executive branch of government. Next to the Departments and the Federal Chancellery, the *Offices* are the primary administrative units. They are subordinated to a Department and usually headed by a director. The Federal Council enjoys wide discretion in defining the portfolio of each Department by regrouping and creating different Offices (Art. 43 RVOG). In every Department a *General Secretariat* assists the head of the Department in planning and coordinating the Department's activities and preparing the meetings of the Federal Council (Art. 42 RVOG). Moreover, a great number of permanent and ad hoc expert committees support the activities of government and administration.[34] 311

Over the years, more and more tasks have been delegated to the Departments and Offices. The burden thus imposed on the heads of Department in their function as administrators has severely impaired the ability of the Federal Council as a collegiate body to adequately perform its role of political leadership. Moreover, the public in general often evaluates members of government pri- 312

---

[33] Enacted 21 March 1997, SR 172.010; abbreviation: RVOG (Regierungs- und Verwaltungsorganisationsgesetz).

[34] They are called extra-parliamentary committees (Art. 57 par. 2 RVOG), as opposed to the parliamentary committees discussed in n. 275 et seq.

marily from the perspective of their performance as heads of department.

313 Statutory law may assign administrative tasks to entities constituted under public or private law or to individuals outside the federal administration (Art. 178 par. 3 Const.). Thus the Swiss Federal Railways is a specialised joint-stock corporation, with the federation and the cantons as shareholders. The two Federal Institutes of Technology (ETH) in Zurich and Lausanne both have separate legal personalities under public law and enjoy wide autonomy.

D. Powers

314 In 1848 and 1874, the framers of the constitution conceived of the Federal Council primarily as a body responsible for implementing legislation and supervising the administration. The growth of state responsibilities, their increasing complexity and dependence on international parameters has since resulted in a shift of power from parliament to government, accentuated in Switzerland by the lack of time and expertise available in a «*militia parliament*».[35]

315 As the highest executive authority, the Federal Council must continuously assess events at home and abroad, *determine the goals of federal government policy* as well as *plan and coordinate* state activities (Art. 180 par. 1 Const.). In doing so, it has to work towards national unity and the preservation of federal diversity (Art. 6 par. 4 RVOG).

316 *Foreign policy* is one of the main tasks of the government, in spite of parliament's increasing responsibility in this field.[36] The Federal Council is responsible for foreign relations, represents Swit-

---

[35] Cf. n. 251.
[36] Cf. n. 289.

zerland abroad, signs and – following approval by parliament or (in case of a referendum) the people – ratifies treaties (Art. 184 par. 1 and 2 Const.).

The Federal Council is a *key player in the legislative process.* Most 317 bills emanate from the government which, on its own initiative or at the request of parliament, proposes constitutional amendments, federal laws and decrees (Art. 181 Const.). Such proposals are normally the result of an intricate preliminary process conducted by the government, but including many actors with the aim of creating consensus at an early stage.[37] Moreover, the Federal Council issues legal norms of its own in the form of *ordinances,* insofar as the constitution or a statute empowers it to do so (Art. 182 par. 1 Const.). Based directly on the constitution, the government is entitled to issue ordinances when the safeguard of the interests of the country so requires (Art. 184 par. 3 Const.), or to guard against existing or imminent grave disturbances to public order or external or internal security (Art. 185 par. 3 Const.). Such ordinances must be limited in duration. Of significantly more practical impact are the numerous ordinances which follow the passing of most federal laws spelling out the application of those laws.[38]

The Federal Council *supervises the federal administration* and other 318 entities entrusted with federal tasks (Art. 187 par. 1 [a] Const.). That federal law be correctly implemented extends to the cantons. However, *relations between the federation and the cantons* (Art. 186 Const.) is distinguished by a spirit of cooperation and mutual respect.

The government's *financial duties* consist in preparing the finan- 319 cial plan, drafting the budget, keeping federal accounts and ensuring correct financial management (Art. 183 Const.).

---

[37] Cf. n. 227.
[38] Cf. n. 532.

320 Another duty of the Federal Council is to regularly *inform the public and parliament* of its activities (Art. 180 par. 2 and Art. 187 par. 1 [b] Const.). Art. 10 par. 2 RVOG specifies that the Federal Council provide consistent, early and continuous information with regard to its assessments, plans, decisions and measures. Such information is coordinated within the Federal Chancellery and is a prerequisite for effective parliamentary supervision and control by the media and the general public.

321 In a few sensitive areas such as external and internal security or diplomatic protection, the Federal Council, not the judiciary, *decides on appeals* (Art. 187 par. 1 [d] Const.).

7. The Federal Supreme Court

A. Comparison with other Federal States

322 The Swiss concept of a federal judiciary contrasts sharply with solutions reached in other federal states: whereas in Austria all jurisdiction emanates from the federation and all judgments are pronounced in the name of the Republic,[39] the powers of Swiss federal courts are essentially limited to the application of *federal law*. For the rest, legal disputes are decided in cantonal courts, and the organisation of the cantonal court system is a cantonal matter.[40]

323 In contrast to the United States, almost all lawsuits begin in cantonal courts even when they concern federal law. An appeal to the Federal Supreme Court is only possible following the decision of a cantonal court of last instance. Though legislation in

---

[39] Art. 82 Austrian Constitution.
[40] Up until now, even the civil and criminal procedures have differed from canton to canton, though a unification of these domains is now in sight; cf. n. 158.

civil and criminal law is almost entirely federal, the bulk of cases in these fields are dealt with by cantonal courts.

Like the Supreme Courts in the United States and Japan, the Swiss Federal Supreme Court decides cases and controversies pertaining to civil, penal, administrative and constitutional law. In contrast to the neighbouring states of Germany, Austria, Italy and France, there is *no special constitutional court* separated from the «ordinary» judiciary. 324

Until recently, the Federal Supreme Court was the only court at the federal level with general competencies in a wide area of law. Apart from the Federal Supreme Court, however, there were a great number of appeals commissions for specific areas of federal administration. Constitutional reform concerning the judiciary passed in 2000 aimed at relieving the pressure on the Federal Supreme Court resulted, among other things, in the creation of a *Federal Criminal Court* and a *Federal Administrative Court*. The former is, since April 2004, the court of first instance for cases that are subject to federal jurisdiction (such as serious cases of organised crime, money laundering and corruption), and also deals with appeals concerning international mutual legal assistance in criminal matters. The Federal Administrative Court commenced duties in January 2007, succeeding the numerous appeals commissions. Its main task is to judge disputes on federal administrative law. In certain cases, the decisions of the Federal Administrative Court can be challenged before the Federal Supreme Court. The administration of justice in military affairs is assigned to special military courts, established by the Military Penal Code. 325

As in other countries based on the rule of law, the *independence of the judiciary* constitutes a fundamental element of the judicial system. In administering justice all courts are independent and subject only to the law (Art. 191c Const.). 326

Part IV – Parliament, Government and the Judiciary

B. Composition and Election

327 The number of judges of the Federal Supreme Court is fixed by statutory law in the Federal Law on the Federal Supreme Court.[41] Pursuant to Art. 1 par. 3–5 BGG, the Federal Supreme Court consists of between 35 and 45 full-time judges and not more than two thirds as many part-time judges, whereby the exact numbers are to be determined in an ordinance enacted by parliament.[42] About 140 law clerks assist the judges in drafting the written judgments.

328 The judges are *elected by the United Federal Assembly* for a term of six years from among Swiss citizens eligible for election to the National Council. This means that any Swiss citizen over the age of 18 not placed under guardianship by reason of mental illness is eligible (Art. 143 in conjunction with Art. 136 Const.). Neither a law degree nor any legal training is required, at least in theory. But in fact parliament elects only experienced jurists with years of practice at court, the bar or as university professors. Another noteworthy peculiarity is the *relatively short term of office, combined with the possibility of re-election.* In order to bolster the independence of the judiciary, other countries avoid judges having to run for re-election, either by stating that they hold office «during good behaviour»,[43] or by electing them for a long but not renewable term.[44] Yet, in practice, Swiss judges seeking re-election are regularly re-elected. Due to the limited powers of the Federal Su-

---

[41] Enacted 17 June 2005, SR 173.110; abbreviation: BGG (Bundesgerichtsgesetz).

[42] Currently there are 38 full-time and 19 part-time judges.

[43] Federal judges of all three levels in the United States; Art. III Section 1 U.S. Constitution.

[44] Thus the judges of the German Constitutional Court are elected for a term of 12 years, whereby neither an immediate nor even a later re-election is permitted; Art. 4 Gesetz über das Bundesverfassungsgericht, enacted 11 August 1995.

preme Court in constitutional matters,[45] Swiss Federal Court judges are less exposed to the political limelight than their colleagues in Washington and Karlsruhe.

Members of the Federal Supreme Court may not simultaneously serve as members of the federal government or parliament. Full-time judges are, moreover, subject to the same restrictions as members of the Federal Council with regard to other offices and gainful occupations.[46] 329

Since March 2003, a Judicial Committee which includes members of both chambers and all parliamentary factions, prepares the elections to all federal courts including the Federal Supreme Court. Vacant posts have to be advertised, and the applications screened by the Judicial Committee. However, political considerations have a great impact. Apart from the legitimate desire to ensure that the different language communities are represented, seats are allocated roughly in proportion to the strength of the leading political parties. 330

C. Organisation

The *President* and the Vice President of the Federal Supreme Court are elected by the United Federal Assembly from among the full-time members of the court for a term of two years; re-election for one additional term of office is admissible (Art. 14 BGG). 331

The judges carry out their respective duties in the *seven Court Divisions*. There are two Public Law Divisions, two Civil Law Divisions, one Criminal Law Division, and two Social Law Divisions. The court's official residence is in Lausanne, but the two Social Law Divisions (which recently replaced the Federal Insurance 332

---

[45] Cf. n. 561 et seq.
[46] Cf. n. 302.

Court) are located in Lucerne. Every two years, at the request of its Administrative Committee, the court decides in plenary session on the composition and chair of each Division (Art. 15 par. 1 [d] BGG).

333 According to Art. 188 par. 3 Const., the court administers itself. This includes a certain *financial autonomy* and enables the court to present budget proposals in parliament without them first being vetted by the federal government and administration.[47] A *General Secretariat* serves as the main office for the personnel as well as for the organisational, administrative and financial matters of the entire court. It also assists the President, the Conference of Division Presidents and the Administrative Committee.

D. Duties

334 The Federal Supreme Court is the *highest federal judicial authority* in Switzerland (Art. 188 Const.).[48] Art. 189 Const. specifies its tasks.

---

[47] The federal courts of first instance (i.e. the Federal Criminal Court and the Federal Administrative Court) are also responsible for organising themselves but are subject to supervision by the Federal Supreme Court. All federal courts are subject to parliamentary control, which has to be exercised with due respect to the independence of the judiciary; cf. n. 292.

[48] The Constitution uses the term *Federal Court (Bundesgericht)*. In view of the creation of lower federal courts (cf. n. 325) the nomenclature *Federal Supreme Court* is, in a comparative context, easier to understand.

> **Art. 189 Const. Jurisdiction of the Federal Supreme Court**
>
> (1) The Federal Supreme Court adjudicates disputes over:
>   a. federal law;
>   b. international law;
>   c. intercantonal law;
>   d. cantonal constitutional rights;
>   e. communal autonomy and other cantonal guarantees in favour of corporations under public law;
>   f. federal and cantonal provisions on political rights.
> (2) It adjudicates disputes between the federation and cantons or between cantons.
> (3) Further competencies of the Federal Supreme Court can be established by statutory law.
> (4) An appeal to the Federal Supreme Court against enactments of the Federal Assembly and the Federal Council is not generally admissible. The law does, however, provide for exceptions.

As a rule, the Federal Supreme Court reviews decisions on *appeal*. Such decisions emanate either from the highest cantonal courts or from federal authorities, such as the Federal Criminal Court or the Federal Administrative Court. Apart from providing legal redress to aggrieved parties, the court ensures the unified application of federal law and contributes to the further development of the law. Exceptionally, in disputes between the federation and cantons or between cantons, the court exercises *original jurisdiction* (Art. 189 par. 2 Const).

The new Federal Law on the Federal Supreme Court, in force since the beginning of 2007, achieved a simplification of appeals available to submit a case to the highest federal court. It replaced the former variety of appeals and admissibility requirements with a uniform type of appeal including three alternative forms: an *appeal in civil matters,* an *appeal in criminal matters,* and an *appeal in matters of public law.* The grounds for complaint and a number of further procedural requirements are roughly the same; however, cantonal laws and decrees can only be directly contested in a public law appeal. Constitutional questions are most likely to be argued within the scope of a public law appeal, but can also arise in civil or criminal law cases. In addition to the three ordinary forms of appeal, the legislator created a *subsidiary constitutional appeal* to challenge cantonal decisions in cases where an ordinary appeal is not possible but the appellant claims that the decision violates constitutional rights. Constitutional jurisdiction will be discussed in more detail in Part VI.

337 In cases of original jurisdiction (Art. 189 par. 2 Const.) the federation or a canton files an *action* before the Federal Supreme Court.

338 On a very small scale the Federal Supreme Court may also enact ordinances. Such rules mainly concern the organisation and administration of the Federal Supreme Court itself.

E. Court Proceedings

339 In civil and criminal cases, only qualified legal practitioners can represent a party (Art. 40 BGG). However, an appellant is not obliged to retain a lawyer. It sometimes happens that a party litigates without legal assistance. The proceedings are conducted in one of the official languages, usually in the language of the contested decision (Art. 54 BGG).[49]

340 For the most part, appeals are deliberated and decided upon by a bench of three judges assisted by a law clerk; the latter may con-

---

[49] In composing the divisions, not only the expertise of the judges in various fields of law, but even a representation of the official languages has to be taken into consideration (Art. 18 par. 2 BGG). Judgments are pronounced in German, French or Italian. In one case, the Federal Supreme Court drew up the judgment in Romansh: BGE 122 I 93, Corporaziun da vaschins da Scuol.

tribute his or her opinion and is responsible for drafting the written judgment after a decision has been reached. In certain cases defined by law (for instance when the admissibility of a cantonal popular initiative is contested) or when requested by a judge, a five judge bench is necessary (Art. 20 BGG). Special quorums are required if a Division wants to decide on a question of law which would not conform with the precedent of another Division (Art. 23 BGG). Decisions are taken by the majority; abstention is not allowed. The president of a Division can declare certain appeals inadmissible, for instance for lack of sufficient grounds or because the time-limit for lodging an appeal has not been observed (Art. 108 BGG).

Deliberations are oral only when ordered by the presiding judge or demanded by one of the participating judges, or when unanimity cannot be achieved (Art. 58 BGG). In these rather rare cases, not only are the hearings open to the public; the judges even debate, vote and come to a decision in open court.[50] Such debates are usually bi- and sometimes even trilingual.

341

---

[50] This is quite common in Swiss courts at cantonal level, but noteworthy in a comparative context.

Part V – Fundamental Rights

1. General Considerations

A. Definitions

In view of the widespread use of imprecise and inconsistent terminology in the field of fundamental rights, some terms are defined here at the outset as they are to be understood in this book. *Fundamental Rights* (synonym: *basic rights*) are the rights of an individual vis-à-vis the state that have their basis either in a constitution or in an international convention. Catalogues of fundamental rights in constitutions and treaties usually encompass those rights considered as *human rights.* However, fundamental rights owe their existence not to natural law, but to *legal rules.* Fundamental rights embrace civil liberties, basic procedural and social rights, equality before the law and further principles that protect individuals in their relations with government authorities.

342

Civil liberties (or: *civil liberties and freedoms*) guarantee individuals a sphere of liberty and freedom and protect them from interference by the state. They safeguard the individual either in his or her personal integrity (such as right to life, personal freedom, privacy, religion) or with respect to interrelations with others (for instance freedom of expression, assembly or association); finally, they can protect an institutions such as marriage and private property. Civil liberties can be traced back to the Magna Carta of 1215. They were the focus of the American and French Bills of Rights at the end of the 18th century. Formerly, they were often regarded as merely «*negative*» or «*defensive*» rights, obliging the state to tolerate only the constitutionally protected spheres of human existence and to refrain from undue interference. In the course of time, the idea that civil liberties embody *guiding princi-*

343

ples for state activities with an impact on all areas of law has been generally accepted in some jurisdictions and is gaining ground in others.[1] Under certain circumstances the government has a *positive* obligation to ensure that individuals can enjoy civil liberties such as the right to life, liberty, property and the freedom of association. This may require legislation, funding, police action or judicial interpretation of civil and criminal law provisions in conformity with standards set by fundamental rights.

344 Usually, *basic procedural rights* are also classified as civil liberties. They figure in ancient as well as contemporary declarations of rights and in most modern constitutions. Essentially, they guarantee everyone a *fair trial*. Art. 6 of the European Convention on Human Rights (ECHR) formulates in relatively detailed terms the essence of such a fair trial, with special emphasis on a minimum of rights for persons charged with a criminal offence. Such procedural safeguards have a long tradition in British and American law.[2] Procedural justice obliges the state to fulfil a number of obligations, for instance to inform a person promptly and in a language which he understands of the reasons for his arrest,[3] or to provide free legal assistance where a person lacks the necessary means.

345 *Equality before the law*, too, developed as an independent guarantee in the United States and in France after their revolutionary periods. The individual has the right to equal treatment by all state authorities. Similar matters have to be dealt with in a similar manner by the legislator, and laws are to be applied equally to everyone.

---

[1] A landmark decision was the *Lüth judgment* of the German Constitutional Court, BVerfGE 7, 198 (1958).
[2] Cf. as examples the English prerogative writ of *habeas corpus;* Sections 8 to 12 of the Virginia Bill of Rights of 12 June 1776, and Amendments IV to VIII of the U.S. Constitution.
[3] Cf. Art. 5 (2) ECHR.

1. General Considerations

Sometimes *political rights* are listed together with classical civil liberties.[4] The rights of individuals to participate in the political process, usually associated with nationality, have been discussed in Part III of this book.

346

Basic social rights, such as the right to education or to housing, entitle the individual to state benefits. Such rights oblige the state to take positive action, often including comprehensive legislative and financial measures. However, as long as they are proclaimed in abstract constitutional norms only, their enforcement is problematic. For this reason, the European Social Charter of 18 October 1961, designed to protect social rights, does not contain self-executing individual rights;[5] its provisions are primarily aimed at binding the legislatures of the contracting states. Similarly, the Federal Supreme Court has held that most provisions in the U.N. Covenant on Economic, Social and Cultural Rights are not directly applicable.

347

B. Comparative Context

There are different ways of enshrining fundamental rights in a constitutional order: originally, the *U.S. Constitution* of 1787, which is still in force, was most reluctant to grant fundamental rights.[6] However, the first ten Amendments of 1791, commonly referred to as the «Bill of Rights» and aimed at restricting federal authorities only, contain a comprehensive list of civil liberties

348

---

[4] Cf. for instance the French Declaration of the Rights of Man and of the Citizen of 26 August 1789 and the U.N. Covenant on Civil and Political Rights of 16 December 1966.

[5] A right is self-executing when it can be given effect without the aid of implementing legislation.

[6] The only pertinent provisions concerned *habeas corpus,* the interdiction of bills of attainder, *ex post facto* laws and laws «impairing the obligation of contracts», trial by jury, and the right of the citizens of each state «to all privileges and immunities of citizens in the several states».

Part V – Fundamental Rights

and basic procedural rights. The «postwar» Amendments included among others an equal protection clause (Amendment XIV Section 1), ratified in 1868, which proved to be most important for bringing fundamental rights to bear even in the individual states.[7]

349 The British approach to fundamental rights contrasts greatly with the American approach. The *United Kingdom* has no written constitution, and until recently the rights of individuals were not set out in any sort of bill of rights, though a number of rights were protected by statute. Then the Human Rights Act 1998, an Act of parliament, incorporated most of the substantive rights of the European Convention on Human Rights (ECHR) into domestic law. The Human Rights Act 1998 places a duty on all courts and tribunals in the United Kingdom to interpret legislation so far as possible in a manner compatible with the ECHR and to take account of decisions of the European Court of Human Rights. Judges are not authorised to invalidate a parliamentary Act which is incompatible with the ECHR. But certain appellate courts may declare an Act incompatible with the ECHR in such cases.[8]

350 *France* cuts yet a different path. Its Constitution of 1958 mentions only very few fundamental rights, such as equality before the law (Art. 1) and personal liberty (Art. 66). But the preamble to the constitution solemnly proclaims solidarity with other documents reaching back to the Declaration of the Rights of Man and of the Citizen of 1789, and the preamble of the Constitution of 1946 that included a number of basic social rights in addition to classical civil liberties. Since 1971,[9] the French Constitutional

---

[7] As a result of the U.S. Supreme Court's jurisprudence, virtually all the provisions of the Bill of Rights have been «incorporated» into the XIV. Amendment and made applicable to the states.

[8] Cf. JOHN WADHAM / HELEN MOUNTFIELD, Blackstone's Guide to the Human Rights Act 1998, Blackstone, London 1999.

[9] Decision 44 DC of 16 July 1971 concerning freedom of association.

1. General Considerations

Council has applied the rights granted in the sources referred to in the preamble when examining the compatibility of legislation and treaties with the constitution. However, these rights do not include the ECHR which, though integrated into the national legal order and superior to ordinary legislation, ranks below the constitution.[10]

The *Basic Law for the Federal Republic of Germany* of 1949 puts a great deal of emphasis on fundamental rights. They are guaranteed in the first part of the Basic Law (Arts. 1 to 19), commencing with the mandate to respect human dignity. The emphasis lies on classical civil liberties and equality before the law. Fundamental social rights are not mentioned as such, but Art. 20 sets forth the basic constitutional principles and states that the Federal Republic is a «democratic and social federal state».

To grant fundamental rights in a special catalogue as part of the constitution has almost become an indispensable attribute of a modern constitution. In the past, the German Basic Law has thereby quite often served as a model. However, more recent European constitutions take the rights covered by the ECHR and other documents, such as the Charter of Fundamental Rights of the European Union, into consideration or even incorporate such rights.

The Swiss Constitutions of 1848 and 1874 only granted some fundamental rights in a piecemeal fashion scattered throughout the documents. By means of judicial interpretation and inspired by constitutional developments in the cantons, the Federal Supreme Court derived so called «unwritten», i.e. implied fundamental rights from the text of the constitution and deduced basic procedural rights from the concept of equality before the law.[11]

351

352

353

---

[10] Decision 54 DC of 15 January 1975 concerning termination of pregnancy.
[11] Cf. n. 39.

This jurisprudence, together with the impact of international conventions, is reflected in the *catalogue of fundamental rights* guaranteed in a separate chapter of the *Swiss Constitution of 1999*.

354 As far as the *substance* of fundamental rights is concerned, a sort of *European common law* has evolved.[12] There are three main reasons for this phenomenon: firstly, fundamental rights are the product of a common history of thought, determined by natural law teachings in the 17th and 18th centuries, the struggle for legislative supremacy in England that resulted in the guarantee of rights and freedoms there in the 17th century, and, in the outgoing 18th century, the French Revolution with the proclamation of human and citizens' rights following American bills of rights. Secondly, the violation of human rights during the Second World War strengthened the need for international protection and resulted, in Europe, in the ECHR providing for an effective mechanism to safeguard these rights and in the development of constitutional jurisdiction. And finally, due to the impact of the ECHR and the resulting Strasbourg case law on national legislation and jurisprudence, a far-reaching harmonisation occurred in this area. As Swiss particularities play a lesser role here, in comparison to the implementation of federalism, democracy and the system of government, we will refrain from analysing every single fundamental right in a comparative context.

C. Sources in Swiss Law

355 In the first place, fundamental rights are based on *federal constitutional law*. Chapter 1 of Title 2 Const. (Arts. 7 to 36) deals with fundamental rights. It contains a *comprehensive catalogue*, starting with the obligation to respect and protect human dignity, fol-

---

[12] PETER HÄBERLE created the term «common European constitutional law» («gemeineuropäisches Verfassungsrecht») as early as 1991; cf. *Europäische Grundrechte-Zeitschrift* 1991, p. 261 et seq.

1. General Considerations

lowed by an equal protection clause, civil liberties and freedoms, basic procedural rights, political rights and – to the extent practicable – basic social rights. The chapter concludes with two general provisions concerning the scope and restrictions of fundamental rights.[13] The fundamental rights as developed by the practice of the Federal Supreme Court[14] are thereby grounded in a modern text.

This catalogue is not to be regarded as a straitjacket, in spite of its elaborate nature. During the parliamentary debates on the new constitution it was repeatedly emphasised that, in future, there would still be room for the judiciary to evolve new spheres of liberty and freedom to be protected by the constitution from undue state interference. The imperative to protect human dignity may even require the recognition of new «unwritten» fundamental rights. Above all, the open-ended wording of many guarantees permits a *dynamic interpretation,* comparable to the practice of the European Court of Human rights with regard to the ECHR.[15]   356

Cantonal constitutions are a further source of fundamental rights. They often set apart such rights in a special chapter. Yet, according to the Federal Supreme Court, such provisions are only practically relevant if they protect the individual on a larger scale than the federal constitution. In view of the amplitude of the federal «Bill of Rights» this is rarely the case.   357

Next to the federal constitution, the *European Convention on Human Rights (ECHR)* is of outstanding importance in determining   358

---

[13] Rights qualified as fundamental can also be found in other parts of the constitution. Thus Art. 127 Const. states the principles of legality and equality in taxation matters and prohibits intercantonal double taxation.
[14] Cf. n. 39.
[15] Cf. with regard to the ECHR as «living instrument» *Tyrer v. the United Kingdom,* Judgment (Chamber), 25 April 1978, Series A, Vol. 36.

the content and scope of civil liberties and freedoms.[16] As Switzerland follows a monistic system, the rights guaranteed by the ECHR automatically became part of the Swiss domestic legal order with the ratification of the ECHR in 1974. Switzerland has also ratified most protocols to the ECHR.[17]

359 In all procedural respects, the rights of the ECHR are applied in the same manner as the fundamental rights granted in the Swiss constitution. They are directly applicable in specific cases, and all state organs must respect them. Their violation can be redressed by the Federal Supreme Court in the context of either an ordinary appeal or a subsidiary constitutional appeal. After exhaustion of domestic remedies, an aggrieved party can appeal to the European Court of Human Rights in Strasbourg.

360 The ECHR establishes a *European minimal standard*. It cannot be construed as limiting or derogating from any of the fundamental rights ensured by domestic law (Art. 53 ECHR). If somebody alleges a violation of both the ECHR and the federal constitution, the guarantee offering the more effective protection to the individual must be applied. Not always, however, does this rule lead to a clear-cut result. The Federal Supreme Court, therefore, strives to bring the contents of the constitution and the ECHR in line, even when national constitutional law quite obviously offers an equivalent protection. The consequence is that decisions of the highest Swiss court giving shape to a constitutional right very often include references to the case law of the European Court of Human Rights. Cases in which the Federal Supreme Court con-

---

[16] For a more detailed account cf. DANIELA THURNHERR, The Reception Process in Austria and Switzerland, in: Helen Keller / Alec Stone Sweet (eds.), A Europe of Rights: The Impact of the ECHR on National Legal Systems, Oxford University Press 2008, p. 311 et seq.

[17] With exception of the protocols no. 1, no. 4 and no. 12.

cludes that the constitution falls below an ECHR guarantee are rare.[18]

In addition to the ECHR, Switzerland has, mostly with a considerable delay, ratified a number of other international conventions pertaining to human rights. The most important ones are the U.N. Covenant on Economic, Social and Cultural Rights, the U.N. Covenant on Civil and Political Rights, the International Convention on the Elimination of All Forms of Racial Discrimination, the U.N. Convention against Torture and Other Cruel, Inhuman or Degrading Treatment or Punishment, the European Convention for the Prevention of Torture and Inhuman or Degrading Treatment or Punishment, and the U.N. Convention on the Rights of the Child. As far as these conventions are formulated clearly enough to have a direct bearing in specific cases, they are directly applicable by courts and administrative agencies. This is, for instance, the case with regard to the U.N. Covenant on Civil and Political Rights and some provisions of the U.N. Convention on the Rights of the Child.

D. Implementation

Art. 35 Const. Implementation of Fundamental Rights
(1) Fundamental rights are to be implemented throughout the entire legal system.
(2) Whoever exercises a state function must respect the fundamental rights and contribute to their implementation.
(3) Public authorities must ensure that fundamental rights, wherever appropriate, also take effect in relationships between individuals.

It is often said that fundamental rights are rights of an individual vis-à-vis the state. This conclusion deserves some specification in

---

[18] Example: BGE 109 Ib 183 (1983), *Reneja*, concerning right to respect for family life (Art. 8 ECHR), decided under the Const. 1874.

Part V – Fundamental Rights

two respects: who exactly is the *subject* of these rights? And who is their *addressee,* in other words, who is obliged to respect and implement them? The first question is easier to answer than the second one.

363 *Natural persons,* i.e. individuals, can be the subject of all fundamental rights. This includes minors, even at a stage where they lack the capacity to conduct proceedings in their own name.[19] *Foreign nationals* can invoke all fundamental rights, with the exception of political rights, the freedom of domicile (Art. 24 Const.) and, depending on their status, economic freedom (Art. 27 Const.). *Public officers* are also beneficiaries of fundamental rights. Their special relationship to the state can, in certain cases, justify specific restrictions in the public interest.

364 *Legal persons constituted under private law,* such as associations or joint stock companies can invoke those fundamental rights that are not exclusively aimed at the protection of an individual sphere of human existence, as would be the case regarding personal liberty or the right to marriage and family. Thus, a legal person can for instance rely on the right to property, economic freedom or equality before the law. *Legal persons constituted under public law,* however, can invoke a fundamental right only under exceptional circumstances, namely when they act under private law and are affected by state activities in the same way as an individual.

365 Fundamental rights are primarily *directed at the state.* By «state» we mean *all state authorities at every level,* i.e. federal, cantonal and communal, irrespective of the nature of the task performed. *Lawmakers* enjoy a wide margin of discretion in realising the community's manifold interests; yet, in appraising and balancing

---

[19] Art. 11 Const. emphasizes that children and young people have a right to special protection and that they may exercise their rights themselves to the extent of their capacity to discern.

these interests, they must take fundamental rights into account, for instance balance the demand for effective law enforcement against the interest of an accused to humane treatment and a fair trial. *Government* and *administration* have to observe fundamental rights not only in their day-to-day application and enforcement of laws, but also when they prepare legislation and enact ordinances. The obligation of *courts* is threefold: to redress violations of fundamental rights; to interpret open-ended provisions in conformity with standards set by fundamental rights; and, finally, to refuse to apply a norm which conflicts with fundamental rights.[20]

State authorities sometimes act under private law, for instance by concluding a contract of sale or a building contract. Or, it can happen that entities constituted under private law are assigned public tasks. Formerly, the relevance of fundamental rights in such constellations was highly controversial. Art. 35 par. 2 Const. has made clear that whoever exercises a state function must respect fundamental rights. This includes state authorities that are parties to private law contracts as well as private entities performing public tasks delegated to them by the state. How far the commitment reaches will depend on the nature of the activity or task in question. 366

The most delicate question with regard to the addressee of fundamental rights is whether they have an *effect between private parties* and not only in relation to the state. Some freedoms are not only threatened by state intrusions, but also put at risk by the conduct of powerful private actors such as business enterprises. Thus economic freedom or the freedom of the press can become illusory for small entrepreneurs if some market participants acquire a monopolistic position and prevent free competition. In the United States the Supreme Court tried to solve this problem 367

---

[20] Except when Art. 190 Const. obliges courts to apply a provision irrespective of its conformity with the constitution; cf. n. 562.

by expanding the notion of «state action» (and therewith the scope of Amendment XIV) to agreements between private individuals as soon as elements attributable to the state could be discerned.[21]

368 Under the influence of German doctrine Switzerland took a different path, developing the concept of «*Drittwirkung*» *(=third-party effect)*. The essence of this concept is that fundamental rights are objective values or guiding principles that affect all areas of law, including private law. However, a too wide-ranging acceptance of such third-party consequences could undermine contractual freedom and potentially allow judicial interpretation to outmanoeuvre civil law. Art. 35 par. 3 Const. therefore uses a prudent formula which accepts, yet at the same time limits, the impact of fundamental rights between private parties.

369 Fundamental rights, according to this formula, have *no direct third-party effect*, i.e. private parties are not directly bound by them.[22] However, public authorities have an obligation to ensure, wherever appropriate, that fundamental rights take effect in relationships between individuals. This has two main consequences: firstly, fundamental rights include a (judicially non-enforceable) *mandate to the legislatures* at federal and cantonal level to protect the values inherent in the catalogue of fundamental rights, for instance by imposing legal sanctions against individuals who violate or threaten the freedom of their fellow citizens. This may require legislation protecting life, property and specific freedoms, or directed against discrimination based on race or gender. Secondly, a so called *indirect third-party effect* is attributed to funda-

---

[21] Famous and most controversial example: *Shelley v. Kramer*, 334 U.S. 1 (1948), where the court regarded the *enforcement* of a restrictive covenant excluding black families from ownership or occupancy of real property as state action violating the equal protection clause.

[22] Except when the constitution presumes such an effect, as in the case of the right of men and women to equal pay for work of equal value granted in Art. 8 par. 3 (3) Const.; cf. n. 455.

mental rights. This means that courts take fundamental rights into account when they apply general clauses or other legal terms which, despite being part of civil or penal law, implicate constitutional concerns and leave room for judicial interpretation. To take an example: in deciding whether a communication in the media violated Art. 28 par. 2 of the Civil Code which prohibits «wrongful» invasion of the right of privacy, the Federal Supreme Court balanced the interests of the private party affected against the task of media to inform the public.[23]

E. Restrictions

Art. 36 Const.   Restrictions on Fundamental Rights

(1) Restrictions on fundamental rights require a legal basis. Grave restrictions must be prescribed by statute. Situations of serious, imminent and not otherwise preventable danger are reserved.

(2) Restrictions on fundamental rights must be justified by public interest or by the need to protect the fundamental rights of others.

(3) Restrictions on fundamental rights must be proportionate to the goal pursued.

(4) The core content of fundamental rights is inviolable.

Art. 36 Const. lists the prerequisites for restrictions on fundamental rights as developed by long-standing court practice under the 1874 Constitution: legal basis, public interest, proportionality and inviolability of the core content. These conditions are *cumulative*; if one of them is lacking, a fundamental right cannot be restricted.

370

---

[23] BGE 132 III 641 (2006), *Kessler-Bösch*. The U.S. Supreme Court does not treat lawsuits against governmental entities for failure to protect life and physical integrity as fundamental rights issues. Cf. *Castle Rock v. Gonzales*, 545 U.S. 748 (2005), where the refusal by the police to enforce a restraining order which a woman had obtained against her violent husband led to the murder of the couple's three children.

Part V – Fundamental Rights

371 The text of Art. 36 Const. covers all types of fundamental rights. Preparatory materials to the framing of the constitution, however, suggest that the restrictions were *aimed at civil liberties only*.[24] With regard to equality before the law or basic social rights the criteria for restrictions indeed make little sense. Moreover, certain basic procedural guarantees, such as the right to be judged by an independent and impartial court (Art. 30 par. 1 Const.), do not tolerate any restriction. The current doctrine and jurisprudence in this matter can be summed up as follows: Art. 36 Const. applies to all civil liberties. Other types of fundamental rights can be relativised, whereby the criteria contained in Art. 36 Const. may be used as an alternative, as long as a right is not regarded as absolute. Thus affirmative action favouring women and discriminating against men can be justified under certain circumstances, but only if the respective measures have a clear legal basis and are proportionate to the constitutional goal (Art. 8 par. 3 Const.) of achieving gender equality in law and in fact.[25]

372 Restrictions on the rights guaranteed in Arts. 8 to 11 ECHR (respect for private and family life, freedom of thought, conscience and religion, freedoms of expression, assembly and association) must have a *legal basis* and furthermore be *necessary* to achieve *public interests* essential in a democratic society and defined in these articles. Art. 36 Const. is in harmony with these standards.[26] As a matter of fact, the proportionality assessment gradually adopted by the European Court of Human Rights, as opposed to the traditional and less stringent reasonableness test, was, origi-

---

[24] Cf. the Federal Council's message on the new constitution in the Federal Gazette, BBl 1997 I 194 et seq.
[25] Cf. n. 454.
[26] Other rights of the ECHR, such as the right to liberty and security (Art. 5 ECHR), are subject to specific limitations.

1. General Considerations

nally, native only to the legal systems of Germany and Switzerland.[27]

373 The requirement of a *legal basis* comprises two elements. First of all, the restriction must be determined by a *legal rule* (i.e. described in general and abstract terms). The rule has to be formulated with sufficient *precision* to permit individuals to act in conformity with it, and to enable them to foresee the legal consequences of their behaviour with a degree of certainty corresponding to the circumstances.[28] This provides for legal security and serves the principle of equal treatment of individuals.

374 Yet, an ordinance enacted by the executive, though containing legal rules, does not suffice as the legal basis for *grave restrictions*. Such limitations of spheres protected by civil liberties and freedoms have to be *prescribed by statute* (Art. 36 par. 1 [2] Const.). Statutes are enacted in a procedure involving the parliament and, through referendum, the people. This provides statutes with an increased democratic legitimacy. Grave restrictions are, for instance, deprivations of liberty, phone tapping, forced medication, or the imposition of taxes. The more a restriction curtails civil liberties, the greater the need to determine the prerequisites for intervention at statutory level and not merely in an ordinance.

375 Obviously, even a visionary legislator can not foresee all dangers which might threaten public safety in the future. Therefore, it may happen that there is at a given time no legal basis for state measures which are indispensable to avert serious and imminent danger. In such cases, the so-called *general police clause*, laid down

---

[27] Cf. HELEN KELLER / ALEC STONE SWEET (eds.), A Europe of Rights: The Impact of the ECHR on National Legal Systems, Oxford University Press 2008, p. 11 and 24.
[28] BGE 117 Ia 472 E. 3e (1991), Social Democratic Party of Basle-City, with reference to Strasbourg case law.

in Art. 36 par. 1 (3) Const., can temporarily replace a legal basis.[29]

376 In addition to a legal basis, restrictions of civil liberties must be justified by *public interest* or by the need to protect the fundamental rights of others (Art. 36 par. 2 Const.).[30] The notion of «public interest» cannot be captured in a simple formula. It changes over time and can even vary regionally. «Public interest» embraces all measures the state (federation, canton or commune) takes within its competencies in pursuing the public weal. An important category of such interests permitting the restriction of civil liberties is labelled «*police interests*» in Swiss jurisprudence. It comprises the protection of public order, peace, safety, health, morals and good faith in business dealings. Other interests, like environmental protection and land-use planning, quite often justify restrictions of the right to property, and socio-political considerations may demand that the economic freedom be limited. The interest of ascertaining the truth in civil lawsuits and criminal prosecutions also constitutes a public interest, sometimes necessitating restrictions of personal freedom and privacy, as in the case of DNA profiling, search and seizure, and arrest. The range of public interests possibly justifying a restriction varies, depending on the affected right. A deprivation of liberty, for instance, is only permitted in the cases enumerated in Art. 5 (1) ECHR.

377 Civil liberties must be limited to some extent so that they can be enjoyed by all; the unchecked freedom of the one shall not become a burden to others. It can therefore happen, as Art. 36 par. 2 Const. presumes, that the restriction of a civil liberty is de-

---

[29] As in BGE 130 I 369 E. 7.3 (2004), where there was no express legal basis for preventing a journalist from travelling to the World Economic Forum in Davos. The police had taken comprehensive measures, including securing the access roads to Davos, in anticipation of violent demonstrations by anti-globalisation activists.

[30] That the state is obliged to protect the freedom of others follows from the nature of fundamental rights as guiding principles. Cf. n. 368.

1. General Considerations

signed to protect the freedom of others. In such cases legislators and courts face the delicate task of balancing conflicting civil liberties in a just manner, such as the freedom of the media (Art. 17 Const.) against the right of individuals whose constitutionally protected privacy (Art. 13 Const.) is threatened by journalists gathering and publishing private information. This aspect has to be kept in mind when applying the principle of proportionality.

Every restriction of a fundamental right must be *proportionate to the goal pursued* (Art. 36 par. 3 Const.). The underlying idea is, loosely expressed, not to overreact. A restriction may go no further than is required by public interest. This is true as soon as three conditions are met cumulatively: 1. A regulatory measure must be *suited* to achieve a legitimate public purpose. 2. The regulation has to be *necessary*. This is not the case if less restrictive means are available to achieve the goal. 3. Finally, the *proportionality of the measure in relation to the public purpose* must be taken into account, in other words, the public and private interests concerned must be balanced against each other. A measure is disproportionate if its negative effect outweighs the public interest. 378

> Example: it often happens that the right to property (Art. 26 Const.) has to be balanced against public interests, such as protection of the landscape. In order to protect a beautiful landscape, a building ban is likely to be a suitable measure. Whether it is also necessary, depends on an appraisal of various elements; perhaps, for example, building restrictions not amounting to a total ban would suffice. Almost certainly, however, a demolition order with regard to inhabited buildings in the area in question would appear to be a disproportionate measure in relation to the goal of protecting the landscape.

The *core content of fundamental rights is inviolable* (Art. 36 par. 4 Const.). This limit on any restriction follows the formulation of 379

Art. 19 par. 2 of the German Basic Law.[31] It had already found its way into Swiss doctrine and case law before receiving a special place in the constitutional text.[32] Measures that disregard human dignity (Art. 7 Const.) are absolutely prohibited. Some guarantees are *per se* inviolable. This holds true for, among others, prohibition of the death penalty (Art. 10 par. 3 (2) Const.) and the prohibition of torture and any other cruel, inhuman or degrading treatment or punishment (Art. 10 par. 3 Const.).[33] In such cases the scope of a guarantee and its inviolable core are congruent.

2. Human Dignity: Basic Value, Guiding Principle and Civil Liberty

Art. 7 Const.   Human Dignity
Human dignity must be respected and protected.

380 The obligation to respect and protect human dignity opens the chapter on fundamental rights. Obviously it was inspired by Art. 1 par. 1 of the German Basic Law,[34] as was the foregoing case law of the Federal Supreme Court acknowledging the importance of human dignity in giving shape to fundamental rights.

---

[31] Art. 19 par. 2 German Basic Law: «In no case may a fundamental right be infringed upon in its core content.»

[32] In BGE 109 Ia 273 E. 7 (1983), *Vest,* the Federal Supreme Court remarked in an *obiter dictum,* i.e. in an observation not essential to the grounding of the decision in the case, that the use of narco analysis (the so called «truth drug») in a criminal prosecution would infringe upon the inviolable content of personal liberty.

[33] Cf. also Art. 15 par. 2 ECHR and protocols no. 6 and no. 13 to the ECHR.

[34] Art. 1 par. 1 German Basic Law: «The dignity of man is inviolable. To respect and protect it is the duty of all state authorities.»

2. Human Dignity: Basic Value, Guiding Principle and Civil Liberty

The positioning of human dignity in the catalogue of fundamental rights (and not in the general provisions of Arts. 1 to 6 Const.) makes it clear that human dignity is a civil liberty, legally enforceable like any other fundamental right. In addition, human dignity is a basic constitutional value permeating the constitutional order, reinforcing other fundamental rights and guiding state action.

381

Art. 7 Const. presupposes a minimal consensus with regard to the substance of human dignity. This substance has gradually developed and been shaped by philosophical and religious ideas, but cannot be narrowed down to a simple abstract formula. All individuals are to be respected in their personality and uniqueness. Human dignity is violated when human beings are treated as mere objects, in a degrading manner, or when they are discriminated against based on suspect classifications such as race, origin or religion.

382

Some specific fundamental rights are narrowly tied to human dignity, for instance, the prohibitions of discrimination (Art. 8 par. 2 Const.) and of torture (Art. 10 par. 3 Const.) as well as the basic social right to receive assistance when in need (Art. 12 Const.), and specific guarantees of fair procedure (Arts. 29 to 32 Const.). In applying these and other fundamental rights to concrete situations, human dignity serves as the guideline.

383

As the protection afforded by specific fundamental rights granted in the constitution and in international conventions is comprehensive, there is little room for deducing additional rights from Art. 7 Const. Yet human dignity, understood as a civil liberty, has some practical impact. Up to now, the Federal Supreme Court has based two civil liberties, which were expressly included in the Const. 1874, directly in the human dignity clause of Art. 7

384

3. Civil Liberties and Freedoms

A. Right to Life and Personal Liberty

> **Art. 10 Const. Right to Life and Personal Liberty**
> (1) Everyone has the right to life. The death penalty is prohibited.
> (2) Everyone has the right to personal liberty, in particular to physical and mental integrity, and to freedom of movement.
> (3) Torture and any other cruel, inhuman or degrading treatment or punishment are prohibited.

385 Personal liberty and the right to life were originally implied civil liberties, derived from other fundamental rights and constitutional principles by judicial interpretation. The *right to life* was invoked for the first time in a case concerning the admissibility of organ transplants at cantonal hospitals.[37] As the termination of a pregnancy is regulated in the Federal Penal Code,[38] there are no «abortion decisions» by the Swiss Federal Supreme Court balancing the right to life of a fetus against the pregnant woman's privacy and autonomy of decision.

386 Switzerland has ratified protocols no. 6 and no. 13 to the ECHR abolishing the death penalty. In accordance with these international obligations, the constitution prohibits the death penalty absolutely, even in wartime.

---

[35] BGE 125 I 300 E. 2a (1999).
[36] BGE 130 I 169 E 2.2 (2004).
[37] BGE 98 Ia 508 E. 4 (1972), *Gross*.
[38] Which is binding on all courts according to Art. 190 Const; cf. 562.

3. Civil Liberties and Freedoms

The right to life includes the right not to be extradited to a state 387
where the person concerned is menaced by the death penalty.[39]
Moreover, it obliges the state to conduct an effective and independent investigation if the death of a person has been caused by the police force.[40]

Physical integrity and freedom of movement in the sense of the 388
liberty to «dispose of one's own body» were in the focus of *habeas corpus* as it developed in British law as a legal remedy to challenge the validity of a person's detention.[41] The insight that mental integrity, too, needs legal protection is more recent.

The *prohibition of torture* encompasses both physical and mental 389
integrity. Art. 10 par. 3 Const. corresponds to the prohibition of torture, inhuman or degrading treatment or punishment in Art. 3 ECHR.

Physical integrity is affected by any intrusion into the body, even if 390
it does not cause pain or damage.[42] Thus, blood tests restrict personal liberty, with the consequence that they cannot be effected against the will of the person concerned if there is no legal basis for this measure. In the case of operations and medical treatment, the patient's informed consent legitimises the intrusion. If a minor is capable of forming his or her own views, these must be given due weight, and the consent of the parents alone will not suffice. This follows from Art. 12 (1) of the U.N. Convention

---

[39] BGE 130 II 217 E. 8.8 (2004), *Wang*.

[40] *Scavuzzo-Hager v. Switzerland,* Judgment of the European Court of Human Rights (Fourth Section), 7 February 2006, no. 41773/98. The same duty is incumbent upon the state when there are indications of degrading treatment by the police; BGE 131 I 455 (2005).

[41] The procedure for issuing a writ of *habeas corpus* was first codified by the Habeas Corpus Act 1679.

[42] Cf. BGE 118 Ia 427 E. 4b (1992), concerning dental treatment.

on the Rights of the Child and Art. 11 Const. regarding the protection of children and young people.[43]

391 The core of *freedom of movement* is the *protection against unwarranted deprivation of liberty*, i.e. the detention of a person against his or her will in a narrowly confined area for a certain period, as in case of arrest, execution of a prison sentence, custody in a closed psychiatric ward, or detention with a view to deportation or extradition. Such deprivations of liberty are only admissible in the cases exhaustively listed in Art. 5 (1) ECHR; moreover, they are subject to specific procedural safeguards.[44] «Freedom of movement» in the sense of Art. 10 par. 2 Const. is even at stake in certain situations not covered by Art. 5 (1) ECHR, for instance, identification measures and interrogations necessitating a short presence at a police station, or the imposition to remain within a restricted area provided for in Art. 74 of the Federal Law on Foreigners. Such measures do not fall under Art. 5 (1) ECHR, but as they restrict personal liberty they require a legal basis and must be justified by a preponderant public interest. However, not every opportunity to move from one place to another enjoys constitutional protection. For instance, speed limits, traffic and customs checks, a cordoned off road at the scene of an accident, or the prohibition on driving a motor boat or wind-surfing on a defined area of a lake cannot be qualified as intrusions into personal liberty.

392 Art. 10 par. 2 Const. includes *mental integrity* in the scope of personal liberty. Hence, the individual is protected against the infliction of mental suffering by the state. Moreover, mental integrity includes, to a certain degree, freedom of choice. Already under

---

[43] In BGE 134 II 235 (2008) the Federal Supreme Court upheld a sentence fining a physician, because he had not respected the will of a 13 year old girl who had refused a painful therapy which was not absolutely necessary.

[44] Cf. n. 473 et seq.

the Const. 1874 the Federal Supreme Court classified the free exercise of will and the freedom to decide on a way of living and even planning leisure time as one element of personal liberty. Later on, in order to meet concerns that this far-reaching formula, reminiscent of the «right to free development of personality» granted in Art. 2 par. 1 of the German Basic Law, might dilute the substance of personal liberty, the court established a narrower and more precise criterion which has henceforward been decisive: Personal liberty protects only the *basic elements of will essential for self-development.*[45] Many decisions of the Federal Supreme Court concern the *conditions of detention*, pertaining, for instance, to daily open-air walks, medical attendance, receiving visitors and gifts or keeping personal belongings in the cell.[46] In a number of these cases, both physical and mental integrity were concerned and human dignity served as guideline for giving shape to personal liberty.

The wording «in particular» in Art. 10 par. 2 Const. offers the possibility of assigning further aspects of personal development and privacy (in addition to physical and mental liberty, and the freedom of movement) to the area protected by personal liberty. However, as Art. 13 Const. explicitly guarantees the right to privacy, which was part of the implied right to personal liberty under the Const. 1874, it is more obvious to invoke both Arts. 10 and 13 Const. when important choices touch an individual's privacy. Both fundamental rights, personal liberty and privacy, are relevant with regard to the following legal issues (to take but a few examples): 393

---

[45] BGE 101 Ia 336 E. 7 (1975), *Verband der Schweizerischen Automatenbranche:* Personal liberty does not include the freedom to play slot machines.

[46] Summary of the relevant case law in BGE 118 Ia 64 (1992), *Minelli.*

Part V – Fundamental Rights

- sexual autonomy of gay couples;[47]
- access to medically assisted procreation;[48]
- right to die;[49]
- right to make dispositions concerning one's own body with effect beyond death.[50]

B. Right to Privacy

> **Art. 13 Const.   Right to Privacy**
> (1) Everyone has the right to privacy in their private and family life, abode, mail and telecommunications.
> (2) Everyone has the right to be protected against the misuse of their personal data.

394 The first paragraph largely corresponds with Art. 8 (1) ECHR, whereas the second paragraph emphasises the protection of data privacy.

395 *Private life* (and data protection) is encroached upon when public roads and squares are monitored with video cameras and the respective records are kept.[51] Therefore, public interest in bringing perpetrators to justice has to be carefully balanced against the right to privacy.

---

[47] BGE 126 II 425 E. 4c (2000), concerning a lesbian couple. In this case, only privacy was invoked.
[48] BGE 119 Ia 460 (1993) and 115 Ia 234 (1989), concerning laws of Basle-City and St. Gall.
[49] However, this right does not include the right to be provided with drugs to commit suicide free of pain: BGE 133 I 58 E. 6.2 (2007).
[50] BGE 129 I 173 (2003), concerning burial in Meilen. In this case the last will of the deceased to be cremated outweighed the opposing interests of family members.
[51] BGE 133 I 77 E. 3.2 (2007), *Diggelmann*.

3. Civil Liberties and Freedoms

Family life is of special practical significance when the expulsion of an alien or the denial of permission to enter the country threatens to disrupt the family. In balancing the goals of national immigration policy against affected private interests, the Federal Supreme Court is anxious to comply with the case law of the European Court of Human Rights.[52]

396

The *inviolability of abode* even covers temporarily inhabited housing space, for instance hotel rooms and mobile homes.

397

Secrecy of mail and telecommunications has become a special concern in view of the importance of electronic communication. The Federal Supreme Court has made it clear that Art. 13 Const. also protects e-mails.[53] Telephone tapping and similar surveillance measures are only allowed in criminal proceedings, and are subject to the tough requirements laid down by federal statutory law.[54]

398

In order to protect the individual against the unlimited collection, storage, use and disclosure of personal data, the German Constitutional Court deduced a *right to informational self-determination («informationelle Selbstbestimmung»)* from the Basic Law.[55] The Swiss Federal Supreme Court adopted this term in a number of cases defining the scope of personal liberty and privacy under the Const. 1874. These include the right to decide what information about one's own personal matters should be communicated to others, and the right to inspect personal data

399

---

[52] Summary of relevant case law in BGE 130 II 281 E. 3 (2004), concerning the right of a resident to be joined by his family.
[53] BGE 126 I 50 E. 6 (2000), *Swiss Online AG*.
[54] Federal Law on the Surveillance of Mail and Telecommunications (Bundesgesetz betreffend die Überwachung des Post- und Fernmeldeverkehrs) of 6 October 2000, SR 780.1.
[55] BVerfGE 65, 1 (91 et seq.), relating to personal information collected during the 1983 census.

kept by the authorities.[56] The new constitution expressly added the right to be protected against the misuse of personal data (Art. 13 par. 2 Const.).

400 The constitutional parameters relating to data protection were implemented in a federal statute. The Federal Data Protection Law[57] contains detailed regulations on the collecting and handling of personal data by federal authorities, individuals and private enterprises, backed up by a right of individual access to personal data and by procedural safeguards, for instance concerning error detection and correction as well as eradication of data after a certain time. The cantons have enacted corresponding legislation, often also establishing an ombudsman for data protection.

C. Right to Marriage and Family

Art. 14 Const.   Right to Marriage and Family
The right to marry and to found a family is guaranteed.

401 The right to marry and to found a family has been interpreted by the Federal Supreme Court as being limited to couples of the opposite sex.[58] This is in line with Strasbourg case law. Gay couples are protected by other fundamental rights (personal liberty, right to privacy). Furthermore, since 2007, they can have their partnership registered, which provides them with the legal and social benefits of a traditional marriage. Nevertheless, they are not permitted to adopt children, and they have no access to medically assisted procreation.

---

[56] Cf. BGE 113 Ia 257 E. 4 (1987) concerning the right to be informed about entries in police records.
[57] Of 19 June 1992, SR 235.1.
[58] BGE 126 II 425 E. 2b (2000); BGE 119 II 264 E. 4 (1993). MÜLLER / SCHEFER, Grundrechte in der Schweiz, p. 221 et seq., argue that the right to a family does not presuppose a marriage.

The Civil Code contains some restrictions on the right to marry 402
which are fairly straightforward: both fiancées must be over the
age of 18 and capable of forming their own will. An already existing marriage as well as a close degree of relationship precludes a
marriage. Formerly, the Civil Code empowered divorce courts to
fix a period (in the case of adultery up to three years) during
which the party «at fault» was not permitted to remarry. The
European Court of Human Rights regarded this regulation as a
violation of Art. 12 ECHR.[59] The Civil Code has since been
amended.

During the parliamentary debates on the new constitution, the 403
right to have a family was added to the draft presented by the
government. The legal situation with regard to family basically
corresponds to the protection conferred by the ECHR: while
Art. 14 Const. and Art. 12 ECHR guarantee the right to *found a
family*, the *integrity of family life* is a concern of Art. 13 par. 1
Const. and Art. 8 ECHR.

D. Freedom of Religion and Conscience

> **Art. 15 Const. Freedom of Religion and Conscience**
> (1) Freedom of religion and conscience is guaranteed.
> (2) Everyone has the right to choose their religion and their philosophical convictions of their own free will and to manifest them either alone or in community with others.
> (3) Everyone has the right to join or belong to a religious community and to attend religious instruction.
> (4) Nobody may be forced to join or belong to a religious community, to perform religious acts or to attend religious instruction.

---

[59] *F. v. Switzerland*, Judgment (Plenary), 18 December 1987, Series A, Vol. 128.

Part V – Fundamental Rights

404 The origins of the Swiss federal state were largely dominated by the struggle to overcome religious antagonism between the mainly protestant liberal and the predominantly catholic conservative cantons.[60] However, it took over one and a half centuries to free the constitution of all traces of the defeat which the catholic cantons had suffered in November 1847 in the *Sonderbund* war: up until 1973 the Jesuit order was banned from any activities in churches and schools, and the establishment of new cloisters and religious orders was forbidden.[61] A constitutional provision requiring federal approval for the institution of new bishoprics was in force until 2001. Today religious majorities and minorities are rather evenly balanced across the cantons between Protestants and Catholics. Central Switzerland and the Canton Ticino are traditionally catholic. The predominance of Protestants in larger cities like Zurich and Berne has faded, mainly due to immigration. Religious strife between Catholics and Protestants is no longer an issue. However, in recent years, the courts have been kept busy with legal proceedings instituted by members of sizable minority religions, foremost by Muslims.

405 According to the population census 2000, the religious composition of the Swiss population is as follows:[62]

–	Roman Catholic	41,8%
–	Protestant	35,3%
–	Muslim	4,3%
–	Orthodox Christian	1,8%
–	Other religion	1,4%
–	No religion	11,1%
–	No indication	4,3%

---

[60] Cf. n. 18.
[61] Arts. 51 and 52 Const. 1874. The repeal of these provisions was a precondition of Switzerland's accession to the ECHR.
[62] Statistical Office, Statistical Data on Switzerland 2006, p. 7.

3. Civil Liberties and Freedoms

The regulation of the relationship between church and state is a cantonal matter (Art. 72 par. 1 Const.). Most of the cantons, except Geneva and Neuchâtel, recognise official churches and endow them with a public law status, thereby favouring the Roman Catholic Church and the Protestant Church. In some cantons, Jewish religious communities have also acquired official status. Officially recognised churches and communities can raise taxes which are collected from their adherents by the state, at the same time as the cantonal and communal taxes. A constitutional initiative calling for a complete separation of church and state was clearly rejected in 1980.

406

Freedom of *religion* protects all forms of an individual's belief relating to the divine transcendent sphere, irrespective of its substance. It even includes atheism, as everyone is free to believe or not to believe in a Supreme Being. The exact meaning of *philosophical convictions*, which are also protected by Art. 15 Const., has never been clarified. As freedom of expression (Art. 16 Const.) protects secular convictions and their manifestation comprehensively, the practical need to draw a clear borderline seems negligible. Freedom of religion and philosophical conviction not only protects believers against restrictions by the state, but even obliges public authorities to observe a certain degree of neutrality in religious matters.[63] This neutrality is of special importance with respect to public schools. In two cases which attracted great interest the Federal Supreme Court found that the required confessional neutrality at public schools had been violated: the first case concerned crucifixes in class rooms at a primary school in

407

---

[63] BGE 118 Ia 46 E. 4e (1992), *Scientology Church Association Zurich*. Absolute neutrality in the sense of the Establishment Clause of the U.S. Constitution, Am. I, is not required. As we have seen, in most cantons catholic and protestant churches are privileged by their recognition as official churches.

Part V – Fundamental Rights

the Canton Ticino.[64] In another judgment the court affirmed a decision of the Geneva government forbidding a Swiss primary-school teacher who had converted to Islam from wearing a headscarf during lessons.[65]

408 A number of other decisions pertain to the rights and duties of Muslims: in 1985 and 1986, 51 and 40 Muslims respectively were serving a prison sentence at Regensdorf. The number of Protestants detained at the same penal institution was only slightly higher (71 in 1985 and 53 in 1986). While Protestants could attend church services every Sunday, Muslims were denied their traditional Friday prayer in community with others. This amounted to a restriction of freedom of religion not justifiable by any public interest.[66] On the other hand, the Federal Supreme Court denied Muslims the right to eternal rest in a public cemetery.[67] The court also rejected a claim by Muslims to have their children exempted from swimming instruction for religious reasons.[68]

409 Freedom of religion includes the right to express and disseminate opinions on religious matters in spoken and written form. In relation to freedom of opinion and information (Art. 16 Const.) and to freedom of the media (Art. 17 Const.), religious freedom is *lex specialis*, i.e. a specific right overriding the more general guarantee. Religious convictions can be manifested in community with others, for instance by attending divine services or partaking in religious processions. Religious freedom is also *lex spe-*

---

[64] BGE 116 Ia 252 (1990), *Comune di Cadro*. Five years later, the German Constitutional Court reached an analogous decision, based on Art. 4 par. 1 Basic Law: BVerfGE 93, 1 (15 et seq.).

[65] BGE 123 I 296 (1997). The European Court of Human Rights declared a complaint against this judgment inadmissible: *Dahlab v. Switzerland*, 15 February 2001, no. 42393/98.

[66] BGE 113 Ia 304 (1987), *Nehal Ahmed Syed*.

[67] BGE 125 I 300 (1999), *Abd-Allah Lucien Meyers*.

[68] BGE 135 I 79 (2009), overruling BGE 119 Ia 178 (1993).

cialis with regard to freedom of association (Art. 23 Const.) as far as the establishment of a religious community, or the right to join or belong to such a community, is concerned.

Nobody may be forced to perform or share in religious acts such as school prayers, field services, baptism, or religious oaths. With regard to religion a person attains their majority at the age of 16.[69] Up until then it is for the parents to decide whether their child will attend religious instruction. 410

In order to meet the concerns of conscientious objectors, Art. 59 par. 1 Const. obliges the legislator to provide for civil service as an alternative to military service. Up to now, an applicant had to undergo a most problematic «conscience test» in order to be exempt from military service which is compulsory for all Swiss men. In future, the willingness to render alternative civil service, which lasts considerably longer than ordinary military service, will suffice as «proof» of an earnest religious or moral conviction. 411

E. Freedom of Expression

Freedom of expression, along with freedom of assembly and other civil liberties, is the *cornerstone of every democracy*. There is no democracy without this freedom. Opinions and information must be able to be freely exchanged by all available means of communication. Persistent criticism of government policy gives opposition groups and political parties the chance to affect change in voter sentiment, which is essential in view of future elections. «The majority cannot artificially turn itself into a permanent majority by eliminating the right of the minority to attempt to become a majority.»[70] In Switzerland, moreover, free- 412

---

[69] Art. 303 Civil Code, SR 210. The general rule (Art. 14 Civil Code) is that a person becomes an adult at 18.
[70] SAMUEL KRISLOV, The Supreme Court in the Political Process, Macmillan Company, New York / London 1966, p. 115.

dom of expression is indispensable for properly making use of the tools of direct democracy and thus permanently and directly influencing political decision-making. In addition to its function as a prerequisite for democracy, freedom of expression safeguards the *basic human need* to freely communicate with other human beings.

413 Whereas the European Convention on Human Rights outlines the scope of and restrictions on freedom of expression in one single Article (Art. 10 ECHR), the Swiss Constitution codifies the essence of freedom of expression in several provisions:[71] Art. 16 Const. guarantees freedom of opinion and information in general, while Art. 17 Const. relates to the media in particular. We include freedom of language (Art. 18 Const.) in this list as a prerequisite for expressing and imparting opinions. Other civil liberties which are closely associated with freedom of expression will be discussed separately.[72]

> **Art. 16 Const.   Freedom of Opinion and Information**
> (1) Freedom of opinion and information is guaranteed.
> (2) Everyone has the right to form, express and impart opinions freely.
> (3) Everyone has the right to receive information freely, to gather it from generally accessible sources, and to disseminate it.
>
> **Art. 17 Const.   Freedom of the Media**
> (1) Freedom of the press, radio and television, and other forms of disseminating opinions and information by means of telecommunications is guaranteed.
> (2) Censorship is prohibited.
> (3) The protection of sources is guaranteed.

---

[71] The Const. 1874 only expressly protected freedom of the press. In BGE 87 I 117 (1961), *Sphinx-Film*, the Federal Supreme Court recognized freedom of expression as a non-textual, implied fundamental right.

[72] Cf. the subsequent chapters on freedom of science and of art, and freedom of assembly.

> **Art. 18 Const.   Freedom of Language**
> Freedom of language is guaranteed.

Art. 16 Const. covers all forms and all types of opinions.[73] In principle, all means of expression are protected: verbal and written communications, banners, audio-storage media, films, caricatures, or messages on the internet. Yet, not all «symbolic speech» is protected. Thus, the Federal Supreme Court found that an attorney who had been disciplined for leaving the court room to protest against the judge's conduct of a case could not invoke the right to freedom of expression.[74] Moreover, Art. 261bis of the Penal Code expressly prohibits speech intended to degrade or incite hate against others because of their race, ethnic origin or religion.

The *transfer of information* enjoys the same protection as the expression of opinion. Art. 16 par. 3 Const. includes the right to gather information «from generally accessible sources», such as public archives. This corresponds with the interpretation of Art. 10 ECHR by the European Court of Human Rights which does not place a duty on state authorities to impart information to the public. In Finland, on the other hand, everyone has a constitutional right of access to public documents and recordings,

414

415

---

[73] However, the Federal Supreme Court assesses restrictions on opinions and information with a commercial objective under economic freedom (Art. 27 Const); as a result more restrictions apply. In contrast, the scope of Art. 10 ECHR extends to such «commercial speech». This ought to be considered while interpreting Art. 16 Const. «Commercial speech» can be given less weight in balancing it against opposed public interests. As the case law of the U.S. Supreme Court shows, the level of scrutiny in interpreting the «free speech clause» of the First Amendment varies, giving political speech more freedom than commercial speech; cf. LAURENCE H. TRIBE, Constitutional Choices, Harvard University Press, Cambridge Mass. / London 1985, p. 210 et seq.

[74] BGE 108 Ia E. 2a (1982).

unless specifically restricted for compelling reasons by statute.[75] However, if Swiss public authorities provide information to the media, they have a duty do so without discrimination. In such cases the right to receive information is a consequence of equality before the law (Art. 8 Const.).[76] Moreover, at the statutory level, the Federal Law on Public Access within the Administration,[77] along with a number of more recent cantonal constitutions, grants individuals a right of access to public documents, with some exceptions justified by preponderant public or private interests.

416 *Freedom of radio and television* (Art. 17 par. 1 Const.) poses specific problems. In this area public interest can justify state intervention to some extent. Although the argument of a finite number of frequencies and channels available for broadcast has lost much of its relevance in the light of more recent developments in communication technology, the fact remains that considerable financial resources are required to operate a radio or a television network, suggesting that only the strongest can succeed. Full liberalisation would therefore increase the risk that programming is primarily determined by economic interests, with a negative impact on the audience's free choice and the quality of programs. On the other hand, state-run radio and television, as it exists in dictatorships, obviously runs the risk of being misused to indoctrinate the public, and does not provide a sufficient (or often any) check on state activities. The European Court of Human Rights decided that the broadcast monopoly of the Austrian Broadcasting Corporation, disallowing any access to private bidders, was a disproportionate restriction of free expression as

---

[75] § 12 par. 2 Finnish Constitution. A similar regulation applies to Sweden, reaching back to the Freedom of the Press Act of 1766.
[76] BGE 104 Ia 377 E. 2 (1978), *Verein Leserkampf*.
[77] Enacted 17 December 2004, SR 152.3 (Bundesgesetz über das Öffentlichkeitsprinzip in der Verwaltung).

guaranteed under Art. 10 ECHR.[78] The Swiss broadcasting system combines state influence with private competition. The Swiss Broadcasting Company (SRG SSR idée Suisse), organised as a private non-profit association but funded largely by the licence fees paid by consumers, is the biggest distributor of programs at the national level. In addition, there are a considerable number of entirely private regional and local television and radio broadcasters. Art. 93 Const. tries to achieve a balance between autonomy of programming and the public's interest in all-round objective information and entertainment which meet certain quality standards. According to Art. 93 par. 2 Const., radio and television contribute to education and cultural development, to the free formation of opinion, and to entertainment, thereby taking the particularities of the country and the needs of the cantons into account. Radio and television stations are obliged to present events with objectivity and to reflect diverse opinions adequately. Within this framework, Art. 93 par. 3 Const. guarantees the independence of radio and television and the autonomy of their programming. Complaints about programs can be submitted to an independent authority (Art. 93 par. 5 Const.).

Censorship in the sense of *prior restraint* of communications 417 would affect the very essence of freedom of expression. It is therefore absolutely prohibited (Art. 17 par. 2 Const.). That does not exclude the civil and penal liability of editors and journalists, for instance in the case of defamation or disclosure of classified material. However, journalistic sources are protected (Art. 17 par. 3 Const.), except in certain cases narrowly defined in Art. 28a Penal Code.[79]

---

[78] *Informationsverein Lentia 2000 and Others v. Austria,* Judgment (Chamber), 24 November 1993, Series A, Vol. 276.

[79] The introduction of protection of journalistic sources was triggered by a judgment of the Strasbourg Court that did not directly affect Switzerland:

418 The special relationship of high-level public officials to the state can justify restrictions on their freedom of expression, setting limits to criticising in public policies or decisions for which their superiors bear political responsibility. Judges, moreover, are obliged to avoid any comment which might cast doubt on their impartiality and independence in forthcoming proceedings. Persons detained and awaiting trial can be subjected to specific restrictions of free expression, if the risk of flight or collusion justifies surveillance measures.

419 In a wider sense, freedom of expression also encompasses the right to address requests or complaints to the competent authorities without suffering prejudice. Art. 33 Const., as is provided for in many other European constitutions, grants this *right of petition* in a separate provision and obliges the authorities to take cognisance of such petitions. Petitions can be useful means of redressing grievances where there is no formal right to appeal against a measure. In Switzerland, however, their use as an instrument to achieve political objectives is relatively small compared with Germany and some other countries. This is partly due to the fact that Swiss citizens have, in the form of referenda and initiatives, much more effective tools to oppose governmental decisions and demand change than those living in a purely representative democracy.

420 *Freedom of language* was originally an «unwritten fundamental right», being a condition precedent for exercising other freedoms, namely freedom of opinion and of the press.[80] Some scholars wondered whether such a right was not superfluous.[81] For, as far as verbal or written *private* communications are concerned, the

---

Goodwin v. the United Kingdom, judgment (Grand Chamber), 27 March 1996, no. 17488/90.

[80] BGE 91 I 480 E. II (1965), *Association de l'Ecole française.*

[81] Cf. ANDREAS AUER, D'une liberté non écrite qui n'aurait pas dû l'être: la «liberté de la langue», in: Aktuelle Juristische Praxis 1992, p. 955 et seq.

3. Civil Liberties and Freedoms

freedom to use any language is obviously inherent in the freedom of expression. However, when restrictions regarding the *official* use of languages are discussed, freedom of language becomes somewhat more complex.

Freedom of language is an especially sensitive issue in Switzerland given its multilingual nature which is a basic feature of Swiss federalism. There are four national languages: German, French, Italian and Romansh.[82] The preservation of and mutual respect for these languages within the country is essential for national unity. The survival of Romansh is endangered; the native language of many people living in the Italian speaking Canton Ticino is not Italian but German, and even in cantons dominated by a German or French speaking population the traditional territorial distribution of languages is blurred. In addition, the high number of foreigners (over 20% of the Swiss population) complicates attempts to preserve traditional linguistic regions. It is in this context that the Federal Supreme Court, in decisions recognising the freedom of language, simultaneously developed the «*territoriality principle*», meaning that the cantons shall ensure the traditional territorial distribution of languages whilst also taking the indigenous linguistic minorities into account. Along with the freedom of language (Art. 18 Const.), the territoriality principle now figures in the constitutional text (Art. 70 par.2 [2] Const.). The practical consequence, among others, is that the use of languages in public life, namely at schools and in legal proceedings, is subject to restrictive measures which aim to protect the language traditionally spoken in a region or commune. Of course, language regulations may not impair the basic procedural rights of defendants, such as the right to be informed of any charges against them in a language which they understand (Arts. 31 par. 2 and 32 par. 2 Const.; Art. 5 [2] ECHR), and the right to the

421

---

[82] Art. 4 Const. Cf. n. 94.

free assistance of an interpreter if they cannot understand or speak the language used in court (Art. 6 [3e] ECHR).

F. Academic Freedom and Freedom of the Arts

> **Art. 20 Const.** **Academic Freedom**
> Freedom of academic teaching and research is guaranteed.
>
> **Art. 21 Const.** **Freedom of the Arts**
> Freedom of the arts is guaranteed.

422 *Freedom of academic teaching* emanates from freedom of expression. By guaranteeing freedom of academic teaching in a separate provision, the constitution underlines the importance of freedom from governmental interference that might impair the mission of a university to discover and disseminate knowledge even if awkward for the authorities. In Germany, the Federal Constitutional Court deduced from the freedom to teach that, with regard to the organisation of a university (namely decision-making authorities in the areas of science, research and teaching), university professors be free to exercise the degree of influence corresponding to their position as teachers.[83] In Switzerland, freedom of teaching has hardly ever given cause for litigation. On the other hand, there are judgments of the Federal Supreme Court relating to *freedom of scientific research* in connection with the use of human reproductive and genetic material.[84] In a more recent case, the

---

[83] BVerfGE 35, 79 (1973), *Group University Case.* Art. 5 par. 3 of the German Basic Law reads as follows: «Arts and sciences, research and teaching shall be free. The freedom of teaching shall not release any person from allegiance to the constitution.»

[84] These questions are now governed by Art. 119 Const. Moreover, a Federal Law on research on embryonic stem cells of 19 December 2003, approved in a referendum, authorizes such research albeit under stringent conditions.

3. Civil Liberties and Freedoms

Court denied a historian, who had invoked freedom of research, the right to inspect the criminal records of the founder of a rock band.[85]

Before *freedom of the arts* was expressly guaranteed in the constitution (Art. 21), the Federal Supreme Court included «art and its emanations» under the concept of liberty of expression. It is indeed almost impossible to draw a clear-cut borderline between artistic and other means of expression. For lack of a generally accepted notion of art, such an attribution depends largely on subjective, time-related value judgments. Under these circumstances, the scope of Art. 21 Const. is to be understood in a broad sense. However, the practical significance of a precise classification is small in Switzerland. For, unlike the situation in Germany under Art. 5 Basic Law,[86] artistic expressions are not privileged compared to other expressions of opinion. In any event, the admissibility of restrictions has to comply with Art. 36 Const.

423

G. Freedom of Assembly and Association

Under the heading «Freedom of Assembly and Association», the European Convention on Human Rights (Art. 11) ensures everyone «the right to freedom of peaceful assembly and to freedom of association with others, including the right to form and to join trade unions for the protection of his interests». The Swiss Constitution guarantees these rights in three separate articles: freedom of assembly (Art. 22), freedom of association (Art. 23), and «freedom of coalition» (Art. 28), meaning the freedom of joint action among employees or among employers.[87]

424

---

[85] BGE 127 I 145 E. 4d (2001), *Wottreng.*

[86] Art. 5 par. 3 Basic Law guarantees freedom of expression in art without reservation. Cf. BVerfGE 30, 173 (1971), *Mephisto Case.*

[87] In German: «*Koalitionsfreiheit*», in French «*liberté syndicale*». Since the employers' freedom of association is also included, the term «freedom to

Art. 22 Const. Freedom of Assembly

(1) Freedom of assembly is guaranteed.
(2) Everyone has the right to organise, to attend or not to attend assemblies.

Art. 23 Const. Freedom of Association

(1) Freedom of association is guaranteed.
(2) Everyone has the right to form associations, to join or belong to them, and to participate in their activities.
(3) Nobody may be forced to join or belong to an association.

Art. 28 Const. Freedom of Coalition

(1) Employees and employers as well as their organisations have the right to co-operate for the protection of their interests, to form associations, and to decide whether to join them or not.
(2) Conflicts are to be settled, as far as possible, through negotiation or mediation.
(3) Strikes and lockouts are permitted when they concern employer–employee relations, and when they, moreover, are not contrary to duties to observe labour peace or to resort to conciliation.
(4) Legislation may prohibit certain categories of persons from striking.

425 *Freedom of assembly* protects meetings in enclosed spaces and outdoors, on private premises as well as in public places, i.e. places to which the public has access. The notion of «assembly» comprises all possible forms of people getting together for a certain purpose and interacting. However, a random gathering of individuals, for instance in the area around an accident, is not an assembly.

426 An assembly can occur at a particular place or be in motion. The latter is often the case when people demonstrate, moving from

---

unionise», sometimes used in English translations of the Swiss Constitution, appears to be too narrow. However, «freedom of coalition» is also somewhat misleading, as the term «coalition» is used in a different sense in connection with politics, government and economics.

one place to another. *Demonstrations* are protected by freedom of assembly as well as freedom of opinion. There is an impressive body of case law relating to demonstrations. The essence of this judge-made law is that demonstrations in places open to the public are subject to further-reaching restrictions than manifestations in private premises, as specific interests of the general public have to be taken into account. Therefore, demonstrations can be subjected to authorisation. However, the authorities issuing such permits have to keep in mind that demonstrators are exercising their civil liberties and that they therefore have a certain claim to make use of public places in order to reach the public effectively. Grounds for declining authorisation include the freedom of others; the outweighing interests of the general public (for instance, in sensitive areas such as busy streets or near railway stations); an imminent danger of violent actions, or the duty of the authorities to protect conference delegates.[88] The demonstration cases show that freedom of assembly and of opinion, like other civil liberties, are not just «negative» rights obliging the authorities to tolerate certain conduct; they also include «positive» state duties, such as making public places available for demonstrations and protecting an authorised demonstration from being disrupted.

Freedom of association protects all groups of individuals organised 427 in a legal entity in order to pursue non-profit interests collectively.[89] Political parties also enjoy the protection of Art. 23 Const. For associations with a religious objective, on the other hand, freedom of religion (Art. 15 Const.) is pertinent. Freedom of association is subject to restrictions in accordance with Art. 36

---

[88] For a concise abstract of the relevant case law and subtle balancing of interests, see BGE 127 I 164 (2001) restricting the freedom of anti-globalisation protesters to demonstrate on the occasion of the 2001 World Economic Forum in Davos.

[89] Profit-oriented entities are protected by Art. 27 Const. (economic freedom).

Const. If the purpose of an association is illegal, the association can be dissolved by a court, as in the case of an association formed for the purpose of squatting.[90] However, the Swiss Constitution contains no provision explicitly prohibiting subversive political parties.[91]

428 By guaranteeing *freedom of coalition* as a separate fundamental right, the constitution emphasises the importance of social partnership. Permanent social dialogue and bargaining between trade unions and organisations representing the employers is essential for peaceful labour relations. Art. 11 (1) ECHR and Art. 22 (1) of the U.N. Covenant on Civil and Political Rights expressly safeguard the right to form and join trade unions. The Swiss Constitution includes employers' associations, and mentions not only strikes but also lockouts as a last resort after negotiation and mediation have failed, albeit under the conditions listed in Art. 28 par. 3 Const. only. The constitutional recognition of the strike as a legitimate measure means that participation in a lawful strike cannot be a ground for dismissal.[92] In this respect freedom of coalition has consequences for private labour relations.

---

[90] BGE 133 III 593 (2007), *Rhino Association*.

[91] Art. 21 par. 2 German Basic Law declares that parties which, by reason of their aims or the behaviour of their adherents, seek to impair or destroy the free democratic basic order or to endanger the existence of the Federal Republic of Germany are unconstitutional, whereby the Constitutional Court decides on the question of unconstitutionality. This provision has its roots in the history of the Weimar Republic.

[92] BGE 132 III 122 E. 4.4 (2006), *Syndicat X*.

H. Freedom of Domicile

> **Art. 24 Const.   Freedom of Domicile**
> (1) Swiss citizens have the right to establish their domicile anywhere in the country.
> (2) They have the right to leave or to enter Switzerland.

In contrast to other fundamental rights, freedom of domicile is 429 restricted to Swiss citizens. This is clear from the explicit wording of Art. 24 Const. However, based on a sectoral agreement with the European Community and its member states concerning the free movement of persons,[93] citizens of EU- and EFTA member states have a right to establish their domicile and to work in Switzerland. Legal entities, too, can invoke this agreement when they transfer the seat of their company to Switzerland; but, as with non-Swiss individuals, they cannot invoke the freedom of domicile as a constitutional right.

The right to sojourn anywhere in the country is included in the 430 right to establish a permanent domicile. Furthermore, freedom of domicile encompasses the right to leave Switzerland at any time and also to have a passport issued.

In certain cases, preponderant public interest can justify restric- 431 tions on the freedom of domicile, for instance when police officers or members of a professional fire brigade are obliged by law to live in the area where they are deployed. The duty of an official to reside at or near his place of employment is even defensible where a close relationship with the population appears to be important for accomplishing a public task, as in the case of primary school teachers or popularly elected office-holders in com-

---

[93] Cf. SR 0.142.112.681.

munes.[94] However, fiscal reasons alone cannot justify the duty of officials to live in the canton or commune where they work and pay taxes.

I. Protection against Expulsion, Extradition and Deportation

> **Art. 25 Const. Protection against Expulsion, Extradition and Deportation**
> (1) Swiss citizens may not be expelled from Swiss territory; they may not be extradited to a foreign authority without their consent.
> (2) Refugees may not be removed by force or extradited to a state in which they would be persecuted.
> (3) Nobody may be removed by force to a state where he or she is threatened by torture or any other form of cruel and inhuman treatment or punishment.

432 The first paragraph of this Article protects *Swiss citizens* from being expelled from their country and, moreover, from being involuntarily extradited to a foreign authority. In the case of expulsion a person is forced to leave the country. An extradition, on the other hand, implies the surrender by one state to another of a person charged with a criminal offence. If a Swiss citizen does not consent in written form to being extradited to another state, he can be prosecuted in Switzerland under Swiss law for crimes committed abroad.[95]

433 Art. 25 par. 2 Const. concerns *refugees* only and implements the *principle of non-refoulement* which is part of *ius cogens* of interna-

---

[94] Summary of relevant case law in BGE 128 I 283 E. 4 (2002) where a court majority upheld a most problematic cantonal regulation obliging recording notaries to live within the canton.

[95] Art. 6 Swiss Penal Code.

tional law.[96] This principle, as defined in Art. 33 par. 1 of the 1951 U.N. Convention Relating to the Status of Refugees, forbids «to expel or return («refouler») a refugee in any manner whatsoever to the frontiers of territories where his life or freedom would be threatened on account of his race, religion, nationality, membership of a particular social group or political opinion».

Art. 25 par. 3 Const. protects *everyone* from being removed by force to a state where he or she is threatened by torture or any other form of cruel and inhuman treatment or punishment. Like Art. 10 par. 3 Const., this prohibition is absolute.[97] 434

J. Right to Property

Art. 26 Const. Right to Property
(1) The right to own property is guaranteed.
(2) Expropriations, and restrictions on property equivalent to expropriation, are to be compensated in full.

The term «property» is to be understood in a wide sense, encompassing not only real and personal property, but also other capital assets such as restricted rights *in rem*, contractual rights of economic value, intangible property rights, or ownership resulting from concessions, for instance water rights. 435

The right to own property guarantees private property as a fundamental institution of the Swiss legal order as well as individual 436

---

[96] As to the notion of such *peremptory norms of international law*, cf. n. 511.
[97] Whereas Art. 33 par. 2 of the U.N. Convention Relating to the Status of Refugees allows for an exception to the non-refoulement principle where there are reasonable grounds for regarding a refugee as a danger to the security of the host country, or where a refugee has been convicted of a particularly serious crime. However, Art. 3 ECHR is absolute in character; cf. *Saadi v. Italy*, Judgment of the European Court of Human Rights (Grand Chamber), 28 February 2008 (not yet reported).

ownership. The guarantee of *private property as an institution* also flows from Art. 36 par. 4 Const., which declares the core content of fundamental rights inviolable. It is directed to lawmakers at all levels, obliging them to preserve the essential rights of an owner to dispose and make use of private property. Replacing real property with state licences of use, or a taxation scheme that is confiscatory in its effect, would undermine private property as an institution and thus violate the constitution. *Individual ownership* is safeguarded by the general requirements on restrictions of fundamental rights as set forth in Art. 36 Const. Moreover, expropriations and comparably grave restrictions of property must be fully compensated.

437 Legal doctrine and court rulings distinguish between formal expropriation, restrictions equivalent to expropriation (so called «material expropriation») and restrictions on property under public law without compensation. These distinctions are of great practical relevance with regard to real property. *Formal expropriation* is the compulsory purchase of private property for public purposes such as constructing roads or railway lines. Here, the ownership is transferred from the individual to the state. A «*material expropriation*» occurs when, though no transfer of ownership takes place, the proprietor is affected in a way that impinges upon his ability to use or dispose of property so severely that it amounts to the taking of his property by the state. This may occur when, for instance, land ear-marked for development is struck by a building ban in order to protect the landscape, whereupon the land becomes useless for the intended purpose (development) and its value drastically diminished. In such cases the affected landowner can claim *full compensation,* i.e. the difference between the fair market value of the building land in the respective area and the value of the land affected with a building

ban.[98] If the restriction on property is judged to be less serious, however, the proprietor will not receive any compensation at all.

K. Economic Freedom

Economic freedom is not a traditional human right. It is neither mentioned in the American Bills of Rights of the outgoing 18th century, the French Declaration of the Rights of Man and of the Citizen of 1789, nor in contemporary international conventions focusing on human rights.[99] Some constitutions protect certain aspects of economic freedom, such as the freedom of contracts,[100] or the right to choose an occupation.[101] However, a comprehensive constitutional guarantee of economic freedom seems to be rather unique.[102] 438

Art. 27 Const., guaranteeing economic freedom as an *individual right,* is closely linked to Arts. 94–107 Const. which allocate the powers relating to the economy. Art. 94 Const., first and foremost, reveals the *institutional function* of economic freedom as a fundamental constitutional *choice for a free market economic system.* In addition, economic freedom fulfils a *federal function* by preventing the cantons from imposing economic protectionism, directing the federation to provide for a unified Swiss economic 439

---

[98] According to the less generous provision of the German Basic Law, Art. 14 par. 3 (3), compensation in the event of expropriation is determined upon just consideration of the public interest and of the interests of the persons affected.

[99] Yet, Arts. 15 and 16 of the Charter of Fundamental Rights of the European Union guarantee the freedoms to choose an occupation, engage in work and conduct a business.

[100] Art. I Section 10 (1) U.S. Constitution.

[101] Art. 12 par. 1 German Basic Law.

[102] For an interesting Swiss / American comparative analysis, cf. MARKUS RÜSSLI, Constitutional Protection of Economic Liberties in Switzerland and the United States, 18 Tulane European & Civil Law Forum (2003), p. 39 et seq.

area and assigning important competencies in the field of economics to the federation.[103]

> **Art. 27 Const.   Economic Freedom**
> (1) Economic freedom is guaranteed.
> (2) It comprises, in particular, free choice of a profession as well as free access to and free exercise of any remunerative private economic activity.
>
> **Art. 94 Const.   Principles of Economic Order**
> (1) The federation and the cantons respect the principle of economic freedom.
> (2) They safeguard the interests of Swiss economy as a whole and, together with the private sector of the economy, contribute to the welfare and economic security of the population.
> (3) Within the limits of their respective powers, they create favourable conditions for the private sector of the economy.
> (4) Deviations from the principle of economic freedom, in particular measures aimed at restraining competition, are allowed only if provided for in the federal constitution, or if based on cantonal monopolies.

440 Economic freedom protects *private* economic activities. State employees, even persons performing professional activities, cannot invoke economic freedom when exercising a state function, for instance as a court appointed counsel or interpreter. Economic freedom covers all private economic activities, secondary occupations included, which have as their *objective to gain profit or income*, no matter whether this objective is achieved or not, or whether profit is the main incentive.

441 Formerly, the Federal Supreme Court denied foreign nationals the right to invoke economic freedom. This practice has successively been modified. To-day, not only foreign nationals with a permanent residency permit, but even those who are entitled to

---

[103] Cf. n. 155.

renew their temporary residency permit and thus have a right to remain in Switzerland, enjoy economic freedom.[104] The same applies to citizens from EU and EFTA member states.

Art. 27 par. 2 Const. stresses three important aspects of economic freedom: free choice of profession, free access to private economic activity, and free exercise of any such activity. Free choice of profession applies to all occupations in the private sector, but does not include a right to be employed by the state or admission to an educational institution.[105] For the rest, economic freedom embraces the free choice of when, where and how to perform private economic activity, including, among others, capital investments, patterns of organisation, use of technical equipment, business relations and advertising. 442

The prerequisites for restricting economic freedom vary greatly, depending on whether a measure deviates from the principle of economic freedom or whether it is consistent with this principle. *Restrictions deviating from the principle of economic freedom*, i.e. measures aimed at restraining competition, are only allowed if the federal constitution itself permits a deviation (Art. 94 par. 4 Const.). The respective constitutional provisions are regularly combined with assigning a matter to the *federation*, for instance with regard to foreign trade (Art. 101 Const.), or structural policy to support economically threatened regions, branches or professions (Art. 103 Const.). However, Art. 94 par. 4 Const. accepts derogations from the principle of economic freedom in the form of traditional *cantonal monopolies*. Such monopolies usually concern natural resources such as mining, hunting or fishing. 443

Restrictions which are compatible with the principle of economic freedom have to comply with the requirements of Art. 36 Const. They need a legal basis, have to be justified by public interest, be pro- 444

---

[104] BGE 123 I 212 E. 2 (1997), *permit for a physiotherapist*.
[105] BGE 125 I 173 E. 3 (1999), *numerus clausus for the study of medicine*.

portionate to the goal pursued and respect the core content of economic freedom. «Police interests»[106] constitute the main category of public interests justifying restrictions, as economic activities may come into conflict with the need to protect health, safety, morals and good faith in business dealings. In addition, the Federal Supreme Court demands that the principle of «*equal treatment of competitors*» be observed. This implies that state regulation of the economy has to be neutral and may not favour one business competitor over another who offers the same goods or services. In this respect, freedom of economy adds to equality before the law and enables the courts to scrutinise economic regulations more carefully. State measures may violate the equal treatment of competitors even if they were compatible with the equal protection clause.[107]

4. Equality before the Law and Other Principles

445 The development of equal protection in Swiss constitutional law gives us a vivid example of how a very abstract constitutional provision has gradually been evolved by court practice, and of how such judge-made law is, in turn, later enshrined in new and more subtle constitutional norms. Art. 4 of the old Swiss Constitution of 1874 only guaranteed equality before the law in general terms and, in 1981, added the equal rights of men and women to the constitutional text. The Federal Supreme Court has deduced quite a number of substantive principles and procedural rules from Art. 4 Const. 1874. These are now, since the total revision of 1999, safeguarded in specific constitutional articles. Thus,

---

[106] As to the notion of «police interests», cf. n. 376.
[107] BGE 121 I 129 E. 3b–d (1995), concerning charges for taxi stands in public places.

equality before the law (Art. 8 Const.) is supplemented by protection against arbitrariness and the principle of good faith (Art. 9 Const.). Furthermore, basic procedural rights, deduced from the old constitutional equality clause in conjunction with Arts. 5 and 6 ECHR and Strasbourg case law, have been absorbed into Arts. 29 to 32 Const., guaranteeing procedural fairness and containing detailed safeguards with regard to *habeas corpus* and criminal law procedure.

A. Equality before the Law

Art. 8 Const. Equality before the Law

(1) Everyone is equal before the law.

(2) Nobody shall be discriminated against, particularly on the grounds of origin, race, sex, age, language, social status, lifestyle, religious, philosophical or political convictions, or because of a physical or mental disability.

(3) Men and women have equal rights. The law provides for their equal treatment in law and in fact, particularly with regard to family, education and work. Men and women are entitled to equal pay for work of equal value.

(4) The law provides for measures to eliminate discrimination against disabled persons.

There is a tense relationship between equality and liberty. Liberty 446 spawns certain inequalities whereas egalitarian state measures have a tendency to reduce the room for individuals to conduct their lives freely. However, historically and ideologically, *equality and liberty are closely connected.* The conviction that human dignity and freedom are to be respected by state authorities with respect to all human beings *alike* is preponderant in natural law teachings and in human rights declarations of the outgoing 18th century, particularly in the French Declaration of the Rights of Man and of the Citizen, which heralded the evolvement of fundamental rights in European constitutions. There is also a close connexion between equality and democracy: universal suffrage for all adult nationals and equal voting rights are prerequisites of a modern democracy.

447 The *general equal protection clause* (Art. 8 par. 1 Const.) binds all state authorities at all levels, lawmakers included. In this respect, the wording «before the law» is too narrow. Not only individuals, but even legal persons constituted under private law can invoke the equal protection clause.[108]

448 Legal rules violate the general equal protection clause if they make legal distinctions for which there are no reasonable grounds, or if they ignore significant factual differences.

> Example: in BGE 115 Ia 277 E. 6 (1989) the Federal Supreme Court upheld a cantonal law which had introduced an official duty for physicians and other medical staff in the event of catastrophes. In such crises the number of injured persons increases drastically, and their timely and appropriate treatment requires the assignment of additional qualified medical personnel. To extend the official duty to unqualified persons with no medical expertise, on the other hand, would have made no sense.

The perception as to when unequal treatment is justified can change over time. In 1887 the Federal Supreme Court still considered it justifiable under the equal protection clause to exclude women from practising law![109] In 1923, long before equal rights

---

[108] The German and French texts, however, in contrast to the equivalent Italian version, speak of human beings only. German: «alle Menschen»; French: «tous les êtres humains»; Italian: «tutti» (= everyone).

[109] BGE 13, 1 (1887), concerning *Emilie Kempin-Spyri*, the first Swiss woman to obtain a doctor's degree at a Swiss law faculty. Fourteen years earlier, the U.S. Supreme Court, in *Bradwell v. Illinois*, 83. U.S. (16 Wall.) 130 (1873), had rejected an attack on Illinois' refusal to license a woman to practice law. In a much-quoted concurring opinion Justice JOSEPH P. BRADLEY even invoked «divine ordinance» to reconcile his conception of the «functions of womanhood» with the equal protection clause of Amendment XIV.

of men and women were expressly included in Art. 4 Const. 1874, the Court overruled its prior disastrous decision by stating that there were no reasonable grounds for excluding women from legal practice.[110]

The Federal Supreme Court exercises great restraint when assessing whether a cantonal law is compatible with the general equal protection clause. It accords lawmakers a wide margin of recognition and only intervenes when a violation is apparent. This restraint is in line with an appropriate role allocation between the judiciary and political authorities. Moreover, it respects the distribution of tasks in a federal state, which would otherwise be jeopardised by judicial activism based on a rather open-ended constitutional provision.

449

The application of the law, too, has to be consistent with the general equal protection clause. This means that statutes and ordinances have to be applied equally to all cases. This has special significance where a legal provision is open-ended or concedes discretionary power to administrative or judicial authorities. As a general rule, the unlawful application of a norm does not give others a right to be treated in the same way. In such cases, the principle of legality has priority over the principle of equality.

450

The *ban on discrimination* (Art. 8 par. 2 Const.) protects against social exclusion and lists some features that are likely to bring about discriminatory practices. These categories mostly concern attributes that are either predetermined, such as race or sex, or, like religion and political conviction, concern the very essence of fundamental rights. The enumeration is exemplary, not exhaustive. Not all attributes have the same significance. Thus differentiation based on age is less suspect than discrimination based on origin, race or sex. Discrimination occurs when people are treated by state authorities in a *derogatory manner* because they belong to

451

---

[110] BGE 49 I 14 (1923), *Roeder*.

Part V – Fundamental Rights

such a category. However, the discriminatory clause does not prohibit differentiating regulations based on attributes listed in Art. 8 par. 2 Const. Quite often such distinctions are highly desirable, for instance a minimal age for the capacity to act in a way as to produce legal consequences, or taking into account the special needs of religious minorities at state schools or disabled persons in buildings. Yet, such differentiated treatment has to be justified on special grounds. That there is room for affirmative action based on gender or disability also results from Art. 8 pars. 3 and 4 Const.

452 *Equality between men and women* was, at least in theory, already granted by Art. 4 Const. 1874. However, in practice, legal inequalities based on gender and determined by traditional role models were often justified as being on «reasonable grounds». A popular initiative, submitted in 1976 and withdrawn later on, resulted in parliament presenting a counter-proposal, which was adopted in 1981 by the people and the cantons, and figures as Art. 8 par. 3 in the new Constitution of 1999. This provision basically guarantees an almost *absolute equality* before the law. «Reasonable grounds» alone can no longer justify unequal treatment based on gender. However, two specific constitutional norms derogate the gender equality clause as *lex spcialis*: only men must render military service (Art. 59 pars. 1 and 2 Const.), and civil defence service can only be made compulsory for men (Art. 61 par. 3 Const.).

453 Art. 8 par. 3 Const. is composed of *three sentences* which distinguish between the functions and addressees of the precept to respect and implement equality between men and women. Each of these three sentences will be discussed in turn: the rule that «men and women have equal rights» (first sentence), is directed to *all state authorities* and confers on affected individuals a *right* which is enforceable by legal action. Gender is not a valid criterion for unequal treatment by the state. Exceptions to this principle can only be justified by inherent necessity, namely where biological

differences absolutely preclude an equal treatment, as in the case of maternity protection.

The second sentence of Art. 8 par. 3 Const. *mandates lawmakers* at every level of state activity to provide for equal treatment in law and in fact. This responsibility covers all subject matters, not only family, education and work. In recent years a lot of legislative measures have been taken to achieve the goal of equality of men and women, for instance in the fields of family law and the acquisition of citizenship as well as in the Federal Act on Gender Equality.[111] This law aims to achieve factual equal treatment of women and men, in particular in working life. Employment relations under civil law are thereby included. Various measures are designed to combat discrimination effectively, such as better protection against dismissal, the establishment of a Federal Office for Gender Equality, as well as procedural devices such as class actions, conciliation processes, and means to facilitate the burden of proof with regard to discriminatory practices. The obligation of legislators to provide for equal treatment not only *in law*, but also *in fact*, causes tension vis-à-vis the first sentence which prescribes the absolute legal equality of men and women. In order to promote factual equality *affirmative action*, taking gender into account and thereby favouring women to the disadvantage of men, can be justified or is even necessary.[112] The Federal Supreme Court applies a balancing test oriented towards the principle of proportionality: affirmative action has to be commensurate with the goal of factual gender equality, i.e. quotas and other measures have to be suited and necessary to achieve this goal as well as balanced in relation to the conflicting interests of those

454

---

[111] Enacted 24 March 1995, SR 151.1.

[112] The U.S. Supreme Court has developed rich case law concerning the admissibility of affirmative action as a means not only to redress prior racial discrimination, but also to maximize the benefits of diversity in areas such as university education. A landmark decision is *University of California Regents v. Bakke*, 438 U.S. 265 (1978).

Part V – Fundamental Rights

who are disfavoured.[113] Gender quota with respect to the composition of popularly elected cantonal bodies are not permitted.[114]

455 The third sentence of Art. 8 par. 3 Const. grants men and women *equal pay for work of equal value*. This right binds not only all state authorities, but also private employers. It thus has a *direct third-party effect*.[115] In giving shape to the term «work of equal value» courts are confronted with intricate questions, sometimes necessitating comparisons between different professional activities based on workplace evaluation.[116] In spite of this clear constitutional requirement, on average women's salaries still lag considerably behind those of men.

456 Art. 8 par. 4 Const. mandates lawmakers to provide for *measures to eliminate discrimination against disabled persons*, for instance with regard to education, employment or accessibility to public buildings and public transport. A federal law of 13 December 2002[117] aims to achieve the better social integration of disabled persons and prescribes a number of measures and procedures to that effect.

---

[113] Summary of case law in BGE 131 II 361 E. 5 (2005), concerning a quota system at the University of Fribourg.
[114] Cf. n. 219.
[115] This term is defined in n. 369.
[116] Summary of case law in BGE 125 II 385 (1999), concerning the job of a physiotherapist.
[117] SR 151.3.

B. Protection against Arbitrariness and Observance of Good Faith

Art. 9 Const. Protection against Arbitrariness and Observance of Good Faith

Everyone has the right to be treated by state authorities in a non-arbitrary manner and in good faith.

The express constitutional *prohibition of arbitrary state acts* crowned the well established case law of the Federal Supreme Court under the old equal protection clause of Art. 4 Const. 1874. Other countries, such as Germany and Austria, deduce a right to be treated by state authorities in an objective and non-arbitrary way from the principle of equality. To our knowledge, only the Spanish Constitution specifically prohibits arbitrariness, not, however, as a constitutional right, but as a basic principle governing state activities next to legality and other attributes of a state governed by law.[118]

All state organs, lawmakers as well as those applying the law, are bound by the prohibition on arbitrariness. An act is arbitrary if it is not only incorrect but *plainly untenable.* In other words: a norm is arbitrary if it cannot be based on serious objective grounds, if it is senseless or useless; an arbitrary application of the law occurs in the case of a clearly wrong interpretation. The prohibition on arbitrariness enhances the scope of review by federal courts adjudicating disputes over federal law, as an arbitrary application of cantonal law concurrently violates federal law. When examining whether the latter is the case, the Federal Supreme Court applies a somewhat higher level of scrutiny compared to the U.S. Supreme Court's rational basis review.[119] However, an appellant is

---

[118] Cf. Art. 9 par. 3 of the Spanish Constitution.
[119] Cf. FELIX UHLMANN, Das Willkürverbot (Art. 9 BV), Stämpfli, Berne 2005, p. 150 et seq.

Part V – Fundamental Rights

in a better position if he can invoke a more specific fundamental right than the prohibition of arbitrariness.

459 The *principle of good faith* demands loyal and trustworthy behaviour in legal relations. It embraces private as well as public law and has occupied a prominent place in civil law for more than a century.[120] Its relevance to public law relations was, as with the prohibition on arbitrariness, regarded as a consequence of equality before the law. The Constitution of 1999 codified good faith as a principle guiding public authorities as well as private persons,[121] and, in Art. 9 Const., as a fundamental right of the individual versus the state to be treated in good faith.

460 As a fundamental right, the observance of good faith means that, under certain circumstances established by case law, an individual can rely on promises or information given by public authorities which create well-founded expectations causing him or her to make dispositions even where a legal basis is lacking.

> Example: if the instructions in a court decision concerning the time to appeal against the decision are incorrect, and the addressee is not represented by counsel, his or her trust in the instructions can justify a failure to appeal within the period prescribed by law, thus prompting the court of appeals to hear the appeal.

5. Basic Procedural Rights

461 In no other area has the European Convention on Human Rights had such an impact on Swiss constitutional law as with regard to basic procedural rights. Art. 29 to 32 Const. guarantee basic rules of fair procedure, some of which the Federal Supreme Court, in its earlier practice, had linked to the equal protection clause.

---

[120] Art. 2 Civil Code of 1907, SR 210.
[121] Art. 5 par. 3 Const.; cf. n. 57.

However, the essence of these procedural safeguards is attributable to Arts. 5 and 6 ECHR which became part of the Swiss domestic legal order with the ratification of the ECHR in 1974. Henceforward, decisions of the Swiss Federal Supreme Court concerning questions of due process have regularly taken the ECHR and the relevant Strasbourg case law into account. When framing the new constitution, these developments were not simply reiterated. In certain respects, the basic procedural rights of the Swiss Constitution exceed the «minimal standard» established by the ECHR.[122]

Basic procedural rights operate to guarantee that individuals are taken seriously and treated with respect. They ensure the legitimacy of decisions attributable to the state. Those who are treated equally and fairly, who are heard and can defend themselves in an orderly procedure, are more likely to accept an adverse decision by a state authority. Furthermore, procedural safeguards enhance the chance of achieving correct and just decisions.

A. Procedural Safeguards in General

> **Art. 29 Const. General Procedural Guarantees**
> (1) Everyone has the right to be treated equally and fairly in judicial and administrative proceedings, and to have their case decided within a reasonable time.
> (2) Parties to a case have the right to be heard.
> (3) Anyone who lacks the necessary means has the right to be exempted from costs of the proceedings, unless their case appears to lack any chance of success. Moreover, they have a right to free legal counsel to the extent necessary to safeguard their rights.

---

[122] However, this minimal standard is being gradually raised by dynamic case law interpreting the ECHR as a «living instrument».

Part V – Fundamental Rights

463 Art. 29 Const. governs all proceedings in which the law is applied to individual cases. It is also relevant to the administrative procedure, in contrast to Art. 30 Const. and Art. 6 (1) ECHR, which set up specific requirements for judicial proceedings only.

464 Art. 29 par. 1 Const. guarantees a *fair procedure* and implies the principle of «*equality of arms*», i.e. the parties must be given a reasonable opportunity to present their case before an independent body, and under conditions that do not put them at a disadvantage vis-à-vis their opponents. Cases have to be decided within a reasonable time. What this means in a specific case depends on a number of criteria including the complexity of a matter and the parties' behaviour. Excessive formalism can also amount to a denial of justice. If, to take an example, an appeal is filed in time, but the appellant has forgotten to sign it or to enclose required duplicates, he ought to be accorded a short grace period to correct the default; to decide otherwise would be excessively formalistic.

465 The *right to be heard* is highlighted in Art. 29 par. 2 Const. This means that parties to a case have access to the files, can ask for new relevant evidence, be present when testimony is given, and give their views on all aspects relevant to the case. As a rule, a violation of the right to be heard renders a decision void. Moreover, decisions affecting a party negatively must state the grounds on which they are based.

466 Obtaining justice should not depend on the financial resources of a party. In a state governed by the rule of law there ought to be no room for the old saying that «the courts are open to everyone – like the Ritz Hotel». For this reason Art. 29 par. 3 Const. gives those who lack the necessary means to conduct legal proceedings a *right to be exempted from costs.* This exemption is provisional and does not exclude a claim for a refund as soon as the party has sufficient financial resources. *Free legal counsel* is only granted if, in addition to a party's indigence, the complexity of the subject mat-

B. Guarantee of Access to the Court

> **Art. 29a Const. Guarantee of Access to the Court**
> Everyone has the right to have legal disputes judged by a judicial authority. The federation and the cantons may, in exceptional cases, by law preclude access to the courts.

This Article was added to the Constitution as part of the module 467 concerning reform of the judiciary.[123] It grants every person access to a judge in a legal dispute. The scope of application is wider than that of Art. 6 (1) ECHR which is restricted to the determination of civil rights and obligations or of criminal charges. At least one cantonal or federal judicial authority must be entitled to a full review of questions of law and of fact; judicial review of discretionary power, however, is not included.

In exceptional cases, and based on statute, access to courts can be 468 precluded. Certain decisions, for instance concerning the grant of a pardon or other issues of an almost exclusively political nature, are not suitable for judicial review. A more incisive limitation of access to a court results from Art. 189 par. 4 Const., stating that enactments of the Federal Assembly and the Federal Council cannot be directly challenged before the Federal Supreme Court, unless provided for by statute.

---

[123] The German Basic Law (Art. 19 par. 4) contains a similar provision.

C. Special Guarantees for Judicial Proceedings

> **Art. 30 Const. Judicial Proceedings**
> (1) Anyone whose case must be decided in a judicial proceeding has the right to a competent, independent and impartial court established by law. Ad hoc courts are prohibited.
> (2) Anyone against whom a civil action is filed has the right to have the case judged by the court at his domicile. Legislation may prescribe a different forum.
> (3) Court hearings and the pronouncement of judgments are public. Legislation may provide for exceptions.

469 In contrast to Art. 29 Const. (general procedural guarantees), Art. 30 Const. applies to *judicial proceedings* only. Par. 1 and par. 3 are in line with the basic requirements set up in Art. 6 (1) ECHR. The *right to be judged at the defendant's domicile* (Art. 30 par. 2), on the other hand, is of lesser importance, and has been constricted by a number of statutory provisions as well as international treaties such as the Lugano Convention on Jurisdiction and the Enforcement of Judgments in Civil and Commercial Matters.[124]

470 In a general way, Art. 191c Const. safeguards the *independence of the judiciary*. In addition to this institutional guarantee, Art. 30 par. 1 Const. confers a specific *fundamental right to an independent and impartial court established by law*. This is essential for a fair trial and a just judgment. *Ad hoc courts,* constituted in contradiction to existing law on a case-by-case basis, are explicitly prohibited.

471 The notion of an «independent and impartial court» has been developed gradually, in accordance with the relevant Strasbourg case law. Courts are considered to be *independent* if their organisation and the status of judges assure that the resolution of legal disputes is based on the law only, and with binding effect. *Impar-*

---

[124] Of 16 September 1988, SR 0.275.11.

tiality means that judges are unprejudiced and unbiased, whereby the mere appearance of bias has to be avoided. It is «of fundamental importance that justice should not only be done, but should manifestly and undoubtedly be seen to be done», as Lord HEWART remarked in a much-quoted dictum.[125] A judge has to be disqualified as soon as, from an objective point of view, certain circumstances indicate the appearance of bias or imply a danger of prejudice.[126]

Secrecy arouses suspicion. Court hearings in public and transparency of judgments are more likely to inspire public confidence. In addition, publicity guarantees that vigilant media and the public in general control the performance of the courts. This, in turn, enhances the chance that all litigants are treated equally and fairly. Therefore, Art. 6 (1) ECHR emphasises that everyone is entitled to a fair and public hearing, and that judgment shall be pronounced publicly, unless special circumstances require that the press and the public be excluded. Art. 30 par. 3 Const. also calls for *public court hearings*. This does not ignore the fact that proceedings before courts of higher instance are quite often in writing.[127] However, where oral proceedings are prescribed, they have to be in public unless outweighing interests, such as those of juvenile delinquents or victims of sexual offenses, demand confidentiality. The requirement that *judgments shall be pronounced publicly* can also be met by making a judgment accessible to the public after its pronouncement.[128]

472

---

[125] *R. v. Sussex Justices, ex parte McCarthy* (1924), 1 King's Bench 256, All England Law Reports 233.

[126] BGE 133 I 1 E. 6.2 (2007), concerning the impartiality of a judge in a divorce case where one party was represented by an attorney holding a part-time judgeship in an appellate court.

[127] Cf. with regard to proceedings before the Federal Supreme Court n. 341.

[128] BGE 119 Ia 411 E. 5 (1993), *Municipal Council Nesslau*.

D. No Deprivation of Liberty without a Due Process

> **Art. 31 Const.   Deprivation of Liberty**
> (1) No one may be deprived of their liberty save in the cases and in the manner prescribed by law.
> (2) Anyone deprived of their liberty has the right to be informed immediately and in a language which they understand of the reasons for their detention and of their rights. They must have the opportunity to assert their rights. In particular, they are entitled to have their next of kin informed.
> (3) Anyone in detention awaiting trial has the right to be brought before a judge without delay. The judge shall decide whether the arrested person must remain in detention or be released. Anyone in detention awaiting trial has the right to be judged within a reasonable time.
> (4) Anyone whose deprivation of liberty has not been ordered by a court is entitled to go to court at any time. The court decides as soon as possible whether the detention is legal.

473 Deprivation of liberty is one of the most incisive coercive measures a state can apply.[129] In British law, *habeas corpus* developed as a legal remedy through which a person can seek relief from unlawful detention.[130] The U.S. Constitution of 1787 specifically included *habeas corpus* in Art. 1 Section 9 (2), the so-called «suspension clause»: «The privilege of the writ of habeas corpus shall not be suspended, unless when in cases of rebellion or invasion the public safety may require it». International conventions pertaining to human rights recognise the great importance of *procedural protection against unlawful deprivation of liberty*. Art. 31 Const. is strongly influenced by Art. 5 ECHR and Art. 9 CCPR.

474 Deprivation of liberty is a grave restriction on the right to personal liberty and therefore has to be prescribed by statute (Art. 36

---

[129] As to the notion of deprivation of liberty, cf. n. 391.
[130] Cf. n. 388.

par. 1 [2] Const.). Art. 31 par. 1 Const. makes it clear that a *legal basis* is necessary with regard to the reasons justifying a deprivation of liberty as well as the manner of accomplishing such a measure. Moreover, the legislator has to take into account that a deprivation of liberty can only be prescribed in the cases enumerated in Art. 5 (1) ECHR.

The right to *immediate information about the reasons for detention and of the rights of the detainee* follows from the right to be heard.[131] Art. 31 par. 2 Const. specifies the consequences of this basic principle in the event of a deprivation of liberty. Those affected must have the opportunity to assert their rights, such as the right to be silent and (an issue not quite uncontested) to consult with an attorney as soon as questioning begins.[132] Evidence obtained in violation of the constitutional rights of a defendant is, with narrowly defined exceptions, inadmissible in criminal proceedings.[133] This is reminiscent of the *exclusionary rule* developed in U.S. constitutional law.[134] 475

Art. 31 par. 3 Const. concerns one form of deprivation of liberty only: *detention awaiting trial*. The detainee has the right to be brought before a judge without delay, as well as the right to be judged within a reasonable time. These rights also follow from Art. 5 (3) ECHR. In the event that a deprivation of liberty has not been ordered by a court, a detainee can demand *judicial review of the legality of the detention* (Art. 31 par. 4 Const.). 476

---

[131] Cf. n. 465.
[132] Parallels with the «Miranda warnings», as a result of the U.S. Supreme Court's landmark decision *Miranda v. Arizona*, 384 U.S. 436 (1966), are striking.
[133] BGE 130 I 126 E. 3 (2004) concerning self-incrimination.
[134] In *Weeks v. United States*, 232 U.S. 383 (1914), the U.S. Supreme Court held that in a federal prosecution the Fourth Amendment barred the use of evidence secured through an illegal search and seizure. This *exclusionary rule* was later extended to all improperly obtained evidence and to state criminal cases; cf. *Mapp v. Ohio*, 367 U.S. 643 (1961).

E. Criminal Proceedings

> **Art. 32 Const.   Criminal Proceedings**
> (1) Everyone is presumed innocent until finally convicted.
> (2) All accused persons have the right to be informed as quickly and completely as possible of the charges against them. They must be given the opportunity to assert their rights to a proper defence.
> (3) All convicted persons have the right to have the sentence reviewed by a higher court, except in cases where the Federal Supreme Court has original jurisdiction.

477 The *presumption of innocence* (Art. 32 par. 1 Const.) is explicitly included in many constitutions and international conventions. Thus, Art. 6 (2) ECHR states that «everybody charged with a criminal offence shall be presumed innocent until proved guilty according to the law». This right already figured in the French Declaration of the Rights of Man and of the Citizen of 1789 (Art. 9). It implies that the burden of proof in criminal trials is on the prosecution which has to present enough compelling evidence to convince the court that the accused is guilty. Otherwise he or she is to be acquitted. The presumption of innocence applies until the accused is finally convicted by a legally enforceable judgment. It even has consequences with regard to the apportionment of court costs: if criminal proceedings are terminated on account of limitation, the presumption is violated if, without the accused having been proven guilty, a decision on the costs implies that he is guilty.[135]

478 Moreover, the presumption of innocence extends beyond judicial proceedings. Political authorities should refrain from statements referring to a suspect or accused as though their guilt were certain. The same is even true with regard to the media; otherwise they risk civil actions for violation of personal rights; in such a

---

[135] *Minelli v. Switzerland*, judgment of the European Court of Human Rights (Chamber), 25 March 1983, Series A, Vol. 62.

case, the presumption of innocence can have an indirect third-party effect.

The *right of an accused to quick and complete information of the charges* (Art. 32 par. 2 [1] Const.) is a consequence of the right to be heard and a prerequisite for an effective defence. Moreover, an accused must have the opportunity to *assert his rights to a proper defence* (Art. 32 par. 2 [2] Const.; Art. 6 (2) ECHR). These include, among other things, the right to defend oneself in person or through legal representation of one's own choosing, to have adequate time and facilities for the preparation of the defence, to confer freely and unguarded with counsel, to call for and cross-examine witnesses, and to have, if necessary, the free assistance of an interpreter. 479

Finally, all convicted persons have a *right to have the sentence reviewed by a higher court* (Art. 32 par. 3 Const.). Since the Federal Criminal Court commenced duties in April 2004,[136] the Federal Supreme Court does not exercise any original jurisdiction in criminal proceedings; the last half sentence of Art. 32 par. 3 Const. has thus become obsolete. 480

6. Basic Social Rights

Only few basic social rights are guaranteed in the constitution. They *entitle the individual to state benefits* and are directly *enforceable in courts*. This contrasts with the legal nature of *social goals:* the objectives listed in Art. 41 Const., such as access to social security, health care or suitable housing on reasonable terms, are intended as guidelines which the authorities on federal and cantonal level shall endeavour to ensure within the scope of their constitutional powers and the means available to them; Art. 41 481

---

[136] Cf. n. 325.

par. 4 Const. leaves no doubt that «no direct right to state benefits may be derived from these social goals». However, these objectives may be taken into account as terms of reference when giving shape to the equal protection clause (Art. 8 Const.) or interpreting legal norms that leave room for considering them.

482 The constitution grants two basic social rights: the right to assistance when in need (Art. 12 Const.) and the right to primary school education (Art. 19 Const.). Some scholars regard further basic rights as social ones, namely the right to free legal counsel and representation (Art. 29 par. 3 Const.),[137] the right to strike (Art. 28 par. 3 Const.),[138] and the right of children and young people to special protection (Art. 11 Const.).[139]

A. Right to Assistance when in Need

Art . 12 Const.   Right to Assistance when in Need
Persons in need and unable to provide for their living have the right to assistance and care, and to the means indispensable for living in dignity.

483 The Constitution of 1874 did not contain any basic social rights. However, in 1995 the Federal Supreme Court recognised, by judicial interpretation, an implied fundamental right to a subsistence minimum.[140] The Court argued that the provision of elementary human necessities such as food, clothing and shelter, is a precondition of human existence and development, indispensable in a democratic society based on the rule of law. This judi-

---

[137] AUER / MALINVERNI / HOTTELIER, Droit constitutionnel suisse, volume 2, p. 691 et seq. Cf. n. 466.
[138] AUER / MALINVERNI / HOTTELIER, Droit constitutionnel suisse, volume 2, p. 713 et seq. Cf. n. 428.
[139] KIENER / KÄLIN, Grundrechte, p. 379 et seq. Cf. n. 390.
[140] BGE 121 I 367 E. 2 (1995), concerning refugees.

cial activism was approved by many legal scholars but met substantial criticism in the political debates surrounding the drafting of the new constitution. As a result, Art. 12 Const. emerged. The tempered wording of this provision clarifies that the right to assistance when in need does not guarantee a certain subsistence minimum, but only extends to the means indispensable for living in dignity; moreover, in line with the principle of subsidiarity, state benefits are only granted to those who do not refuse to take appropriate employment and are unable to provide for their living.

The right to assistance when in need is absolute. It cannot be restricted on the basis of Art. 36 Const., as it is closely linked to the essence of human dignity. Indeed, the state may grant benefits under the condition that the recipient takes an active part in an employment program provided by the state. On the other hand, the aid cannot be denied on inappropriate grounds, for instance because a rejected asylum seeker obliged to leave the country refuses to cooperate with the authorities in the manner required by the legislation relating to aliens.[141] 484

B. Right to Primary School Education

> **Art. 19 Const.   Right to Primary School Education**
> The right to a sufficient and free primary school education is guaranteed.

The responsibility for education lies mainly with the cantons, but the federal constitution establishes some benchmarks.[142] With regard to primary school education, Art. 62 par. 2 Const. obliges the cantons to provide sufficient, compulsory and free education 485

---

[141] BGE 131 I 166 E. 4.5 (2005).
[142] Cf. n. 149.

under state direction or supervision;[143] in addition, Art. 62 par. 3 Const. prescribes an adequate education for handicapped children and young people. In accordance with these responsibilities, all children (represented by their parents) have the right to a primary school education that complies with the constitutional requirements.

486 The right is confined to *primary school education*. This means nine years of obligatory school education until the age of 15.[144] Furthermore, the state has to bear the costs of transportation if the way to school on foot would be unreasonably long or dangerous for a child of a given age.

487 High schools are not covered by the right to *free education*, not even for pupils who are still of compulsory school age.[145] School fees can therefore be charged for education at all high school levels without violating the constitution. However, cantons may legislate to extend the right to a free education. Art. 29 par. 2 of the Constitution of the Canton of Berne, for instance, guarantees every child a free school education consistent with their talents and abilities. In March 1973, a comprehensive social right to education to be anchored in the Federal Constitution, which was backed by a majority of the citizens voting nationwide, failed to achieve the necessary approval by the majority of cantons.

488 Art. 13 of the U.N. Covenant on Economic, Social and Cultural Rights recognizes the right of everyone to education and states in par. 2(b) that, according to the intentions of the contracting parties, even «secondary education in its different forms ... shall be

---

[143] Basically, the principle of compulsory and free primary school education under state direction reaches back to 1874 (cf. Art. 27 par. 2 Const. 1874). One intended side effect was to reduce the dominance of the church in education.

[144] An intercantonal treaty aims at adding two years of kindergarten to the compulsory education.

[145] BGE 133 I 156 E. 3 (2007), concerning a junior high school.

made generally available and accessible to all by every appropriate means, and in particular by the progressive introduction of free education». The Federal Supreme Court does not regard this programmatic provision as directly applicable to specific cases. However, it conceded in a dictum that the objective inherent in the norm might be taken into account where there is room for judicial interpretation.[146]

---

[146] BGE 130 I 113 E. 3.3 (2004), concerning tuition fees at the University of Basle.

Part VI – Rule-Making, Treaties and Constitutional Jurisdiction

In Swiss constitutional law there are basically three levels in the 489
hierarchy of federal norms:[1] *constitutional provisions*, subject to a mandatory referendum and the approval of a «double majority» (people and cantons); *federal statutes* (ordinary legislation) which, having been passed by parliament can be brought to a popular vote via an optional referendum; and *ordinances*, adopted by a state authority (usually the executive) and not subject to referendum. Constitutional norms have priority over ordinary legislation, and federal statutes over ordinances.[2]

In France and in Spain, there is a layer between the constitution 490
and ordinary laws: *organic laws (lois organiques; leyes orgánicas)* which have to comply with the constitution, but rank above ordinary statutes.[3] As far as municipal law is concerned, such an intermediate level does not exist in Switzerland. International law, however, specifically in the form of conventions pertaining to human rights, occupies a rank (at least) superior to that of statutory law.[4]

An important function of *constitutional jurisdiction*, i.e. judicial 491
review of constitutional matters, is to ensure the validity of the constitution. In Switzerland, this function is severely hampered by the obligation of courts to give effect to federal statutes.[5]

---

[1] The situation in the cantons is roughly the same.
[2] In this chapter we are also going to discuss *federal decrees*, a form of parliamentary enactment reserved for decisions on specific matters. Cf. n. 516 and n. 528 et seq.
[3] Art. 46 of the French Constitution; Art. 81 of the Spanish Constitution.
[4] Cf. n. 550.
[5] Art. 190 Const.; cf. n. 562 et seq.

Part VI – Rule-Making, Treaties and Constitutional Jurisdiction

1. Revision of the Constitution

492 The Federal Constitution may be totally or partially revised at any time (Art. 192 par. 1 Const.). The distinction between total and partial revision is crucial for determining which amendment procedure is to be followed. In the case of a total revision, the procedure is more cumbersome.

A. Distinction between Total and Partial Revision

493 The relevant criterion for distinguishing the two methods of constitutional amendment is predominantly a formal one. A *total revision* is required where all the articles of a given constitution are put up for debate with the object of reformulating and, as appropriate, amending them, irrespective of the degree of innovation achieved. Such total revisions occurred in Switzerland in 1874 and in 1999.[6] In both cases the basic structure of the constitutional order remained unchallenged, and the reforms were rather moderate. In the case of a *partial revision*, only one or some interconnected provisions are enacted, amended or repealed, whereby new or revised articles are integrated into the given constitutional document. In Austria, on the other hand, the total revision *(«Gesamtänderung»)* of the constitution is regarded as necessary when a reform involves basic principles of the constitutional order, even if only one single provision is to be amended.[7]

494 However, Swiss political practice lacks consistency. The reforms concerning the judiciary (2000) and direct democracy (2003)[8],

---

[6] Cf. n. 23 and n.27.

[7] Cf. PETER PERNTHALER, Österreichisches Bundesstaatsrecht, Verlag Österreich GmbH, Vienna 2004, p. 678 et seq. The distinction is particularly important in Austria, as only total revisions are subject to a mandatory referendum.

[8] Cf. n. 28.

each of which comprised a few articles only, were handled as total revisions. In 1947, on the other hand, the revision of the Swiss economic order with a distinctive shift towards more state intervention, by means of various articles, was achieved by a partial revision. In 2005, another partial revision, this time concerning education, affected ten constitutional provisions and implied a substantial reform of the distribution of competencies between the cantons and the federation.

B. Total Revision

> **Art. 193 Const. Total Revision**
> (1) A total revision of the Federal Constitution may be proposed by the people or by either of the two chambers, or be decreed by the Federal Assembly.
> (2) If the initiative emanates from the people or if the two chambers disagree, the people decide on whether a total revision should be carried out.
> (3) If the people vote for a total revision, new elections to both chambers must be held.
> (4) Peremptory norms of international law are inviolable.

The voters of a number of cantons, for example Aargau, Basle-Land and Zurich, decided to convene special assemblies when they totally revised their constitutions in recent years. Such *constitutional conventions* relieve parliaments of extra duties and enable the active participation of a broad spectrum of society; on the other hand, they can also impair the chances of approval by drifting too far from political realities.[9]

---

[9] Art. V of the U.S. Constitution even provides an option for two thirds of the state legislatures to call for a national convention with the task of proposing amendments, i.e. partial revision of the constitution. However, this alternative route has never been taken. Successful amendments have always been proposed by a two-third majority in each house.

Part VI – Rule-Making, Treaties and Constitutional Jurisdiction

496 The Swiss Federal Constitution, however, does not provide for such constitutional conventions. Total as well as partial revisions basically follow the legislative process. They are always debated in parliament. Nonetheless, special constitutional and statutory provisions ensure the increased involvement of the people and of the cantons in comparison with the passing of ordinary legislation.

497 Impulses for a total revision can come from within parliament (individual members, parliamentary committees or factions), but also from the government, cantons or members of the public. An *initiative*, i.e. a proposal which *ipso iure* triggers off the amendment procedure, can only be launched by a decree of the Federal Assembly, a proposal by one of the chambers, or by *popular initiative*. At least 100,000 citizens entitled to vote can demand a total revision of the constitution. In order to succeed, the necessary signatures have to be collected within 18 months of the official publication of the initiative (Art. 138 par. 1 Const.). A popular initiative demanding a total revision can only take the form of a general proposal, and not of a fully formulated draft. It must be submitted to a vote of the people (Art. 193 par. 2 in conjunction with Art. 140 par. 2 [a] Const.). In the event that there is disagreement between the two chambers, a preliminary decision on whether a total revision should be carried out is also required (Art. 193 par. 2 in conjunction with Art. 140 par. 2 [c] Const.).

498 If the people vote in favour of a total revision, the Federal Assembly is dissolved and new elections to both chambers of the Federal Assembly have to be scheduled (Art. 193 par. 3 Const). This means new elections to the Federal Council, too, as their members are to be elected «following each full renewal of the National Council» (Art. 175 par. 2 Const.). The *requirement of new elections before the regular terms of office of the respective bodies have expired*, conceives of a total revision as something outstanding, hence justifying a departure from characteristic features

of the Swiss political system such as the election of government and parliament for fixed terms.

The idea underlying Art. 193 par. 3 Const. is that, in the event of disagreement between the people and parliament (or, respectively, one of its chambers) on the question of a total revision, the people must have the opportunity to elect a parliament which is more open-minded vis-à-vis constitutional reform. In practice, this complicated regulation has been irrelevant up to now. 499

The drafting of a completely new constitution is the task of parliament, and is accomplished in the same manner as ordinary legislation. The totally revised constitution comes into force after having been approved by the people and the cantons.[10] 500

C. Partial Revision

> **Art. 194 Const. Partial Revision**
> (1) A partial revision of the Federal Constitution may be requested by the people, or be decreed by the Federal Assembly.
> (2) The partial revision has to respect the principle of the unity of subject matter and may not violate peremptory norms of international law.
> (3) The popular initiative for partial revision must, in addition, respect the principle of the unity of form.

Impulses for a partial revision can come, as in the case of a total revision, from various political actors (citizens, parliament, government, cantons). However, a formal *initiative* requires either a decree of the Federal Assembly or a popular initiative signed by at least 100,000 citizens entitled to vote. Unlike the procedure 501

---

[10] Art. 195 Const.; cf. n. 506.

for total revision, one chamber alone cannot bring about a popular vote on a partial revision of the constitution.

502 A partial revision must respect the principle of the *unity of subject matter* (Art. 194 par. 2 Const.). This unity is preserved if a sufficient interrelationship exists between different components of a proposed amendment, i.e., if they are interrelated as regards content. The purpose of this requirement is to guarantee the clear expression of the voter's will when adding his or her signature to a popular initiative and, foremost, when voting on a partial revision (whether proposed by parliament or by popular initiative). If several unrelated matters were incorporated in one single proposal, voters could only accept or reject the whole package, without being able to differentiate.

> Example: In 1977, the Federal Assembly invalidated a popular initiative against inflation which included measures in the areas of economic and social policy, environmental protection, agriculture and tax law, combined with guarantees concerning employment and housing.[11] Such invalidation due to a violation of the unity of subject matter occurs very rarely.

503 A popular initiative demanding a partial revision can take the form of either a *general proposal* or a *fully formulated draft* (Art. 139 par. 2 Const.). In practice, most popular initiatives are accurately phrased as legal norms. This has the advantage that they have to be submitted to a vote of the people and the cantons unmodified, i.e. parliament has no right to alter the text. However, the Federal Assembly debates the initiative and recommends its approval or rejection. Moreover, it can submit its own *counter-proposal*.[12]

504 The procedure for processing a general proposal is more complicated: if parliament agrees with the initiative, it drafts the partial

---

[11] BBl 1977 II 501 et seq.
[12] In this case, the people may vote in favour of both proposals and indicate a preference on the ballot in case both proposals are accepted.

revision on the basis of the initiative and submits it to the vote of the people and the cantons. However, if it rejects such an initiative, a preliminary vote of the people on the initiative is required. Only where the people (a majority of the cantons is not necessary) vote in favour of the general proposal is the Federal Assembly obliged to draft a corresponding text (Art. 139 par. 4 Const.), and submit it to a vote of the people and the cantons.

As the amendment procedure to be followed depends on the form of the initiative (general proposal or formulated draft), it is not permissible to combine the two forms in the same initiative. In other words, the popular initiative for partial revision has also to respect the principle of the *unity of form* (Art. 194 par. 3 Const.). 505

The final stage of every constitutional revision is a *nationwide vote* requiring a *double majority*. A constitutional amendment can only come into force after having been approved «by the people and the cantons» (Art. 195 Const.). Hence, in addition to a majority of the national popular vote, a majority of popular votes in at least twelve cantons is necessary. The result of a popular vote in the canton determines the «vote of the canton», whereby six of the 26 cantons (Obwalden, Nidwalden, Basle-City, Basle-Land, Outer and Inner Appenzell) have half a cantonal vote each (Art. 142 Const.). 506

Since the introduction of the popular initiative for partial revisions of the constitution in 1891, up until 1 July 2009, two hundred and seventy-two popular initiatives have attained the necessary number of signatures (50,000 until 1977; now 100,000). Of the 169 initiatives actually voted upon, less than 10% (16 altogether) have been approved by the people and the cantons. Some more recent examples are: a moratorium on new nuclear power plants (1990); a provision declaring the Federal National Day (1 August) a public holiday (1993); the protection of alpine regions from transit traffic (1994); accession to the United Nations 507

Part VI – Rule-Making, Treaties and Constitutional Jurisdiction

(2002); correctional measures for particularly dangerous criminals (2004), and the non-applicability of the statute of limitation for sexual offenses against children (2008).

508 However, the indirect success of popular initiatives, even if they are eventually defeated, is most impressive. Sometimes they encourage government and parliament to present a counter-proposal which partly meets the concerns voiced in the initiative but which has a better chance of attracting the popular vote. In such cases the original initiative is then quite often withdrawn. Other initiatives bring about changes of statutory law. Political scientists believe that about one third of the initiatives leave their mark on federal legislation.[13]

509 In November 1989 the people and the cantons had to vote on a popular initiative demanding the complete abolition of the Swiss Army. The voters, with a high turnout of 68.6%, rejected this initiative. However, the fact that one third of them as well as a majority in two cantons (Geneva and Jura) voted in favour of the initiative had a strong impact on future debates and led to a number of overdue reforms.

510 Who are the initiators? Sometimes impulse and support come from a political party. Even parties which have strong representation in parliament and a seat in the government sometimes launch initiatives. In recent years, right-wing parties have launched several initiatives directed against foreigners,[14] while the Social Democrats were behind initiatives concerning the extension of social insurance. By means of such initiatives, political parties hope to widen their voter base in forthcoming elections, even if their initiative is defeated at the polls. Of course, associations representing economic or idealistic interests, insofar as they can mobilize sufficient adherents, make use of the popular initiative. Even the threat of launching an initiative can sometimes

---

[13] WOLF LINDER, Die schweizerische Demokratie, p. 265.
[14] Cf. n. 209.

motivate the legislator to act. However, not only powerful political parties and associations which can afford the costly publicity have the chance to win an initiative campaign. The internet has facilitated campaigning as well as the collecting of signatures. The initiative aimed at the non-applicability of the statute of limitations for sexual offenses against children which succeeded at the polls in November 2008, was fought through by a dedicated Genevan housewife.

D. Barriers to Constitutional Amendments

Peremptory norms of international law (so called *ius cogens*) constitute a barrier to constitutional revision (Arts. 139 par. 2, 193 par. 4 and 194 par. 2 Const.). Peremptory norms of international law are norms accepted and recognised by the international community of states as a whole as norms from which no derogation is permitted.[15] Although there is no clear agreement on which norms reach the status of international *ius cogens*, it is generally accepted that this category includes the prohibition of genocide, slavery, and torture, as well as the main features of international humanitarian law and the principle of *non-refoulement*.[16]

511

> Example: in 1996, the Federal Assembly invalidated a popular initiative which stipulated that persons seeking asylum who had entered Switzerland illegally were to be removed by force immediately and without any right of appeal. This violated the principle of non-refoulement. Although the constitution at the time did not yet explicitly mention peremptory norms of international law as a barrier to constitutional amendments, parliament rightly argued that such norms had to be respected in any event.[17]

---

[15] Cf. Art. 53 of the Vienna Convention on the Law of Treaties of 23 May 1969.
[16] As to the contents of this principle, cf. n. 433.
[17] Cf. BBl 1996 I 1355; BBl 1997 I 433 et seq. and 446.

512 To what extent human rights are to be included in this list, is controversial. A number of Swiss scholars have suggested that the notion «peremptory norms of international law» ought to be attributed in a wider sense in Swiss constitutional law, encompassing not solely those norms recognised by the international community of states as a whole as non-derogatory. Up to now, government and parliament have refrained from such a problematic extension and adhered to the standards established in international law.

513 In recent years, popular initiatives which have raised concerns as to their compatibility with international law have increased in number. If such initiatives do not violate *ius cogens*, they have to be submitted to a vote of the people and the cantons. Most initiatives falling into this category were defeated at the polls. However, if such an initiative is accepted, its implementation poses an awkward alternative: either to interfere with the intention of the initiators,[18] or to run the risk of violating international law. In order to avoid such an embarrassment, a process of constitutional revision enabling the strict scrutiny of popular initiatives which could possibly be incompatible with international obligations, ought to be seriously considered.

514 Two other barriers expressly established in the constitution apply to partial revisions only: the *unity of subject matter*[19] and the *unity of form*.[20] For the rest, the constitution deliberately does not contain any provisions limiting constitutional amendments. In particular, it does not declare certain fundamental principles as absolutely rigid, i.e. it does not bind constitutional amendments to any national principles.[21]

---

[18] This was the case with regard to the implementation of a popular initiative concerning correctional measures for particularly dangerous criminals, which conflicted with Art. 5 par. 4 ECHR.

[19] Cf. n. 502.

[20] Cf. n. 505.

[21] Other constitutions do contain such provisions, the most noteworthy

Though not mentioned in the constitutional text, the *feasibility* of a proposal constitutes a further barrier. The recommended norm must be capable of being carried out and not demand the impossible. However, the impossibility has to be manifest. Simple practical difficulties in implementing a popular initiative do not justify its invalidation.

515

> Example: in 1955, the Federal Assembly invalidated a popular initiative demanding a 50% reduction of the defence budget which was to take effect before a popular vote could be arranged. On the other hand, a popular initiative aimed at the complete abolition of the Swiss Army[22] was not regarded as infeasible.

2. Statutes, Decrees and Ordinances

A. Form of Legal Norms and Other Acts

> **Art. 163 Const. Form of Enactments of the Federal Assembly**
> (1) The Federal Assembly enacts legal norms in the form of a federal statute or ordinance.
> (2) Other acts are promulgated in the form of a federal decree. A federal decree that is not subject to a referendum is named a simple federal decree.

Art. 163 Const. thus distinguishes between several categories of enactments: *legal norms*, i.e. legally binding rules governing an indeterminate number of cases, organising federal authorities or

516

---

being Art. 79 par. 3 German Basic Law (cf. n. 33). Some constitutions of former monarchies protect the republican form of government against constitutional changes, for example, Art. 89 par. 5 of the French Constitution and Art. 139 of the Italian Constitution. Art. V (in fine) of the U.S. Constitution determines that no state, without its consent, shall be deprived of its equal suffrage in the Senate.

[22] Cf. n. 509.

establishing procedures are promulgated either in the form of a *federal statute* or (parliamentary) *ordinance*. Only the former is subject to a referendum (Art. 140 par. 1 [c] and Art. 141 [a and b] Const.). Other acts, i.e. *decisions concerning specific matters* such as federal spending or the validity of a popular initiative, are promulgated in the form of a *federal decree*. Here again, there is a subdivision depending on whether or not an optional referendum can be requested.

517 The Federal Council also enacts legal norms in the form of ordinances (Art. 182 Const.). Based on statutory law, departments and other administrative agencies as well as federal courts can issue ordinances.

B. Federal Statutes

518 Art. 164 par. 1 Const. determines that all *important legal norms* must be enacted in the form of a federal statute, and adds an exemplary list of matters which, due to their importance in a democracy governed by the rule of law, require a statutory basis.

Art. 164 par. 1 Const. Legislation

(1) All important legal norms have to be enacted in the form of a federal statute. These include, in particular, fundamental provisions on:
 a. the exercise of political rights;
 b. restrictions on constitutional rights;
 c. the rights and obligations of individuals;
 d. persons subject to taxes or duties as well as the basis of assessment and the method of calculation;
 e. the tasks and services of the federation;
 f. the obligations of the cantons in implementing and enforcing federal law;
 g. the organisation and procedures of federal authorities.

2. Statutes, Decrees and Ordinances

The purpose of this article is to ensure that the people can initiate referendums concerning such important legal norms. This provides such norms with a *heightened democratic legitimacy*.

519

An *initiative* to enact, alter or abrogate statutory norms can come from a member of one of the two chambers of parliament (National Council or Council of States) or from a parliamentary committee or faction. Moreover, the Federal Council as well as each canton has the right to submit initiatives to the Federal Assembly. The people, however, have no such right with regard to ordinary legislation. As a consequence, a somewhat excessive use is made of popular initiatives demanding constitutional amendments, which in turn contributes to the insertion of provisions into the constitution which ought to be placed in a statute.

520

> In 2003 the people and the cantons adopted a new Art. 139a Const. which provides for an overall popular initiative («allgemeine Volksinitiative») allowing 100,000 citizens entitled to vote to present an initiative in the form of a general proposal, thereby leaving it to parliament to decide whether its implementation was to be accomplished by amending the constitution or on the level of ordinary legislation, and to draft the norms. However, this provision has never entered into force, as parliament and government realised that the new instrument would require complicated procedures and was ill-suited to improve direct democracy. Government and parliament therefore propose to abrogate Art. 139a Const.[23]

521

The executive branch of government is engaged significantly in the process of preparing new legislation.[24] Most bills are drafted within the federal administration, which, in more important

522

---

[23] BBl 2008, 2903 et seq.; BBl 2009, 13 et seq.

[24] A distinguished Swiss politician, who served as a Federal Councillor for fifteen years, observed recently that: «The Federal Council initiates, organises, coordinates and moderates the legislative process.» Cf. KASPAR VILLIGER, Eine Willensnation muss wollen – Die politische Kultur der Schweiz: Zukunfts- oder Auslaufmodell, Verlag Neue Zürcher Zeitung, Zurich 2009, p. 194.

cases, is assisted by *expert committees* appointed by the Federal Councillor who heads the responsible department. A first draft is subjected to a *consultation procedure,* whereby the cantons, political parties, associations and other groups with a particular interest in the subject matter are invited to express their views (Art. 147 Const.). Apart from making expert knowledge available, expert committees, as well as the consultation procedure, fulfil an important political function: to *negotiate a compromise which has a fair chance of surviving a referendum.*[25] A second draft takes the results of the consultation process into account. The preliminary process conducted within the executive concludes with a *governmental proposal* consisting of a bill as well as detailed commentary, and is published in the Federal Gazette.[26]

523 The bill is then debated and, if necessary, adjusted in the competent *parliamentary committee* which makes a recommendation to the respective chamber. In rare cases, a parliamentary committee even composes the initial draft, for which it can call upon the expertise of the federal administration.[27]

524 After having been *approved by both chambers*[28], the statute is published in the Federal Gazette. Within 100 days of publication, either 50,000 citizens entitled to vote or eight cantons can request that a popular ballot be held (Art. 141 [a] Const.). If such an *optional referendum* comes about, the statute has to be approved by a nationwide majority of voters. Unlike constitutional amendments, federal statutes do not need the backing of a majority of cantons.

525 Since 1874, in only about 7% of cases where an optional referendum was possible did referendum committees succeed in col-

---

[25] Cf. n. 227.
[26] The commentaries are a valuable source in the historical and teleological interpretation of federal norms.
[27] So-called *«parliamentary initiative»;* cf. Art. 107 – 114 ParlG.
[28] Concerning the parliamentary procedure, cf. n. 258.

lecting the required number of signatures leading to a popular ballot. However, in almost 50% of these cases the adherents of the referendum gained a victory at the polls, thus vetoing a parliamentary act.[29] In the years 1971 to 2007, referendum committees have been successful in collecting signatures on 88 occasions and won at the polls 28 times, which amounts to an almost one in three level of success.[30]

Ordinary federal legislation cannot enter into force before either the deadline for requesting a referendum (100 days from publication in the Federal Gazette) has expired, or, in the event that a referendum committee succeeds in collecting the necessary signatures, the statute has been accepted at the polls. This solution would be most unsatisfactory where legislative measures tolerated no delay. Art. 165 Const. therefore provides for an abrogate (instead of suspensive) referendum in cases of urgency. This implies that a statute declared to be urgent can be put into force immediately but could be repealed at the polls at a later date.

526

Art. 165 Const. Urgent Legislation

(1) A federal statute whose coming into force cannot be delayed can be declared urgent by a majority of the members of each of the two chambers and put into force immediately. Its duration is to be limited.

(2) If a referendum is demanded on an urgent federal statute, the statute ceases to apply one year after its adoption by the Federal Assembly, unless it is approved by the people in the meantime.

(3) An urgent federal statute which has no constitutional basis ceases to apply one year after its adoption by the Federal Assembly, unless it is approved by the people and the cantons in the meantime. The duration of such a statute is to be limited.

(4) An urgent federal statute that is defeated in a popular vote cannot be re-enacted.

---

[29] WOLF LINDER, Schweizerische Demokratie, p. 250.
[30] SWISS FEDERAL CHANCELLERY, The Swiss Confederation – a brief guide 2008, p. 17.

A precondition for declaring a federal statute urgent is that a legislative measure ought to have immediate effect in order to achieve the goals pursued. A qualified majority in both chambers (i.e., a majority of all the *members* of the respective Councils) is required to declare an act urgent. Moreover, the duration of urgent legislation must be limited.

527 Art. 165 Const. distinguishes between two kinds of urgent federal statutes: those that are in conformity with the constitution and those that have no basis in the constitution, for instance, because a federal competency is lacking. As urgent legislation not based on the constitution amounts to a modification of the constitutional order, the respective urgent federal statutes are subject to a mandatory referendum and acceptance by a double majority of the people and the cantons if they are to remain in force for over one year (Art. 165 par. 3 Const.). Under the new constitution, only a small number of urgent federal statutes have been enacted, all having a constitutional basis.

C. Federal Decrees

528 Federal decrees are *acts of parliament not embodying legal rules* but concerning specific matters. In certain cases, the constitution expressly states that the Federal Assembly decide in the form of a federal decree. This, for instance, is the case with regard to the approval of modifications to the territory of a canton (Art. 53 par. 3 Const.).[31] In such cases, the decree is subject to an optional referendum.

529 Sometimes a federal statute subjects a specific decision of parliament to an optional referendum, such as the Federal Law on Nuclear Energy[32] with regard to the approval of authorisation for a

---

[31] Cf. n. 113.
[32] Of 21 March 2003, SR 732.1, Art. 48 par. 3.

nuclear power plant. This means that the Federal Assembly decides in the form of a federal decree subject to a referendum.

Where there is no explicit constitutional or statutory reference to 530
the form of a federal decree, the Federal Assembly decides on concrete issues in the form of a «simple federal decree» not subject to referendum (Art. 163 par. 2 Const.). Thus, no referendum is available with regard to elections, the adoption of the budget, the approval of cantonal constitutions, or decisions on the validity of popular initiatives.

D. Ordinances

The term «ordinance» comprises all legal rules not enacted in the 531
form of a constitutional amendment or a federal statute. In Swiss constitutional law, as far as the federal level of government is concerned, this is equivalent to *legal norms not subject to a (mandatory or optional) referendum.* Such secondary norms can emanate from the Federal Assembly, the Federal Council, an administrative agency or a federal court. Most ordinances come from the executive branch. Ordinances of the Federal Assembly and the Federal Supreme Court are mainly destined to regulate matters concerning their internal administration in more detail.

According to Art. 164 par. 2 Const., legislative powers may be 532
delegated by federal statute unless this is excluded by the constitution. However, explicit delegation is not regarded as necessary insofar as the norms in the ordinance are merely destined to *spell out the application of a statute.* The duty of government and administration to ensure the implementation of legislation (Art. 182 par. 2 Const.) includes the framing of such accessory rules.

However, if an ordinance is intended to *supplement a statute*, for 533
instance by regulating matters left open in the statute, a delegation of legislative power is required. In order to be in harmony with the division of powers underlying the constitutional order

and to provide a norm with democratic legitimacy, such a delegation has to comply with certain requirements: the delegation has to be based on a statutory provision and be confined to a subject area circumscribed in the statute. The degree to which the statute itself (and not an ordinance) ought to determine the application of the law varies, depending on the affected rights. Grave restrictions on fundamental rights, for instance, have to be prescribed by statute[33] thus leaving little room for a delegation. Moreover, Art. 164 par. 1 Const., which states that all important legal norms have to be enacted in form of a federal statute, has to be kept in mind.[34]

534 In some situations calling for immediate measures the Federal Council is empowered to issue ordinances based directly on the constitution. This, for instance, is the case if an ordinance is required to safeguard the interests of the country or to counter imminent threats to public order and security.[35]

3. Treaties

A. Definitions

535 A treaty is an international agreement concluded between states and governed by international law.[36] International or supranational organisations can also be parties to a treaty.[37]

---

[33] Cf. n. 374.
[34] Cf. n. 518. It is not quite clear what falls under the category of «fundamental provisions».
[35] Cf. n. 317.
[36] Cf. Art. 2 par. 1 (a) of the Vienna Convention on the Law of Treaties of 23 May 1969.
[37] As in the case of Switzerland's sectoral agreements with the European Community and its member-states; cf. n. 82.

Some treaties *settle a specific matter*, for instance a boundary ad- 536
justment. Others *unify legal rules* for the participating states. They
automatically become part of the Swiss domestic legal order
upon ratification, as Switzerland follows a monistic system.[38]
Treaties that establish rights and obligations for individuals may
either be «*self-executing*» or «*non self-executing*». In the first case,
they are directly applicable by courts and other state authorities.
Such direct applicability is only possible if a norm is formulated
with such clarity that it can have a direct bearing in a specific
case.[39] Otherwise, as in the case of programmatic declarations to
unify the law, a provision is regarded as «non self-executing» and
therefore requires implementing legislation. The division is not
always clear.

B. Treaty-Making Procedure

Based on Art. 54 par. 1 Const., the federation has a comprehen- 537
sive competency to conclude treaties, even if the subject-matter
falls within the domain of cantonal powers. Cantonal treaties are
permitted in matters not covered by federal treaties. They usually
concern relations among neighbours, whereby the procedures for
concluding such treaties involve federal authorities.[40] In the following, the focus will be on *federal treaties*.

The tasks and competencies in the treaty-making process are dis- 538
tributed between the executive and the legislature. Due to the
treaty referendum, even the people may be involved. The Federal
Council decides whether to initiate *negotiations*, formulates the
policies for these negotiations, appoints and instructs the agents
and may also decide to drop a treaty project. In spite of the asser-
tion that the Federal Assembly «participates in shaping foreign

---

[38] Cf. n. 37.
[39] Example: the rights of the ECHR; cf. n. 358.
[40] This is discussed in n. 147.

policy» (Art. 166 par. 1 Const.), the ability of parliament to influence the shaping of a treaty by giving directions is very limited. The *signing* of the negotiated text is subject to subsequent ratification.

539 The government has to obtain *legislative approval* after signing a treaty and before ratifying it. However, certain categories of treaties – which might be compared with «executive agreements» in the United States – can be concluded by the Federal Council without parliamentary approval, namely if there is an accordant basis in a federal statute or in a prior treaty approved by the Federal Assembly (Art. 166 par. 2 Const.; Art. 24 par. 2 ParlG). The Federal Law on the Organisation of Government and Administration (RVOG) lists exemptions from parliamentary approval in Art. 7a par. 2 (a–d): agreements which impose no new obligations upon Switzerland and do not implicate a waiver of existing rights; agreements executing prior agreements; agreements concerning matters which, in municipal law, the Federal Council is competent to regulate alone, and agreements dealing with secondary questions of an administrative-technical nature and not causing substantial costs.

540 Ordinarily, i.e. when legislative approval is required, the Federal Council submits the treaty together with explanatory observations to the Federal Assembly. Parliament can only either approve or reject a treaty. If both chambers reach a positive decision, the treaty is approved and the Federal Council authorised to ratify it. However, legislative approval does not create an obligation to ratify. The government remains free to withhold ratification.

541 Direct democracy has also left its mark on the treaty-making power. Switzerland probably has the most democratic treaty-making procedure in the world. Based on a popular initiative, a treaty referendum was introduced in 1921. The increased importance of treaties for the legal order was thereby accompanied by

an extension of popular participation in treaty-making. The constitution provides for two sorts of treaty-referendum: compulsory and optional.

A *compulsory treaty referendum* is required for accession to organisations for collective security or supranational communities (Art. 140 par. 1 [b] Const.). Such far-reaching decisions require, like constitutional amendments, a «double majority», i.e. they have to be approved by the people and the cantons. This procedure was followed when Switzerland joined the United Nations.[41] Membership of the European Union, too, would necessitate the approval of the citizens nationwide and in a majority of cantons, as the EU is a «supranational community». 542

Art. 141 par. 1 (d) Const. provides for an *optional treaty referendum* in three circumstances: if a treaty is of unlimited duration and may not be terminated; in the case of accession to an international organisation; and, finally, if a treaty contains important legal norms or requires implementing federal legislation. When Switzerland ratified the European Convention on Human Rights in 1974, the issue had not been submitted to a prior popular vote, which, in retrospect, seems amazing. However, at that time the constitution did not require a referendum for all treaties containing important legal norms. 543

After a treaty has been approved by parliament and, in the event of a referendum, by the people, it is up to the Federal Council to ratify the treaty (Art. 184 par. 2 Const.). *Ratification* is an act by which the government declares that it accepts the content of the treaty and promises to observe the obligations contained therein. With the exchange of the instruments of ratification between the contracting parties the treaty enters into force and becomes binding under international law. As previously mentioned, treaty pro- 544

---

[41] Cf. n. 88. The U.N. falls under the category of «organisations for collective security».

visions which are not self-executing have to be transformed by the legislature.[42]

545 Swiss authorities are anxious to follow the principle «pacta sunt servanda» and to delay the ratification of a treaty until any incompatibilities within the national legal order have been removed.

C. Relationship between Treaties and Domestic Law

546 Treaties are binding upon the parties and must be performed by them in good faith. A party may not invoke provisions of its internal law to avoid responsibility for the observance of its treaty obligations (except in case of a manifest violation of internal law regarding competence to conclude treaties).[43] However, international law leaves it to the parties to decide *how* to fulfil their treaty obligations, and, in particular, what rank treaties occupy in relation to domestic law.

547 Art. 5 par. 4 Const. emphasises the obligation of the federation and the cantons to respect international law.[44] Art. 5 Const. highlights the rule of law, but was not intended to establish a precedence of international law over domestic law. When the new constitution was drafted, there was no consensus in favour of the primacy of international law. The only concession made in this respect was the recognition of peremptory norms of international law as a barrier to any constitutional amendment.[45]

---

[42] Cf. n. 536.
[43] Cf. Arts. 26, 27 and 46 of the Vienna Convention on the Law of Treaties of 23 May 1969.
[44] Cf. text of Art. 5 Const. in n. 57.
[45] Cf. n. 511.

3. Treaties

Art. 190 Const. obliges the Federal Supreme Court and other authorities to apply federal statutes as well as international law (irrespective of their constitutionality).[46] In other words, federal statutes and treaties are equally binding for the courts. However, in the event of conflict between a treaty and a federal statute, it is logically and practically impossible to apply both. The question whether, in such a situation, the statute or the treaty is to prevail, remains unanswered and has to be decided as the case arises.

First and foremost, if a conflict with international law is conceivable, a court will endeavour to interpret domestic law in such a way that it is compatible with international law. If this is not possible and the statute is older than the treaty, it is generally recognised that the treaty, as «*lex posterior*», abrogates the statutory norm. Moreover, it is uncontested that a treaty is on a higher level («*lex superior*» rule) and therefore supersedes all cantonal law as well as federal ordinances. The really controversial issue is whether courts have to apply a federal statute which conflicts with a *treaty provision already in existence when the law was passed*. This question has generated complex case law by the Federal Supreme Court, sometimes lacking the desirable consistency. In an old decision, named the «Schubert case» and largely criticized in legal doctrine, the court decided that the later statutory provision was to prevail if parliament had *intentionally* departed from the treaty; even if such a deviation could not modify obligations under international law, it was regarded as binding on the court.[47]

In a number of more recent decisions, the Federal Supreme Court has generally accepted that treaty provisions, especially when they protect human rights, override statutory norms, even if these are more recent. In a landmark decision the Federal Supreme Court emphasised the primacy of the European Convention on Human Rights by not applying a federal statute which excluded a

---

[46] Cf. n. 562.
[47] BGE 99 Ib 39 E. 4 (1973), *Schubert*.

court appeal in violation of Art. 6 (1) ECHR.[48] However, the «Schubert case» has never been explicitly overruled. It is somewhat implausible that the Federal Supreme Court would apply a statutory provision which clearly violated the ECHR. Yet it is an open question how the court would decide if a statute deliberately violated a lesser international treaty.

4. Constitutional Jurisdiction

A. Essence and Forms

551 In a wider sense, «constitutional jurisdiction» includes all forms of review by an independent court of government action as to its compatibility with the constitution. In a narrower sense, this term refers to the review by the courts of the constitutionality of legislation.[49] Constitutional jurisdiction is widely regarded as the most effective means of protecting the constitution, as courts are independent of the state authorities responsible for the government action under scrutiny and, moreover, as court proceedings increase the chances of reaching an objective judgment independent of the day's political majorities.

552 Constitutional jurisdiction basically fulfils two functions: to protect individuals, especially with regard to state infringements on their fundamental rights; and, secondly and equally importantly, to safeguard the constitutional order and to ensure the increased validity of the constitution in the legal hierarchy. However, adjudicating constitutional issues is not a mechanical process of laying «the article of the Constitution which is invoked beside the statute which is challenged and to decide whether the latter

---

[48] BGE 125 II (417) (1999), *Partiya Karkêren Kurdistan*.
[49] In the United States the term «judicial review» is frequently used in this connection.

squares with the former».[50] Constitutional interpretation cannot be completely disinterested and neutral, as it necessarily involves value judgments and contributes to evolving the written text.[51]

Various *types of constitutional jurisdiction* can be distinguished. In the case of *abstract judicial review,* the constitutionality of norms (contained in a statute, treaty or ordinance) is reviewed by a court in the absence of a concrete case of application. If the court finds the norms unconstitutional, these will either not come into effect *(preventive judicial review),* or will be repealed *(repressive judicial review).* 553

By contrast, *concrete judicial review* occurs subsequent to an individual act such as an arrest or the seizure of property. If such an act is based on possibly unconstitutional legislation, the court may conduct a preliminary review in order to determine the constitutionality of the legal norm upon which the concrete decision has been based. Should the court determine the norm to be unconstitutional, it will refuse to apply it and consequently annul the contested individual act. The norm itself will not necessarily be rescinded.[52] 554

There are other forms of constitutional jurisdiction apart from examining the constitutionality of legislation or of other norms which rank below the constitution. The tasks of constitutional courts usually include deciding on jurisdictional conflicts between the highest state organs. In federal states, differences between the rights and duties of the federation and the member-states can give rise to constitutional adjudication. Sometimes constitutional courts are empowered to adjudicate charges against high governmental officials aimed at their removal from 555

---

[50] As Justice OWEN J.ROBERTS argued in *United States v. Butler*, 297 U.S. (1936) 62 et seq.
[51] Cf. n. 40.
[52] The consequences depend largely on whether the system is centralised or diffuse; with regard to this distinction cf. n. 558.

Part VI – Rule-Making, Treaties and Constitutional Jurisdiction

office, or to review the legality of popular elections and referenda.

B. Comparative Context

556 Concrete judicial review, exercised to decide actual cases and controversies, is much older than abstract judicial review and other forms of constitutional jurisdiction. The birth of judicial review is often (not quite correctly!) considered to be the decision of the U.S. Supreme Court in *Marbury v. Madison*,[53] drafted by Chief Justice JOHN MARSHALL.[54] The justification for judicial review of ordinary legislation was closely related to the concept of the superiority of a written constitution. To this day, the U.S. Supreme Court exercises this form of constitutional jurisdiction only.

557 Austria was the first country to create, in 1920, a special constitutional court with the power to annul unconstitutional legislation.[55] In the aftermath of the Second World War, some countries in Western Europe established special constitutional courts not serving as regular appellate courts, with a jurisdiction focused entirely on constitutional issues and regularly including abstract judicial review. Most significant were the provisions for constitutional jurisdiction by the German Constitutional Court *(Bundesverfassungsgericht)* under Arts. 93 and 94 of the German Basic Law. In Central and Eastern Europe constitutional jurisdiction experienced a real renaissance after the iron curtain separating the West from the communist world had been dismantled. To-

---

[53] 5 U.S. (1 Cranch) 137 (1803).

[54] More than 200 years earlier, the British Judge Sir EDWARD COKE had claimed that «the common law will control Acts of Parliament, and sometimes adjudge them to be utterly void». Cf. *Dr. Bonham's Case*, 8 Co. Rep, 114 (Court of Common Pleas, 1610).

[55] This concept was prominently influenced by HANS KELSEN, one of the main architects of Austrian constitutional law and renowned world-wide for his «pure theory of law».

day, all countries bordering Switzerland (France, Germany, Italy, Austria and Liechtenstein) as well as numerous others have special constitutional courts.

The impact of constitutional jurisdiction on constitutional development can be considerable even where there is no special constitutional court. This is especially true with regard to the role of the U.S. Supreme Court. In the United States as well as in Canada, Japan and Switzerland – to take just a few examples – the Supreme Court is the final court of appeal in the national justice system, with jurisdiction extending to civil, penal, administrative and constitutional law. Under this model (the so-called «diffuse system»), even inferior courts are quite often empowered to review norms on their compatibility with the constitution and not to apply them if found to be unconstitutional. By contrast, when a legal system provides for a special constitutional court, legislative review is likely to be concentrated in such a court, i.e. only the constitutional court is authorised to review the constitutionality of a statutory norm, and in the event of unconstitutionality to declare the norm invalid (the so-called «centralised system»). Other courts can call upon the constitutional court and, in conjunction with a concrete case, obtain judgment on the constitutionality of the provision pertinent to the case. 558

Example: Art. 100 par. 1 German Basic Law states that where a court considers a law the validity of which is relevant to its decision unconstitutional, the proceedings shall be stayed and a decision obtained from the Federal Constitutional Court if the matter concerns a violation of the Basic Law. (If conformity with the constitution of a member state is doubtful, a decision shall be obtained from the state court competent for constitutional disputes).

There are many ways to conceive of abstract judicial review of the constitutionality of norms. As a rule, recourse to the constitutional court presupposes that the legal norms have been promulgated and are being appealed against within a certain period following official publication. In the event of unconstitutionality, 559 the court will repeal the norm *(repressive judicial review)*. The French Constitutional Council *(Conseil Constiutionnel)*, however, exercises a *preventive judicial review*. This means that legal norms are subjected to court review prior to entering into force. A provision declared unconstitutional will be neither promulgated nor implemented.[56] A corresponding prior review may be launched with regard to treaties; if they contain clauses found by the Constitutional Council to be contrary to the constitution, authorisation to ratify them may be given only after amending the constitution.[57] For this reason, France could only accede to the *Treaty of Maastricht* after accomplishing a constitutional revision which took into account the findings of the Constitutional Council in the «*Maastricht I Decision*» of 9 April1992.[58]

560 Abstract judicial review quite often allows a *parliamentary minority* to initiate a review of legislation in the absence of a concrete case. In Germany, apart from the Federal Government, even one-third of the *Bundestag* members as well as the government of a member-state can demand judicial review as to the formal and material compatibility of an Act with the constitution.[59] In France, since a constitutional amendment of 1974, sixty members of the National Assembly (out of 577) or 60 senators (out of 321) can bring about judicial review of treaties or ordinary laws prior to their entering into force.[60] This gives the parliamentary opposition a chance, having lost a political battle, to continue the dispute in court with legal arguments. Moreover, the threat of sub-

---

[56] Arts. 61 and 62 of the French Constitution.
[57] Art. 54 of the French Constitution.
[58] 92–308 DC.
[59] Art. 93 (2) German Basic Law.
[60] Art. 54 and 61 par. 2 of the French Constitution. Moreover, the President of the Republic, the Prime Minister and the Presidents of both Houses of Parliament may refer a statute to the Constitutional Council. Organic laws (cf. n. 490) are submitted to an obligatory scrutiny; Art. 61 par. 1 of the French Constitution.

sequent judicial review is likely to have an indirect, anticipatory influence on the legislative process, as it encourages government and parliament to bear in mind the risk of defeat before the constitutional court. It may even contribute to consensus building within the legislative assembly.

C. Swiss Model: Overview

In Switzerland the democratic principle dominates the political landscape, and citizens' participatory rights have a tendency to be overemphasised, even at the expense of the rule of law.[61] A deeply rooted distrust vis-à-vis a judiciary making decisions on politically controversial issues fits into this picture. This philosophy has left its mark on the constitution and affected statutory provisions governing constitutional jurisdiction. 561

Art. 190 Const. unconditionally obliges the Federal Supreme Court and other law-applying authorities to apply federal statutes and international law. 562

> **Art. 190 Const. Applicable Law**
> Federal statutes and international law are binding on the Federal Supreme Court and other law-applying authorities.

This means that *federal statutes have to be applied even when they conflict with the constitution* and cannot be construed so as to conform to the constitution. This seems to exclude judicial review of federal statutes. However, Art. 190 Const. is interpreted narrowly by the Federal Supreme Court in the sense that, although it must apply the statute, it can declare that a statutory norm is incom- 563

---

[61] By contrast, in countries where constitutional jurisdiction is most significant, other basic values are preponderant: in Germany, for instance, the *Rechtsstaat*, and in the United States the concept of separation of powers between three co-equal branches of government.

patible with the constitution.[62] Moreover, treaty provisions protecting fundamental rights have priority over federal legislation.[63]

564 The main reason for severely limiting constitutional jurisdiction in Art. 190 Const. can be seen in the Swiss concept of popular democracy. Sometimes it is even argued that the people themselves, through legislative referendum, can repeal unconstitutional laws and thus substitute judicial review. This contrasts with the fact that the constitutionality of a contested statute hardly ever plays a significant role when a referendum is launched or defended in subsequent campaigns. At any rate, Art. 190 Const. largely shields the popularly elected parliament from judicial scrutiny, thereby conceivably increasing its responsibility for legislating in conformity with the constitution.

565 For the rest, all Swiss courts are entitled and even required to exercise *concrete judicial review* with regard to norms below the level of a federal statute. If, for instance, a norm in a federal ordinance or cantonal statute relevant to a case appears contrary to the constitution (or to another provision occupying a superior rank), the court will not apply that norm but base its decision on other provisions.[64] For all practical purposes, this non-application in an individual case will, as in the United States, result in the rescission of the norm in future cases.

566 In Switzerland, parliament carries out important judicial functions which, in other countries, are assigned to constitutional ju-

[62] In the United Kingdom, appellate courts are also confined to «declarations of incompatibility» if legislation cannot be interpreted so as to comply with the ECHR. It is then up to the government to take remedial action. Cf. Human Rights Act 1998, Sections 4 and 10.

[63] The relationship between treaties and domestic law is discussed in n. 546 et seq.

[64] A proposal by the Federal Government to complement this diffuse form of judicial review with a centralised review of federal statutes, to be carried out by the Federal Supreme Court in concrete cases, was blocked in the National Council in 1998.

risdiction. These functions relate to decisions on jurisdictional conflicts between the highest federal authorities and on the validity of popular initiatives.[65] At least, the Federal Supreme Court adjudicates disputes between the federation and the cantons or between cantons after either the federation or a canton has filed an action (Art. 189 par. 2 Const.). However, as federal statutes are binding on the court even in this context, the cantons have no effective means of defending their competencies against the federal legislature in a legal procedure.

Abstract judicial review is strictly *limited to cantonal norms*. Cantonal laws and decrees can be contested in a public law appeal by any individual who has «virtual standing», i.e. it suffices that the appellant might be adversely affected in interests warranting protection by a future application (Arts. 82 [b] and 89 par. 1 BGG). If, to take an example, a cantonal law issues a ban on masking one's feature at a public demonstration, individuals residing in the respective canton can file, within thirty days from the official cantonal publication, an appeal with the Federal Supreme Court against the regulation, asserting a violation of the freedoms of assembly and of opinion.[66]

567

By far, most of the cases raising constitutional issues which find their way to the Federal Supreme Court concern the *constitutionality of individual decisions* emanating from cantonal or federal authorities. Such cases are usually argued within the scope of a public law appeal or a subsidiary constitutional appeal.[67] In order to have standing to sue, an appellant must show that he or she is particularly affected by the contested decision. Appeals are directed either against the cantonal court of last resort, the Federal

568

---

[65] Cf. n. 293.
[66] BGE 117 Ia 472 (1991), *Social Democratic Party of Basle-City.* In this case, an appeal had also been launched by the cantonal section of a political party.
[67] Cf. n. 336.

Administrative Court or another federal authority. However, individual decisions taken by the Federal Assembly (for instance on the validity of a popular initiative) or the Federal Council (for example, concerning information brochures prior to a federal referendum) are excluded from judicial review, with very few exceptions. This creates a conflict with the guarantee of access to court granted in Art. 29a Const.[68]

569 In spite of all these restrictions, constitutional jurisdiction in Switzerland has played a *formidable role in developing constitutional law and advancing fundamental rights.*[69] It may be that the cautious model of a severely restricted constitutional jurisdiction which, to a large extent, keeps the Federal Supreme Court out of ongoing national political controversies and debates, favours a rather more audacious case law which interprets the constitution as a living instrument, thus going beyond the text or «original understanding» of constitutional provisions. Indirectly, this case law even influences federal legislation as a point of reference when federal statutes are drafted or amended.

---

[68] Cf. n. 467.
[69] Cf. n. 39.

Index

References are made to the respective numbers.

A

Academic freedom 422
Affirmative action *See* Equality
Aliens 157, 203–211
- from EU and EFTA member-states 211
- fundamental rights 205–207, 363, 396, 441
- political rights 204, 219
- residency permits 208–210
- statistics 94, 203

Arbitrariness, protection against 457, 458
Asylum 157, 433, 484, 511
Australia 31
Austria 32, 101, 322, 493, 557

B

Basic rights *See* Fundamental rights
Bicameral parliament 252–255 *See* also Federal Assembly, bicameral system
Bills of rights 343, 350, 354, 438, 446, 477
Budget 290, 319

C

Cantonal constitutions 100, 115–120
- as source of fundamental rights 357
- compliance with federal law 116, 117
- constitutional conventions 495
- democratic constitution 61, 118, 219
- federal approval 119, 293, 530
- reviewability 119

Cantons 97–104 *See also* Cantonal constitutions
- autonomy 99, 100, 165
- boundaries 114, 179
- competencies 96, 100, 154, 187, 189, 194, 406, 537, 538

- courts 322, 323
- equality 98, 100
- federal guarantees 109-120
- «half-cantons» 98, 103, 104, 506
- implementation of federal law 100, 130, 142, 165, 175, 318
- number and status 5, 15, 16, 92, 110-112
- participation in federal decision-making 64, 102-104, 145, 146, 256, 506
- protection of inner security 121
- size 93
- territory 110, 111, 113, 120, 528

Censorship 417
Checks and balances *See* Division of powers
Children and young people, right to special protection 363, 390, 482, 485 *See also* U.N. Convention on the Rights of the child
Church and state 107, 149, 406
Citizenship 68, 183-202
- acquisition by law 185, 188, 190
- avoidance of statelessness 186, 187, 200-202
- cantonal 100, 183, 184, 190, 194
- communal 183, 184, 190, 194
- competencies 187-189
- integration 186, 193
- legal status 183
- loss 188, 200-202
- naturalisation 185, 187, 188, 191-198
- nullification 192, 202
- reinstatement 199
- rights and duties 184, 429, 432

Civil defence 148, 452
Civil law 158, 162, 189, 402, 459
Civil liberties *See also* Fundamental rights
- definition 343
- functions 343
- restrictions 371 *See also* Fundamental rights, restrictions

Communes 5, 68, 92, 93, 105-108, 142
Communication 152
Competencies: distribution between federation and cantons 24, 34, 122-160
- allocation in general 64, 122-128
- cantonal competencies *See* Cantons, competencies
- comprehensive 126, 134

Index

- concurrent 127, 138, 147
- exclusive 127, 139
- federal competencies: overview 143–160, 187–189
- parallel 128, 140, 175
- partial 126, 135
- principle of subsidiarity 129
- Swiss method of assigning tasks 129–142
- task and revenue sharing 28, 100, 159, 160, 174
- to establish a framework 126, 136, 150

Concordance democracy 227, 247, 317, 522
Confederate Treaty 16, 22, 97
Confederation 13, 20, 63, 95
Conference of Cantonal Governements 182
Conflicts between highest state organs 259, 293, 555, 566
Congress of Vienna 16, 71, 111
Conscientious objectors 411
Constitution
- basic principles 55–76, 85
- comparative context 29–34
- functions 34
- historical development 13–24
- interpretation 39–54, 552 *See also* Interpretation
- normative openness 34
- of 1848 1, 20, 226
- of 1874 23, 227, 493
- of 1999 25–27, 39, 493
- preamble 69, 76, 78
- qualified procedure 29, 31, 489
- rank 29, 489
- revision *See* Constitutional revision
- sources of constitutional law 27, 28, 35–39, 445

Constitutional jurisdiction 26, 336, 551–569
- abstract judicial review 553, 557, 559, 560, 567
- and democracy 561, 564
- centralised system 558
- comparative context 556–560
- concrete judicial review 554, 556, 565
- constitutional courts 324, 557, 558
- definition 551
- diffuse system 558
- federal controversies 555, 566
- functions 491, 552

- impact 9, 558, 569
- obligation to apply federal statutes and international law 9, 30, 57, 163, 548, 562–564
- preventive judicial review 553, 559
- repressive judicial review 553, 559
- types 553–555

Constitutional revision 492–515
- barriers 33, 511–515
- double majority 31, 103, 229, 489, 506, 527
- initiative 497 *See also* Popular initiative
- partial 24, 492–494, 501–510
- total 492–500
- unity of form 514
- unity of subject matter 502, 514

Consultation procedure 104, 522
Cooperation between federation and cantons 100, 175 *See also* Federalism, cooperative
Council of Europe 80
Council of States 270–272
- composition 98, 104, 253, 256, 270
- election 257, 271, 498
- function 270
- incompatibilities 262, 272
- term of office 257, 272

Court system 26, 28, 158, 322–326
Criminal law 158, 432
Cross-border cooperation 147, 175
Culture 94, 149
Cumulation 266
Custom 38

D

Data protection 399, 400
Death penalty 379, 386, 387
Declaration of general application 174
Delegation of legislative power 532, 533
Democracy
- and fundamental rights 412
- and judicial review 561, 564
- democratic principle 17, 58–61, 116, 118

- direct 7, 26, 28, 58–60, 213, 221–233, 247, 519 *See also* Popular initiative; Referendum
- semi-direct 59, 213
- representative 118, 213

Demonstrations 426
Departement 310, 312
Deportation 433, 434
Detention, conditions of 392, 418, 475, 476
Diet 13, 15, 18, 22
Diplomatic protection 184
Disabled persons 451, 456
Discrimination *See* Equality, ban on discrimination
Districts 108
Division of powers 6, 21
- and historical analysis 46
- and rule of law 56
- in a parliamentary system 239
- in cantonal constitutions 118
- in France 244
- in Switzerland 249, 250, 286, 292, 533
- in the United States 241, 242

E

Economic freedom 153–155, 438–444
Education 106, 142, 149, 165, 175, 181, 407, 421, 494 *See also* Social rights, right to primary school assistance; Universities
Elections
- majority vote 263, 264, 271
- presidential 241, 244
- proportional 24, 220, 239, 263–267, 271

Energy 152
Environmental protection 150
Equality 39, 345, 415, 445–456, 481
- affirmative action 371, 451, 454
- and democracy 446
- and liberty 446
- ban on discrimination 195, 206, 361, 382, 383, 414, 451, 456
- equal treatment of competitors 444
- gender equality 24, 50, 216, 371, 448, 452–455
- general equal protection clause 446–450

European Community *See* European Union

Index

European Convention on Human Rights (ECHR) 80, 543
- Art. 3 389
- Art. 5 376, 391, 421, 461, 473, 474, 476
- Art. 6 344, 421, 461, 467, 469, 472, 477, 479, 550
- Art. 8 394–398, 403
- Art. 10 413, 415, 416
- Art. 11 424, 428
- Art. 12 402, 403
- as source of fundamental rights 36, 354, 358–360
- direct applicability 359
- impact on Swiss law 2, 78, 117, 461, 550
- protocols 358, 386
- restrictions 372

European Court of Human Rights 39, 356
European Economic Area (EEA) 81, 84
European Free Trade Association (EFTA) 81, 211, 429
European Social Charter 347
European Union (EU) 62, 79–87, 103, 229, 542
- fundamental rights 352
- sectoral agreements 36, 82, 211, 429, 441

Execution by substitution 169
Expert committees 522
Expropriation 436, 437
Expulsion 184, 396, 432–434
Extradition 184, 387, 432–434

F

Fair procedure *See* Procedural rights
Familiy life, protection of 396, 403
Federal Administration *See* Department; Federal Council; Office
Federal Administrative Court 325, 335, 568
Federal Assembly *See also* Council of States; National Council; United Federal Assembly
- bicameral system 6, 20, 64, 104, 256–259
- committees 258, 275, 277, 282, 289, 330, 523
- decisions 258, 284
- equal powers of both chambers 258, 259
- factions 278
- form of enactments 516
- immunity 283
- incompatibilities 249

- initiative 104, 281
- interpellation 281
- meetings 280–284
- militia system 251, 285, 314
- motion 281
- ordinary question 281
- parliamentary services 279
- postulate 281
- powers 61, 119, 168, 178, 259, 285–294, 538–540, 566
- presidency 274
- quorum 284
- secretary general 279

Federal Chancellery 266, 299
Federal Council 245, 246, 295–321
- collegiate principle 297, 308
- composition 248, 296–299
- decisions 298
- dual function 295, 310, 312
- election 230, 296, 300–307, 498
- eligibility 300, 301
- incompatibilities 249, 302
- magic formula 305–307
- meetings 298
- powers 168, 260, 289, 310, 314–321, 522, 534, 538, 539, 544
- presidency *See* Federal President
- quorum 298
- term of office 300

Federal Criminal Court 325, 335, 480
Federal decree 113, 497, 501, 516, 528–530
Federal guarantees *See Cantons,* federal guarantees
Federalism 3, 5 *See also* Federal state
- as a basic principle 62–68, 94
- cooperative 66, 181, 182 *See also* Treaties, intercantonal
- «executive» 125
- federal comity 120, 176
- fiscal federalism 159, 160

Federalist Papers 20, 123
Federal President 245, 297, 309
Federal state *See also* Federal Assembly, bicameral system
- creation 1, 20, 95
- federal coercion 168, 169
- federal supervision 165–167

255

- notion 62–64, 95, 96
- primacy of federal law 117, 161–164

Federal statute 38, 489, 516, 518–527, 562–564
Federal Supreme Court 322–341
- composition 327
- election 328, 330
- financial autonomy 333
- incompatibilities 249, 329
- jurisdiction 142, 166, 334–337, 468, 567, 568
- organisation 331–333, 338
- proceedings 339–341
- term of office 328

Finances 290, 319
Finland 415
Foreigners *See* Aliens
Foreign relations 72, 76–87, 99, 142, 144–147, 289, 316 *See also* Treaties
France 60, 223, 243, 244, 350, 490, 559, 560
Freedom of assembly 424–426
Freedom of association 424, 427
Freedom of coalition 424, 428
Freedom of domicile 184, 205, 429–431
Freedom of expression 407, 412–418, 420, 423
Freedom of information 413, 415
Freedom of opinion *See* Freedom of expression
Freedom of religion 404–411
Freedom of the arts 423
French Revolution 2, 14, 21
Fundamental rights 342–488 *See also* Civil liberties; Equality; Political rights; Procedural rights; Social rights
- addressee 365–369, 447, 453–456
- cantonal 100, 357
- catalogue 8, 57, 352, 353, 355, 356
- comparative context 348–354
- core content 379, 436
- definitions 342–347
- functions 368, 369, 426, 453–455
- implementation 362–369
- implied rights 353, 356, 385, 420, 483
- restrictions 370–379, 533
- sources 355–361

- subject 205-207, 363, 364, 429, 440, 441, 447
- third-party effect 367-369, 455

G

Gay couples 193, 393, 401
Gender quota 219, 454
General 259
German Basic Law
- barriers to constitutional revision 33
- basic principles 115
- bicameral parliament 254
- constitutional jurisdiction 557, 558, 560
- fundamental rights 351, 352, 379, 380, 392, 399, 422, 423
- relation between federation and member-states 125, 127, 168
- system of government 240

Good faith, observance of 459, 460

H

Habeas corpus 388, 445, 473
Head of State 239, 240, 245
Health 135, 156, 165, 181
Helvetic Republic 14
Human dignity 33, 379-384, 484
Human rights 342

I

Immunity 283
Independence of the judiciary 56, 57, 292, 326, 328, 470, 471
Initiative *See* Popular initiative
Intercantonal bodies 173, 179
International Law 36, 37, 57, 162 *See also* Treaties
- interpretation in harmony with 54, 549
- monistic system 37, 358, 536
- peremptory norms 33, 78, 433, 511, 512, 547
- rank in relation to domestic law 490, 546-550, 562, 563

International Monetary Fund 90
Interpretation 40-54
- combination of methods 53, 54
- historical analysis 45-48, 53
- in harmony with the constitution and with international law 54, 549

- nature and task 40, 41
- systematic analysis 44
- teleological analysis 51, 52
- topical analysis 49, 50
- verbal analysis 42, 43, 53

Inviolability of abode 397
Italy 221, 240, 252
Ius cogens *See* International law, peremptory norms
Ius sanguinis 185
Ius soli 185

J

Judicial review *See* Constitutional jurisdiction
Judiciary *See* Constitutional jurisdiction; Court system; Federal Supreme Court
Jura 24, 97, 111, 120

L

Landsgemeinde 50, 232, 236
Languages
- freedom of language 413, 420, 421
- national 5, 94, 421
- official 43, 94, 339
- territoriality principle 421

Legality 57, 373–375, 474, 533
Legislative process 213, 288, 317, 496, 522

M

Magic formula *See* Federal Council, magic formula
Magna Carta 343
Mediation 15
Military 121, 148, 169, 184, 325, 452, 509
Mobility 82, 154, 211, 429
Monopoly 155, 443
Muslims and freedom of religion 408

N

National Council 260–269
- composition 256, 260

- election 257, 263–267, 299, 498
- eligibility 261
- incompatibilities 262
- term of office 268

Neutrality 71–73, 88
Non-refoulement principle 433, 511

O

Office 312
Ordinance 317, 338, 374, 489, 516, 517, 531–534, 565
Organisation for Security and Cooperation in Europe 80

P

Pacta sunt servanda 545
Panachage 266
Pardon 259, 468
Parliament *See* Federal Assembly
Parliamentary control 292
Personal liberty 385, 388–393 *See also* Detention, conditions of; Habeas corpus; Procedural rights, deprivation of liberty; Right to life; Right to privacy; Torture, prohibition of
- freedom of movement 388, 391
- mental integrity 389, 392, 393
- physical integrity 388–390

Police 121, 148, 165
Police clause 375
Political parties 239, 248, 263, 269, 277, 278, 305–307, 330, 427, 510
Political rights 112, 184, 212–237, 346 *See also* Elections; Popular initiative; Referendum
- cantonal 204, 219, 220, 231, 232
- communal 204, 219, 220, 233
- elections 184
- freedom of decision 219, 234–237
- nationals living abroad 216–218
- notion 212
- postal voting 217
- right to vote 214–220
- voting register 218

Popular initiative 24, 196, 497, 520, 521
- and international law 511–513

- counter-proposal 503, 508
- for constitutional revisions 3, 226, 228, 503-510
- function 209, 213, 224, 228, 510
- in the cantons 118, 231
- validity 293, 530, 566

Presumption of innocence *See* Procedural rights
Procedural rights 47, 344, 383, 461-480
- access to court 467, 468, 480, 568
- criminal proceedings 477-480
- deprivation of liberty 473-476
- equality of arms 464
- exemption from costs 466, 482
- free legal counsel 466, 482
- functions 462
- general guarantees 463-466
- judicial proceedings 469-472 *See also* Independence of the judiciary
- presumption of innocence 477, 478
- public court hearing 472
- right to a proper defence 479
- right to be heard 195, 465, 475, 479

Properity, right to 378, 435-437
Proportionality 169, 378, 454
Public aims 70, 76, 78, 94, 131
Public interest 376, 444
Public works 151
Publicity 320, 341, 415, 472

R

Radio and television 52, 152, 416
Recall 225
Rechtsstaat *See* Rule of law
Referendum
- abrogate 221, 526
- administrative 230
- fiscal 230
- function 213, 228, 247
- in the cantons 118, 231
- mandatory 31, 98, 103, 222, 226, 229, 230, 489, 527, 542
- optional 23, 31, 104, 113, 174, 222, 227, 229, 290, 489, 516, 524, 525, 528, 529, 543
- plebiscite form 60

- suspensive 221, 526
- treaty referendum *See* Treaties, treaty referendum
Refugees *See* Asylum
Regeneration 17
Research 137, 149, 422
Restoration 16
Right of petition 419
Right to a decent burial 384
Right to be heard *See* Procedural rights, right to be heard
Right to die 393
Right to informational self-determination 399
Right to life 385–387
Right to marriage 401, 402
Right to privacy 393–400
Right to vote *See* Political rights
Rule of law 56, 57, 197

S

Schengen/Dublin accords 82, 83
Secrecy of mail and telecommunications 398
Separation of powers *See* Division of powers
Social goals 70, 78, 131, 481
Social rights 8, 70, 347, 481–488 *See also* Social goals
- definition 481
- right to assistance when in need 383, 482–484
- right to primary school assistance 482, 485–488
Social securitiy 70, 141, 156
Sonderbund 18, 22, 176, 404
Spain 252, 457, 490
Statutory law *See* Federal statute
Strike 428, 482
Sustainable development 74–76
Swiss citizenship *See Citizenship*
System of government 238–251
- parliamentary 239, 240, 247
- presidential 241, 242
- semi-presidential 243, 244
- Swiss system 6, 87, 227, 245–251

Index

T

Tagsatzung *See* Diet
Taxation 106, 140, 159, 290, 406, 436
Torture, prohibition of 361, 379, 383, 389, 434, 511
Traffic 151
Treaties 535–550
- competencies 145, 147, 537, 538
- definitions 535, 536
- implementation 147, 536, 544–546
- intercantonal 170–180
- legislative approval 539, 540
- negotiations 538
- rank in relation to domestic law 546–550, 559
- ratification 316, 540, 544, 545
- treaty-making procedure 147, 537–545
- treaty referendum 88, 103, 177, 229, 541–543

U

Unitary state 14, 20, 63
United Federal Assembly 275, 291, 303, 309, 328, 331
United Kingdom 29, 37, 56, 349, 388, 473
United Nations 73, 88, 103, 507, 542
Unitiy of subject matter 237 *See also* Constitutional revision, unity of subject matter
Universities 140, 149, 181, 313
U.N. Convention on the Rights of the Child 361, 390
U.N. Covenant on Civil and Political Rights 117, 361, 428, 473
U.N. Covenant on Economic, Social and Culture Rights 78, 347, 361, 488
Urgent legislation 284, 526, 527
U.S. Constitution
- constitutional jurisdiction 45, 324, 556, 558
- fundamental rights 348, 367, 473, 475
- impact on Swiss constitution 2, 20, 21, 104, 253, 255
- relation betrween federation and member-states 62, 115, 124, 125, 168, 323
- system of government 241, 242

W

World Bank 90
World Trade Organisation 89

Z

Zoning and building 106, 142, 150, 165, 169, 437